THE LAST
AMERICAN MAN

ALSO BY ELIZABETH GILBERT

Pilgrims

Stern Men

ELIZABETH GILBERT

THE LAST AMERICAN MAN

VIKING

VIKING

Published by the Penguin Group

Penguin Putnam Inc., 375 Hudson Street,

New York, New York 10014, U.S.A.

Penguin Books Ltd, 80 Strand,

London WC2R 0RL, England

Penguin Books Australia Ltd, 250 Camberwell Road, Camberwell,

Victoria 3124, Australia

Penguin Books Canada Ltd, 10 Alcorn Avenue,

Toronto, Ontario, Canada M4V 3B2

Penguin Books (N.Z.) Ltd, Cnr Rosedale and Airborne Roads, Albany,

Auckland, New Zealand

Penguin Books Ltd, Registered Offices:

Harmondsworth, Middlesex, England

First published in 2002 by Viking Penguin,

a member of Penguin Putnam Inc.

10   9   8   7   6   5   4   3   2   1

CIP data available

ISBN: 0-670-03086-4

Printed in the United States of America

Set in Minion

Designed by Francesca Belanger

For the two most brilliant women I know—
My big sister Catherine Murdock
and my dear friend Deborah Luepnitz.
Your influence is beyond measure.

The result is that to the frontier the American Intellect owes its striking characteristics. That coarseness and strength combined with acuteness and inquisitiveness: that practical, inventive turn of mind, quick to find expedients; that masterful grasp of material things, lacking in the artistic but powerful to effect great ends; that restless, nervous energy; that dominant individualism, working for good or for evil, and withal that buoyancy and exuberance which comes from freedom—these are the traits of the frontier . . .

—*Frederick Jackson Turner*

THE LAST
AMERICAN MAN

# CHAPTER ONE

What a wild life! What a fresh kind of existence!

—Henry Wadsworth Longfellow, considering the possibility of writing an epic poem about the American explorer John Frémont

By the time Eustace Conway was seven years old, he could throw a knife accurately enough to nail a chipmunk to a tree. By the time he was ten, he could hit a running squirrel at fifty feet with a bow and arrow. When he turned twelve, he went out into the woods, alone and empty-handed, built himself a shelter, and survived off the land for a week. When he turned seventeen, he moved out of his family's home altogether and headed into the mountains, where he lived in a teepee of his own design, made fire by rubbing two sticks together, bathed in icy streams, and dressed in the skins of the animals he had hunted and eaten.

This move occurred in 1977, by the way. Which was the same year the film *Star Wars* was released.

The following year, when he was eighteen, Eustace Conway traveled the Mississippi River in a handmade wooden canoe, battling eddies so fierce, they could suck down a forty-foot tree and not release it to the surface again until a mile downriver. The next year, he set off on the two-thousand-mile Appalachian Trail, walking from Maine to Georgia and surviving almost exclusively on what he hunted and gathered along the way. And in the years that followed, Eustace hiked across the German Alps (in sneakers), kayaked across Alaska, scaled cliffs in New Zealand, and lived with the Navajo of New Mexico. When he was in his mid-twenties, he decided to study a primitive culture more closely in order to learn even more ancient skills. So he flew to Guatemala, got off the plane, and basically started asking, "Where are the primitive people at?" He was pointed toward the jungle, where he hiked for days and days until he found the remotest village of Mayan Indians, many of whom had never before seen a white person. He lived with the Maya for about five months, learning the language, studying the religion, perfecting his weaving skills.

But his coolest adventure was probably in 1995, when Eustace got the notion to ride his horse across America. His younger brother, Judson, and a close family friend went with him. It was a mad act of whim. Eustace wasn't sure if it was possible or even legal to ride a horse across America. He just ate a big Christmas dinner with his family, strapped on his gun, hauled out an eighty-year-old U.S. Cavalry saddle (rubbed so thin in places that he could feel the heat of the animal between his legs as he rode), mounted his horse, and headed out. He reckoned that he and his partners could make it to the Pacific by Easter, although everyone he told this to laughed in his face.

The three riders galloped along, burning away nearly fifty miles a day. They ate roadkill deer and squirrel soup. They slept in barns and in the homes of awestruck locals, but when they reached the dry, open West, they fell off their horses every night and slept on the ground where they fell. They were nearly killed by swerving eighteen-wheelers when their horses went wild on a busy interstate bridge one afternoon. They were nearly arrested in Mississippi for not wearing shirts. In San Diego, they picketed their horses along a patch of grass between a mall and an eight-lane highway. They slept there that night and arrived at the Pacific Ocean the next afternoon. Eustace Conway rode his horse right into the surf. It was ten hours before Easter. He had crossed the country in 103 days, setting, while he was at it, a world record.

From coast to coast, Americans of every conceivable background had looked up at Eustace Conway on his horse and said wistfully, "I wish I could do what you're doing."

And to every last citizen, Eustace had replied, "You can."

But I'm getting ahead of my story here.

Eustace Conway was born in South Carolina in 1961. The Conways lived in a comfortable suburban home in a new neighborhood full of the same, but there was a fine patch of woods, standing right behind their house, that had not yet been cleared for development. It was, in fact, a wild, undisturbed, first-growth forest without so much as a trail cut through it. It was an old world forest, still filled with quicksand and bears. And it was here that Eustace Conway's father—whose name was also Eustace Conway and who knew everything—used to take his young son to teach him how to identify the plants, birds, and mammals of the American South. They would wander together in those woods for hours, looking up into the trees and discussing the shapes of the leaves. So these are Eustace Conway's first memories: the cosmic scope of the woods; the stipple of sunlight slanting through a verdant natural awning; the enlightening voice of the father; the loveliness of the words *locust, birch,* and *tulip poplar;* the new intellectual pleasure of study enhanced by the distinct physical sensation of his wobbly toddler's head tilting so far back that he might have toppled over from the effort of looking up so hard at so many trees for such a long time.

As for the rest, and over the years, it was his mother who taught Eustace. She taught him how to camp, bait a hook, build a fire, handle wildlife, weave grasses into rope, and find clay in river bottoms. She taught him how to read books with wonderful titles, like *Davy Crockett: Young Adventurer* and *Wild Wood Wisdom.* She taught him to sew buckskin. She taught him how to execute every task with ardent perfection. Eustace Conway's mother was not exactly like the other mothers of the day. She was a little gutsier than the average mom in the American South in the early 1960s. She'd been raised like a boy at a summer camp that her family had owned in the mountains of Asheville, North Carolina. She was an unrepentant tomboy, a proficient horseback rider, and a capable woodsman who, at the age of twenty-two, had sold her silver flute for passage to Alaska, where she lived in a tent by a river with her gun and her dog.

By the time Eustace was five years old, the forest behind his house had been leveled by the real estate market, but the family soon moved to a four-bedroom home in another suburban development. It was in Gastonia, North Carolina, and had its own dense forest standing behind it. Mrs. Conway let Eustace and his young siblings have the run of the woods from the time they could walk—barefoot and shirtless and without supervision—from sunup to sundown, every moment of their childhood, except for those few interruptions for mandatory schooling and churchgoing (because it wasn't as though she were raising *savages*).

"I suppose I was a bad mother," Mrs. Conway says today, not very convincingly.

The other mothers of Gastonia naturally were horrified by this childrearing technique, such as it was. Some of them, alarmed, would call Mrs. Conway on the telephone and say, "You can't let your babies play in those woods! There are poisonous snakes out there!"

Thirty years later, Mrs. Conway still finds their concern amusing and adorable.

"For heaven's sake!" she says. "My children always knew the difference between poisonous snakes and regular snakes! They did just fine out there."

Briefly, the history of America goes like this: there was a frontier, and then there was no longer a frontier. It all happened rather quickly. There were Indians, then explorers, then settlers, then towns, then cities. Nobody was really paying attention until the moment the wilderness was officially tamed, at which point everybody wanted it back. Within the general spasm of nostalgia that ensued (Buffalo Bill's Wild West Show, Frederic Remington's cowboy paintings) there came a very specific cultural panic, rooted in the question *What will become of our boys?*

The problem was that, while the classic European coming-of-age story generally featured a provincial boy who moved to the city and was transformed into a refined gentleman, the American tradition had evolved into the opposite. The American boy came of age by *leaving* civilization and striking out toward the hills. There, he shed his cosmopolitan manners and became a robust and proficient man. Not a gentleman, mind you, but a man.

This was a particular kind of man, this wilderness-bred American. He was no intellectual. He had no interest in study or reflection. He had, as de Tocqueville noticed, "a sort of distaste for what is ancient." Instead, he could sterotypically be found, as the explorer John Frémont described the *über*-frontiersman Kit Carson, "mounted on a fine horse, without a saddle and scouring bare-headed over the prairies." Either that, or whipping his mighty ax over his shoulder and casually "throwing cedars and oaks to the ground," as one extremely impressed nineteenth-century foreign visitor observed.

In fact, to all the foreign visitors during the eighteenth and nineteenth centuries, the American Man was a virtual tourist attraction in his own right, almost as fascinating as Niagara Falls or that ambitious new railroad system or those exotic Indians. Not everybody was a fan, of course. ("There are perhaps no people, not even excepting the French, who are so vain as the Americans," griped one British observer in 1818. "Every American considers that it's impossible for a foreigner to teach him anything, and that his head contains a perfect encyclopedia.") Still, for better or worse, everyone seemed to agree that this was a new kind of human being and that what defined the American Man more than anything else was his resourcefulness, born out of the challenges of wrenching a New World from virgin wilderness. Unhindered by class restrictions, bureaucracy, or urban squalor, these Americans simply got more done in a single day than anyone had imagined possible. That was the bottom line: nobody could believe how fast these guys worked.

German-born Gottfried Duden, who traveled to the West in 1824 to identify suitable homesteads for German families interested in immigrating to America, reported home in wonder: "In North America, construction jobs which the European countries do not accomplish in centuries are completed in a few years, through the voluntary cooperation of individual citizens." At the time of Duden's visit, for instance, the farmers of Ohio were busy constructing a 230-mile-long canal without the help of a single licensed engineer. Duden saw "beautiful cities" thriving where not even towns had stood two years before. He saw new roads, new bridges, "thousands of new farms," and "a hundred more steamships"—all new, handmade, ingeniously designed, and perfectly operative. Did the American Man need something done? Well, then, he simply made it happen.

It was such an attractive idea, this notion of the bold and competent New World citizen. The English travel writer Isabel Bird, famous for her cool and detached prose, seemed scarcely able to keep from exclaiming *hubba-hubba* as she checked out the rugged men she kept encountering on her trip to America in the 1850s:

"It is impossible to give an idea of the 'Western Men' to anyone who has not seen one at least as specimen . . . tall, handsome, broad-chested, and athletic, with aquiline noses, piercing grey eyes, and brown curling hair and beards. They wore leather jackets, leather smallclothes, large boots with embroidered tops, silver spurs, and caps of scarlet cloth, worked with somewhat tarnished gold thread, doubtless the gifts of some fair ones enamored of the handsome physiognomies and reckless bearing of the hunters. Dullness fled from their presence; they could tell stories, whistle melodies, and sing . . . Blithe, cheerful souls they were, telling racy stories of Western life, chivalrous in the manners and free as the winds."

Look, I wasn't there. It's hard to know how much of this rhetoric was based on truth and how much was the product of an excitable foreign press eager to testify on the Next Big Thing. What I do know is that we, the Americans, bought the hype. We bought it and added it to the already hearty stew of our homegrown self-mythology until we cooked up a perfectly universal notion of who the American Man was and how the American Man was made. He was Pecos Bill. He was Paul Bunyan. He altered the course of rivers with the help of his mighty blue ox, he broke wild horses using rattlesnakes as reins, and he was an omnipotent hero created through revelatory communion with the frontier. Everyone knew that.

So Frederick Jackson Turner wasn't the only person who got nervous when the news came in 1890 from the Census Department that the American frontier was suddenly and officially closed. But he was the first to ask what this closure would mean to future generations. His nervousness spread; the questions expanded. Without the wilderness as proving ground, what would become of our boys?

Why, they might become effete, pampered, decadent.

Lord help us, they might become *Europeans*.

I first met Eustace Conway in New York City, of all places. This was 1993.

I met Eustace through his brother Judson, who is a cowboy. Judson and I used to work together on a ranch out in the Wyoming Rockies. This was back when I was twenty-two years old, acting as if I were a Western cowgirl—an act that took considerable pretense, given the inconvenient reality that I was actually a former field hockey player from Connecticut. But I was out there in Wyoming because I was seeking an education and an authenticity that I thought could not be found anywhere but on the American frontier, or what remained of it.

I was searching for this American frontier as earnestly as my parents had sought it two decades earlier, when they'd purchased three acres of land in New England and pretended to be pioneers—raising chickens and goats and bees, growing all our food, sewing all our clothing, washing our hair in a rain barrel, and heating our house (and only two rooms of it) with hand-split firewood. My parents gave me and my sister as rugged a nineteenth-century upbringing as they could manage, even though we were living out the Reagan years in one of Connecticut's wealthiest communities and our insular little frontier farmhouse happened to be located on a major highway only a mile away from the country club.

Well, what of it? My sister and I were encouraged to ignore this reality. We picked blackberries in the ditches alongside that highway in our handmade dresses while the cars raced by and the passing eighteen-wheelers shook the ground. We went to school with goat's milk dried on our sleeves from the morning chores. We were taught to disregard the values of the culture that surrounded us and to concentrate instead on this sacred and more ancient American tenet: Resourcefulness Is Next to Godliness.

It is probably not surprising, then, that when I turned twenty-two I decided that I would not be satisfied by going on to graduate school or settling into some respectable career. I had other aspirations. I wanted to learn the boundaries of my own resourcefulness, and these, I believed, I could learn only in a place like Wyoming. I was inspired by the example of my parents and by Walt Whitman's stirring advice to American boys of the nineteenth century: "Ascend no longer from the textbook! Ascend to your own country! Go to the West and the South! Go among men, in the spirit of men! Master horses, become a good marksman and a strong oarsman . . ."

I went to Wyoming, in other words, to make a man of myself.

I loved ranch work. I was a trail cook. I was ridin' horses into the wilderness, I was sittin' around campfires, I was drinkin' and tellin' stories and cussin' and droppin' all my g's and basically puttin' on a classic act of phony authenticity. When strangers in Wyoming asked me where I hailed from, I'd say, "Lubbock, Texas." As long as nobody asked a single follow-up question, I was generally able to pass as an authentic cowgirl. The other wranglers on the ranch even had an authentic cowgirl nickname for me. They all called me Blaze.

But only because I'd asked 'em to.

I was a complete and thoroughgoing faker. But this fakery, I submit, was merely my right and privilege as a young American citizen. I was following the national ritual. I was no more counterfeit than Teddy Roosevelt had been a century earlier, when he left New York City as a cosseted dandy and headed West to become a robust man. He sent the most self-satisfied and self-conscious letters back home, boasting about his rugged experiences, as well as his macho wardrobe. ("You would be amused to see me," Roosevelt wrote to one Eastern friend, "in my broad sombrero hat, fringed and beaded buckskin shirt, horsehide chaparajos or riding trousers, and cowhide boots, with braided bridle and silver spurs.") I know this letter. I wrote it myself, dozens of times, to dozens of people. ("I bought a pair of rattlesnake boots last week," I wrote to my parents from the ranch in 1991, "and I've beat them to shit already doing chores in the corral, but, hell, that's what they're for.")

I met Judson Conway the first day I came to the ranch. He was the first thing I set eyes on after that long drive up that big Wyoming mountain, and I kind of fell in love with him. I didn't fall in love with Judson like "Let's get married!" I fell in love with him like "Mercy!" Because here was Judson Conway at that moment: slim, handsome, hidden slightly under a cowboy hat, and appealingly dusty. All he had to do was stroll by me with his sexy swagger (classically executed, in the Hollywood manner of Pardon-me-ma'am-but-I-just-came-off-a-long-ride), and I was a believer.

I was attracted to Judson because I was a girl and he was beautiful and I wasn't friggin' blind, but I also recognized in him an immediate commonality. Like me, Judson was twenty-two years old and a complete and thoroughgoing faker. He was no more authentically Western than his new friend Blaze. Nor were we more authentically Western than Frank Brown, the other twenty-two-year-old cowboy working on the ranch. He was a college kid from Massachusetts currently going by the moniker Buck. And then there was our head cowboy Hank, who'd always holler, "Let's pound leather, y'all!" when it was time to ride out, but whose father happened to be the assistant attorney general of Utah. We were all putting on the same show.

But Judson was my favorite, because he enjoyed the show better than anyone. He did have the slight cultural advantage of at least being from the South, so he could drawl. He was so damn cool. Walt Whitman would've loved how Judson was living. He was mastering marksmanship and oarsmanship, but he had also traveled across America in boxcars and hitchhiked back, had kissed girls from everywhere, and had learned to be a great storyteller and a talented hunter. And so lucid a horseman! He'd taught himself tricks like swinging his body up and off his horse while it was running along, and many other diversions that weren't entirely practical for ranch work but were most entertaining.

He and I had a ball together two years in a row, out there in Wyoming, and then we went our separate ways. But we stayed in touch. Like a good Civil War soldier, Judson corresponded eloquently and loyally by post. Never called; always wrote. And he had a lot to write about, because this was the excellent life he'd made for himself: he spent his springtimes dove-hunting at home in North Carolina, summers as a fishing guide in Alaska, autumns as an elk-hunting guide in Wyoming, and winters helping tourists catch trophy fish in the Florida Keys.

"Intent on learning how to fish saltwater and in hopes of getting a job on a charter boat," he wrote to me, on his first trip to Florida. "I'm staying with a couple I took horseback riding one day in Wyoming. Got to talking, and here I am . . . Been spending a lot of time in the Everglades National Park, birdwatching and wrestling alligators."

"Not making a living," he wrote, on his first trip to Alaska, "just *living*."

Judson always swore he'd come and see me sometime in New York City, where I had since moved. ("Does the Hudson have fish in it?") But the years passed, and he didn't swing by, and I never quite expected him to. ("Gettin' married, huh?" he finally wrote, after a long letter of mine. "Guess I waited too long to visit . . .") And then one day, years after we'd last spoken in person, he called. This was in itself astonishing. Judson doesn't use telephones, not when there are perfectly good stamps to be had. But the call was urgent. He told me he was flying to New York the very next day, to visit. Just a whim, he said. Just wanted to see what a big city was like, he said. And then he added that his older brother, Eustace, would be coming along, too.

Sure enough, the Conway boys arrived the next morning. They stepped out of a yellow cab right in front of my apartment and made the most outrageous, incongruous sight. There was handsome Judson, looking like a young swain from "Bonanza." And there, right beside him, was his brother, Davy Fuckin' Crockett.

I knew this was Davy Fuckin' Crockett because that's what everyone on the streets of New York City started calling the guy right away.

"Yo, man! It's Davy Fuckin' Crockett!"

"Check out Davy Fuckin' Crockett!"

"King of the wild motherfuckin' frontier!"

Of course, some New Yorkers mistook him for Daniel Fuckin' Boone, but everyone had something to say about this curious visitor, who moved stealthily through the streets of Manhattan, wearing hand-made buckskin clothing and carrying an impressive knife on his belt.

Davy Fuckin' Crockett.

So that's how I met Eustace Conway.

Over the next two days, against the unlikely backdrop of New York City, I heard all about Eustace Conway's life. One night, Judson and Eustace and I went drinking in a lowdown bar in the East Village, and while Judson kept busy dancing with all the pretty girls and telling thrilling stories of life on the range, Eustace sat in a corner with me and quietly explained how he had been living for the last seventeen years in a teepee, hidden away in the Southern Appalachian Mountains of North Carolina. He called his home Turtle Island, named for the Native American creationist legend of the sturdy turtle who carries the entire weight of the earth on his back. Eustace told me he owned a thousand acres of land back there in the woods—a perfectly contained and unspoiled basin, with a protected watershed.

It seemed curious to me that somebody who eats possum and wipes his butt with leaves could have managed to acquire a thousand acres of pristine wilderness. But Eustace Conway was, as I would discover, a most cunning man. He had amassed that property slowly and over time with money he made by going into the local school systems and talking to riveted schoolchildren about eating possum and wiping one's butt with leaves. Land, he declared, was his only major expense in life. Everything else he needed he could make, build, grow, or kill. He hunted for his own food, drank water from the ground, made his own clothing . . .

Eustace told me that people tended to romanticize his lifestyle. Because when people first ask him what he does for a living, he invariably replies, "I live in the woods." Then people get all dreamy and say, "Ah! The woods! The woods! I love the woods!" as if Eustace spends his days sipping the dew off clover blossoms. But that's not what living in the woods means to Eustace Conway.

Some years ago, for instance, out hunting for his winter deer, he came upon a gorgeous eight-point buck grazing through the brush. He shot. The buck went down. Not knowing if he had killed the animal, he waited and waited to see whether it would struggle up from where it had fallen and try to run. There was no movement. Slowly, quietly, Eustace crept toward the spot where the animal had gone down and found the massive buck, lying on its side, breathing a thin, red vapor of blood through its nose. The animal's eyes were moving; it was alive.

"Get up, brother!" Eustace shouted. "Get up and I'll finish you off!"

The animal didn't move. Eustace hated to see it lying there, alive and injured, but he also hated to blow off its beautiful head at point-blank range, so he took his knife from his belt and stabbed into the buck's jugular vein. Up came the buck, very much alive, whipping its rack of antlers. Eustace clung to the antlers, still holding his knife, and the two began a wrestling match, thrashing through the brush, rolling down the hill, the buck lunging, Eustace trying to deflect its heavy antlers into trees and rocks. Finally, he let go with one hand and sliced his knife completely across the buck's neck, gashing open veins, arteries, and windpipe. But the buck kept fighting, until Eustace ground its face into the dirt, kneeling on its head and suffocating the dying creature. And then he plunged his hands into the animal's neck and smeared the blood all over his own face, weeping and laughing and offering up an ecstatic prayer of thanksgiving to the universe for the magnificent phenomenon of this creature who had so valiantly sacrificed its life to sustain his own.

That's what living in the woods means to Eustace Conway.

The morning after our conversation in the bar, I took the Conway brothers on a walk through Tompkins Square Park. There, I lost Eustace. I couldn't find him anywhere, and I got worried, concerned that he was out of his environment and therefore helpless and vulnerable. But when I found him, he was in pleasant conversation with the scariest posse of drug dealers you'd ever want to meet. They had offered Eustace Conway crack, which he had politely declined, but he was engaging with them, nonetheless, about other issues.

"Yo, man," the drug dealers were asking as I arrived, "where'd you buy that dope shirt?"

Eustace explained to the drug dealers that he had not, in fact, bought the shirt; he had made it. Out of a deer. He described exactly how he'd shot the deer with a black powder musket, skinned the deer ("with this very knife!"), softened the hide with the deer's own brains, and then sewed the shirt together, using strands of sinew taken from alongside the deer's spine. He told the drug dealers that it wasn't such a difficult process, and that they could do it, too. And if they came to visit him in his mountain home of Turtle Island, he'd teach them all sorts of marvelous ways to live off nature.

I said, "Eustace, we gotta go."

The drug dealers shook his hand and said, "Damn, Hustice. You something *else*."

But this is how Eustace interacts with all the world all the time—taking any opportunity to teach people about nature. Which is to say that Eustace is not merely a hermit or a hippie or even a survivalist. He does not live in the woods because he's hiding from us, or because he's growing excellent weed, or because he's storing guns for the imminent race war. He lives in the woods because he belongs there. Moreover, he tries to get other people to move into the woods with him, because he believes that is his particular calling—nothing less than to save our nation's collective soul by reintroducing Americans to the concept of revelatory communion with the frontier. Which is to say that Eustace Conway believes that he is a Man of Destiny.

Eustace created Turtle Island—the thousand-acre perfect cosmos of his own design—as the ultimate teaching facility, a university-in-the-raw, a wild monastery. Because, after years of studying primitive societies and after countless experiences of personal transformation within the wilderness, Eustace has formed a mighty dogma. He is convinced that the only way modern America can begin to reverse its inherent corruption and greed and malaise is by feeling the rapture that comes from face-to-face encounters with what he calls "the high art and godliness of nature."

It is his belief that we Americans, through our constant striving for convenience, are eradicating the raucous and edifying beauty of our true environment and replacing that beauty with a safe but completely faux "environment." What Eustace sees is a society steadily undoing it-self, it might be argued, by its own over-resourcefulness. Clever, ambi-tious, and always in search of greater efficiency, we Americans have, in two short centuries, created a world of push-button, round-the-clock comfort for ourselves. The basic needs of humanity—food, clothing, shelter, entertainment, transportation, and even sexual pleasure—no longer need to be personally labored for or ritualized or even under-stood. All these things are available to us now for mere cash. Or credit. Which means that nobody needs to know how to *do* anything anymore, except the one narrow skill that will earn enough money to pay for the conveniences and services of modern living.

But in replacing every challenge with a shortcut we seem to have lost something, and Eustace isn't the only person feeling that loss. We are an increasingly depressed and anxious people—and not for noth-ing. Arguably, all these modern conveniences have been adopted to save us time. But time for *what*? Having created a system that tends to our every need without causing us undue exertion or labor, we can now fill these hours with . . . ?

Well, for one thing, television—loads of it, hours of it, days and weeks and months of it in every American's lifetime. Also, work. Amer-icans spend more and more hours at their jobs every year; in almost every household both parents (if there *are* two parents) must work full-time outside the home to pay for all these goods and services. Which means a lot of commuting. Which means a lot of stress. Less connec-tion to family and community. Fast-food meals eaten in cars on the way to and from work. Poorer health all the time. (America is certainly the fattest and most inactive society in history, and we're packing on more pounds every year. We seem to have the same disregard for our bodies as we do for our our other natural resources; if a vital organ breaks down, after all, we always believe we can just buy a new one. Somebody else will take care of it. Same way we believe that somebody else will plant another forest someday if we use this one up. That is, if we even notice that we're using it up.)

There's an arrogance to such an attitude, but—more than that—there's a profound alienation. We have fallen out of rhythm. It's this simple. If we don't cultivate our own food supply anymore, do we need to pay attention to the idea of, say, seasons? Is there any difference between winter and summer if we can eat strawberries every day? If we can keep the temperature of our house set at a comfortable 70 degrees all year, do we need to notice that fall is coming? Do we have to prepare for that? Respect that? Much less contemplate what it means for our own mortality that things die in nature every autumn? And when spring does come round again, do we need to notice that rebirth? Do we need to take a moment and maybe thank anybody for that? Celebrate it? If we never leave our house except to drive to work, do we need to be even remotely aware of this powerful, humbling, extraordinary, and eternal life force that surges and ebbs around us all the time?

Apparently not. Because we seem to have stopped paying attention. Or this is what Eustace Conway perceives when he looks around America. He sees a people who have fallen out of step with the natural cycles that have defined humanity's existence and culture for millennia. Having lost that vital connection with nature, the nation is in danger of losing its humanity. We are not alien visitors to this planet, after all, but natural residents and relatives of every living entity here. This earth is where we came from and where we'll all end up when we die, and, during the interim, it is our home. And there's no way we can ever hope to understand ourselves if we don't at least marginally understand our home. That is the understanding we need to put our lives in some bigger metaphysical context.

Instead, Eustace sees a chilling sight—a citizenry so removed from the rhythms of nature that we march through our lives as mere sleepwalkers, blinded, deafened, and senseless. Robotically existing in sterilized surroundings that numb the mind, weaken the body, and atrophy the soul. But Eustace believes we can get our humanity back. When we contemplate the venerable age of a mountain, we get it. When we observe the superb order of water and sunlight, we get it. When we experience firsthand the brutal poetry of the food chain, we get it. When we are mindful of every nuance of our natural world, we finally get the picture: that we are each given only one dazzling moment of life here on Earth, and we must stand before that reality both humbled and elevated, subject to every law of our universe and grateful for our brief but intrinsic participation within it.

Granted, this is not a radical concept. Every environmentalist in the world operates on a philosophy based on these same hypotheses. But what sets Eustace Conway apart from every other environmentalist is the peculiar confidence he's had since earliest childhood that it is his *personal* destiny to snap his countrymen out of their sleepwalk. He has always believed that he alone has this power and this responsibility, that he was to be the vessel of change. One man, one vision.

And this was his precise vision—that, one by one, Americans would come to his mystical utopia in the woods. There, under his guidance, they would shed the frailty, ignorance, and pettiness brought about by their contemporary upbringing. Using his charisma as a lure, he would lead people back into the wilderness, uncoil their blindfolds, point them toward the stunning vista of the unspoiled frontier, and say, "Behold!" Then he would stand back and watch the awakening.

Eustace always envisioned groups of children coming to participate in primitive summer camps, but he would also welcome adults— apprentices—who, for extended periods of time, would seriously study a natural way of life under his leadership. Of course he knows it's impossible to drag every single American into the woods with him, which is why he is also committed to going out into the world with his message and delivering the woods directly to the people himself—carrying the very smell of the wilderness in his hair and on his skin and within his words. He would preach and teach his doctrine in every school, at every state fair, in every mall and parking lot and gas station he could find. He would passionately speak to any businessman, baby-sitter, housewife, hooker, millionaire, and crackhead in America.

With Eustace's energy and through his example—he has always been certain of it—Americans would gradually be transformed. They would grow and learn and once again be strong and resourceful. Then they would leave Eustace's side and disseminate their newfound knowledge among their brethren. In this evangelical manner, Eustace Conway's vision of perfect concordance with nature would spread and spread across families, towns, counties, and states until we would all be living like Eustace—growing our food, fabricating our clothes, making fire with two sticks, and recognizing our blessed humanity. Thus both our grand nation and our sacred planet would be saved.

That was his plan, anyway.

Audacious? Sure. Still, there *is* something about the guy . . .

Eustace is not easily dismissed. As his brother Judson would attest in awe, and as I later came to witness in person, Eustace's skills in the wilderness are truly legion. He is wildly competent. He is physically and intellectually predestined to acquire proficiency. He has perfect eyesight, perfect hearing, perfect balance, perfect reflexes, and perfect focus. He has long muscles on a light but strongly constructed frame, like a natural middle-distance runner. His body can do anything he asks of it. His mind, too. He has to be exposed to an idea or shown a process only once to get it right, to lock it in, and immediately begin improving on its principles. He pays closer attention to his surroundings than anyone I've ever seen. His mind operates, as Henry Adams wrote of the minds of the earliest American settlers, like "a mere cutting instrument, practical, economical, sharp, and direct."

And that kind of mind makes for a hard honesty. So that when I once asked him, "Is there anything you *can't* do?" Eustace replied, "Well, I've never found anything to be particularly difficult." In other words, he's got the self-assurance to back up his conviction that he can change the world. That, in addition to the unshakable will and airtight world view of a natural-born reformer. And he's got charisma, too, which he unleashes brazenly in every interaction he has with anyone.

I first visited Eustace at Turtle Island back in 1995. Midway through my stay, Eustace had to leave the mountain, and I went with him. He had to leave the woods, as he often does, to teach *about* the woods, to make some money and spread the gospel. So we drove across North Carolina to a small summer camp that specialized in environmental education. A group of teenagers skulked into the camp's dining room for the evening's event, and to me they all looked like jerks—loud, disrespectful, shoving, shrieking, laughing. Eustace was supposed to get these kids excited about nature.

I thought, *This is not gonna end well.*

Eustace, wearing jeans and a plaid shirt, not buckskin, walked across the stage toward the microphone. Around his neck hung two large coyote teeth. On his belt, the knife.

The shoving and shrieking and laughing continued.

Eustace, thin and serious, stood at the microphone with his hands in his pockets. After a long moment, he said, "I am a quiet-spoken man, so I am going to have to speak quietly tonight."

The shoving and shrieking and laughing stopped. The jerky teenagers stared at Eustace Conway, riveted. Just like that—dead silence. I swear it. It was like goddamn *To Sir with Love*.

"I moved into the woods when I was seventeen years old," Eustace began. "Not much older than you are today . . ." And he talked about his life. Those kids were so transfixed, you could have operated on them and they wouldn't have noticed. Eustace told them about wilderness survival and his adventures, but he also gave his speech about the difference between the world of boxes and the world of circles.

"I live," Eustace said, "in nature, where everything is connected, circular. The seasons are circular. The planet is circular, and so is its passage around the sun. The course of water over the earth is circular, coming down from the sky and circulating through the world to spread life and then evaporating up again. I live in a circular teepee and I build my fire in a circle, and when my loved ones visit me, we sit in a circle and talk. The life cycles of plants and animals are circular. I live outside where I can see this. The ancient people understood that our world is a circle, but we modern people have lost sight of that. I don't live inside buildings, because buildings are dead places where nothing grows, where water doesn't flow, and where life stops. I don't want to live in a dead place. People say that I don't live in the real world, but it's modern Americans who live in a fake world, because they've stepped outside the natural circle of life.

"I saw the circle of life most clearly when I was riding my horse across America and I came across the body of a coyote that had recently died. The animal was mummified from the desert heat, but all around it, in a lush circle, was a small band of fresh green grass. The earth was borrowing the nutrients from the animal and regenerating itself. This wasn't about death, I realized; this was about eternal life. I took the teeth from that coyote and made myself this necklace right here, which always circles my neck, so I'd never forget that lesson.

"Do people live in circles today? No. They live in boxes. They wake up every morning in the box of their bedroom because a box next to them started making beeping noises to tell them it was time to get up. They eat their breakfast out of a box and then they throw that box away into another box. Then they leave the box where they live and get into a box with wheels and drive to work, which is just another big box broken up into lots of little cubicle boxes where a bunch of people spend their days sitting and staring at the computer boxes in front of them. When the day is over, everyone gets into the box with wheels again and goes home to their house boxes and spends the evening staring at the television boxes for entertainment. They get their music from a box, they get their food from a box, they keep their clothing in a box, they live their lives in a box! Does that sound like anybody you know?"

By now the kids were laughing and applauding.

"Break out of the box!" Eustace said. "You don't have to live like this because people tell you it's the only way. You're not handcuffed to your culture! This is *not* the way humanity lived for thousands and thousands of years, and it is *not* the only way you can live today!"

Another hour of this, then uncontained applause, like at a revival meeting. After the talk, Eustace sat on the edge of the stage, drinking from the glass jug filled with fresh Turtle Island spring water that he carries with him everywhere. The teenagers approached reverently, awed, as the camp director gave Eustace an enthusiastic handshake and a discreetly enveloped generous check. The teenagers gathered around more closely. The toughest, baddest-ass gangsta boy of them all came to stand right beside Eustace. He put his fist on his heart and announced, with real solemnity, "You rule, man. You da *bomb*." Eustace threw back his head and laughed. The other campers lined up to shake his hand and then detonated with questions.

"Could you make fire right now if you had to?"

"Yes."

"If someone dropped you naked into the middle of Alaska, could you survive?"

"I suppose so. But it'd be a lot easier if I had a knife."

"Were you scared when you first moved into the woods?"

"No. The civilized world is much scarier than the woods."

"Were your parents mad at you when you moved into the woods?"

"My father didn't know why I'd want to leave a comfortable modern house, but my mother understood."

"Do you ever get sick?"

"Rarely."

"Do you ever go to the doctor?"

"Never."

"Do you know how to drive a car?"

"How do you think I got here tonight?"

"Do you use any modern tools?"

"I use chain saws all the time to take care of my land. I use telephones. And plastic buckets. My God, but plastic buckets are great! I've made plenty of my own baskets and containers out of tree bark and grasses—I mean, I know how to do it and I've used those primitive means of hauling water around lots of time—but I tell you, there's nothing like a plastic bucket to get the job done faster. Wow! Plastic buckets! Glorious! I love 'em!"

"Do you have a toothbrush?"

"Not at the moment."

"Do you have a hairbrush?"

"I used to have a porcupine hairbrush. I don't have it anymore, though."

"What's a porcupine hairbrush?"

"A hairbrush made out of porcupine bristles."

"Where'd you get *that*?"

"A porcupine saved my life once when I was hiking on the Appalachian Trail, so I made the hairbrush out of its bristles, to honor it."

"How could a porcupine save your life?"

"By giving me something to eat when I was starving to death."

Here, there was an extended silence, as the kids tried to figure that one out. Then they all kind of said, "Ohhh . . ." at the same time, and the questioning continued.

"Why were you starving to death?"

"Because there wasn't any food."

"Why wasn't there any food?"

"Because it was winter."

"What's the longest you've ever gone without eating?"

"Probably the two weeks before I killed that porcupine."

"Can you show us your porcupine hairbrush?"

"I don't have it anymore. I brought it to a demonstration like this one, to show it to some kids your age, and somebody stole it. Can you imagine how sad that made me feel?"

"Do you have a gun?"

"I have several guns."

"Have you ever killed a person?"

"No."

"Are you married?"

"No."

"Why not?"

"I guess I haven't found the right woman yet."

"Do you wish you were married?"

"More than anything in the world."

"Do you ever get lonely out there in the woods?"

Eustace hesitated, smiled wistfully. "Only in the evenings."

Later that night, when we were alone, Eustace told me how heartbroken he gets whenever he spends time around modern American teenagers. Yes, he can communicate with them, but people never understand that it rips him up inside to see how ignorant the kids are, how undisciplined in their personal interactions and how disrespectful of their elders, how consumed they are by material desire and how helplessly incompetent in a way that you would never see with, say, *Amish* children.

But I wasn't listening carefully to Eustace's lament, because I had another question on my mind. "Hey, about what happened there tonight. Do you get that kind of response everywhere you speak?"

"Yes."

"From all age groups; from all backgrounds?"

"Yes."

I thought this over. "So tell me specifically. Why do you think these particular teenagers were so hypnotized by you tonight?"

Eustace's reply was so immediate, so uncompromising, and so coldly delivered that it sent a quick little chill right through me.

"Because," he said, "they recognized right away that I was a real person. And they've probably never met one before."

CHAPTER TWO

My son, my executioner,
I take you in my arms,
Quiet and small and just astir,
And whom my body warms.

—"My Son, My Executioner," Donald Hall

In the winter of 1975, when Eustace Conway was fourteen, he began a new diary and wrote this statement, by means of an introduction:

"I, Eustace Conway, live in a fairly large house in Gastonia, North Carolina. I have a mother and a father living at this time, and I also have two brothers (Walton and Judson) and one sister (Martha). I have a very strong hobby of Indian crafts and lore. I have organized an Indian dance team of four people, including myself. The people are: me, my brother Walton, who is the older of my two brothers, Tommy Morris, who is a close friend living about two blocks away, and also Pete Morris, who is his brother. Their father killed himself about two years ago but their mother is going to remarry soon. I go to the Scheile Museum of Natural History every chance I get because I love it there and I love the people there. I have nearly become a member of the staff . . . My bedroom is itself a museum. I have covered it with Indian paintings and pictures, bear skins from my uncle in Alaska, and many Indian crafts I have made. There is no room in my room for anything else and it is really stuffed and I have many more things that I can't put in."

He was an unusual kid. He was busy all the time. He went to school every day, of course, but only because they made him go. After school, he would ride his bicycle over to the Scheile Museum, a small natural history museum filled with dusty World War I–era dioramas of North Carolina flora and fauna. And that was where the day's real schooling started for Eustace; Mr. Alan Stout, the museum's director, had taken a liking to him and always welcomed him into the marvelous inner asylum of the Scheile.

Eustace was hard to resist. The kid had a wonderful big smile, on the occasions when he'd actually crack one. Such an uncommonly focused child! So highly motivated and interested in geology, anthropology, history, biology—anything you could offer him. Mr. Stout used to let Eustace hang around in the back rooms of the museum for hours every day, to the boy's supreme bliss. ("Mr. Stout knows more about Indians than anyone I know," Eustace raved in his diary. "And he is a very good watercolor painter, and paints scenes of Tennessee, where he was born and raised.") Eustace was like no child Mr. Stout had ever met; indeed, like no child he would ever meet again. If you gave him a book to look at, he'd study it, ask a dozen questions, and then request another book the next afternoon. If Mr. Warren Kimsey, the museum's resident taxidermist, showed Eustace how to skin and flesh a rabbit, he'd do it with a fanatical perfection and ask for another rabbit so that he could try to improve on the skill.

"Warren is new," Eustace confided to his diary, "but he has swiftly become closest to me. In fact, I like him more than any other person in this world."

And he was a terrific helper. A regular eager beaver. Always happy to sweep out the storage rooms or take over any chore nobody else would do. Mr. Stout even let Eustace use the museum as a practice space for his Indian dance troupe. Eustace was the president of the troupe, but Mr. Stout coached the dancers, drove them to competitions, helped show the boys how to sew and bead the intricate, traditional Indian dance costumes. As Eustace got older, Mr. Stout took him on canoe trips on the Catawba South Fork River, to collect water samples for government environmental studies. He took Eustace on camping trips all alone sometimes, and watched in wordless admiration as the teenager caught, killed, skinned, cooked, and ate rattlesnakes.

Mr. Stout more than liked Eustace; he respected him. He thought he was brilliant. He carefully observed the development of Eustace Conway much as Thomas Jefferson had carefully observed the development of a young neighbor named Meriwether Lewis (a child whom the president would always recall as having been "remarkable, even in infancy, for enterprise, boldness and discretion"). And, anyway, Mr. Stout had a sense that Eustace had a desperate need for someplace to go in the afternoons, someplace other than home. He didn't know the details of the family situation, but he had met the father, and it didn't take any genius to recognize that life was not easy in that fairly large house on Deerwood Drive.

So Eustace would spend his afternoons at the museum and then take off and hit the little forest behind his house. Check his traps, hunt for turtles, create trails. He made notes of what he saw during those forays into the woods. He'd been keeping a diary for years, but it wasn't so much a means of personal expression as a compulsive chronicle of everything he had accomplished that day (whether related to wildlife or to the more mundane) and a long list of what he intended to accomplish the next day.

"Today I fed worms to my baby snapping turtle. I watched a movie about a boy and a homing pigeon, practiced on the hoop dance, and started working on the feathers for my coup stick. Then I was developing my skills in table tennis. I have become quite good. I am going to read my Bible every night until I finish it. I may make a feather crest out of real turkey tail feathers."

"Today I found a cougar track that was 3 days old. I caught a corn snake that was 5½ feet. I also set a snare for a coon where I saw 3-day old coon tracks. I hope to catch it for the skin."

"I began reading a book, *Fighting Indians of the West*. After a while of that, I mounted two deer feet . . . Martha told me that a squirrel had been hit on Gardner Park Drive. I skinned it, but froze it to flesh later."

A whole page in one of his childhood diaries was headlined FROGS, full of information and observation on the same. ("Today I caught 3 tree frogs and put them in my 10-gallon terrarium. The next day I found some bunches of eggs in the water bowl. I also caught a salamander and put him in there with the frogs. One of the frogs is thought to be dead, for I have not seen three of them together at the same time for a while . . .")

It was as though Eustace were some kind of baby Thoreau. Or maybe not. Although he was attentive to his environment, Eustace didn't have then, and never would develop, Thoreau's languid communion with nature. (For instance: "Sometimes, in a summer morning, having taken my accustomed bath," Thoreau mused, "I sat in my sunny doorway from sunrise till noon, rapt in reverie, amidst the pines and hickories and sumacs, in undisturbed solitude and stillness.") No way would Eustace Conway endure that kind of decadent repose. Even as a child, he was far too compulsive to sit for weeks on end to watch the light change. Instead, Eustace was driven to *engage*. It's more to the point to say that he was like the young Teddy Roosevelt, another energetic and determined child, who also studied under a master taxidermist, who also zealously created a natural history museum in his bedroom, and who also wrote conscientious, academic observations in preadolescent diaries. Like Teddy Roosevelt, the young Eustace Conway could be described as having been "pure act."

Eustace didn't have a lot of friends. He wasn't much like anybody else, and he already knew this, even at the age of ten. When he looked at other boys his age, he saw kids who spent hours watching television, talking about what they saw on television, and imitating characters from television. None of their references made any sense to him.

The other boys also had strange hobbies. In the cafeterias, they'd play this elaborate pencil-breaking game, trying to steal each other's pencils and snap them in half, keeping score of how many pencils each boy broke. This was both puzzling and upsetting to Eustace. How could anyone have such disrespect for property? Pencils were made out of trees, after all, and were worth something. He also watched boys in his classroom fritter away whole semesters by drawing picture after picture of race cars in their school notebooks—and using only one side of the paper, too! Eustace, even back then, would think, *What a waste of time . . . and what a waste of paper.* These boys just seemed so damn bored. All they could think of doing was to fight and wreck stuff. But Eustace could always think of something useful; there weren't enough hours in the day for all he wanted to do and learn.

Many children in the neighborhood knew Eustace and were involved with his life, but they weren't friends in the typical way of children; they were more like early versions of apprentices. Eustace used to do things like traipse down his sidewalk with a massive black rat snake draped around his neck, which naturally garnered attention. The kids would gather and ask questions and he'd tell them about the habits and nature of the snake, enlist them to gather food for the animal, or—if they demonstrated more interest—take them back into the woods and show them how to catch snakes of their own. Even the children who were older than Eustace would follow him into the woods to build forts under his supervision or wade through swamps to find food for his turtles.

But in school? Eustace had no friends. Without the conversation piece of a snake, without the backdrop of a forest as proof of his expertise, Eustace was pretty hopeless at connecting with his peers. He'd sit at the lunch table with the other outcasts—the mentally retarded children, the children with the braces on their legs, and the sad children of Gastonia's poorest families. He wasn't friends with these kids. They didn't even know one another's names. They would eat together every day but then look away in shameful relief when someone else was singled out for bullying.

There was this one boy, though. Randy Cable, who was new to Gastonia. His parents were hill people, rural Appalachian people, who had moved down from the mountains to this affluent suburban town to find work in the local mills. Randy didn't know anybody, either. One day during seventh grade, Randy was, as usual, playing alone at recess on the periphery of the playground, where the pavement stopped and the woods began. The other kids were involved in a loud baseball game, but Randy Cable didn't know how to play baseball. So he was kicking around near the woods and found a turtle. He was messing with it, poking at it, when Eustace Conway, a thin, dark, serious boy, came over.

"You like turtles?" asked Eustace.

"Sure," said Randy.

"I know everything about turtles. I have more than a hundred turtles in my backyard," Eustace said.

"No, you don't."

"Yes, I do. If you come over to my house, I'll show you."

Randy Cable thought, *Yeah, right.*

But he rode his bike over there that afternoon, and found that it *was* true. In the backyard of Eustace's house was a vast, orderly turtle community. Irrigated and shaded, it was a network of dozens of cages and crates filled with more than a hundred turtles, of different breeds, that Eustace had been feeding and tending to, on a carefully documented rotational system, since he was six years old.

Eustace loved turtles. He loved their character, their calmness, their perfect spiritual balance, and their comforting and ancient aura. Eustace had a genius for turtles. He could find turtles anywhere. He could spot a turtle hidden in dense camouflage with only one fingernail-size piece of its shell showing. Several times in his young life, Eustace had *heard* turtles. Walking silently through the woods, he could hear the almost soundless hiss of air made by a turtle quickly pulling its head and legs into its shell. Then Eustace would stop, freeze, and look around until he spotted it. Sure enough, there was a small box turtle, three feet away, hidden in the forest duff, all tucked up in itself.

Eustace had even developed a system for capturing skittish painted turtles out of ponds and lakes. He'd lurk in the woods at the edge of the water with a rod-and-reel fishing pole, baited with a large chunk of fatback bacon. He'd cast the bacon a few feet in front of the sunning turtle and then slowly drag it before the animal's eyes until the turtle smelled the bait and eased itself into the water to follow. Inch by inch, Eustace would lure the turtle closer to the shore and then jump out of the woods, leap into the water with a net, and snag the turtle before it dove in fear.

Back home, he'd put his new find in one of his plywood pens, each custom-designed with the appropriate balance of shade, water, and grass for the species. He had mud turtles, musk turtles, box turtles, painted turtles. He fed them crawfish and vegetables and worms (harvested from under the dozens of orderly logs Eustace had arranged in the woods behind his yard), and his turtles were so content in their habitats that they bred while in captivity. And he had snakes housed back there in his yard, too, as well as an orphaned baby fox named Sputnik. (Mr. Stout had given Eustace the fox after a local Gastonian found the animal and brought it into the Scheile Museum for care.) This well-ordered empire was what he showed his new friend Randy Cable that afternoon. And all of it was, for a rural kid like Randy, something close to heaven. The two boys became good buddies.

"Today for the first time I went to Randy Cable's house," Eustace wrote in his diary not long after the turtle display. "He showed me his woods and a stream where we saw muskrat, coon, bird, and cat tracks. He showed me a muskrat den in a clay bank. We built a bird trap out of a basket and baited it with bread. We used a long string and a wooden pull-trigger. We had a lot of blackbirds walking around it, but we never caught one because they never went in. We made a set of deadfall trigger sticks. I skinned a cottontail rabbit for a vest."

And so it went for months and years. Randy remembers Eustace as a strange and fascinating kid, full of knowledge and keenly sensitive to his world in a way unlike most other twelve-year-olds. His focus was intense on the smallest detail. For instance, Eustace told Randy, "Do you like chocolate? Do you want to know the best way to eat it? Just put a tiny square of it under your tongue and let it melt there. That way, you'll get the most flavor over the longest time and never take any of it for granted."

Eustace was crazy about Randy Cable and about Randy's father, a mountain-raised man who knew everything about hunting and fishing and what kind of wild greens you could collect from the river banks for food. Eustace went to Randy's house as often as he could. Randy visited the Conways' place far less often. It wasn't as comfortable there. Mrs. Conway was nice, but Mr. Conway was scary. Dinnertime was an especially terrifying event. The children rarely spoke during the meal and neither did their mom. Mr. Conway, seated at the head of the table, was stern and sarcastic, with a hair-trigger temper. All his attention, it seemed, was concentrated on Eustace. If the boy even started to speak, Mr. Conway would ridicule his grammar. If the boy mentioned something about his day, Mr. Conway would laugh it off as "ridiculous, childish." If Mr. Conway asked Eustace how he'd done on a recent math test, and got an answer he didn't like, he would release a barrage of insults and ridicule.

"You are stupid," Eustace recalls his father saying. "I've never met a child more dimwitted. I don't know how I could have sired so idiotic a son. What are we to surmise? I believe you are simply incompetent and will never learn anything."

And then Mr. Conway would encourage the younger children to laugh along with him at the ludicrous stupidity of their worthless older brother. Which they would willingly do, in the manner of the outcast kids at the lunch table with the braces on their legs who are always relieved to see another child bullied in their stead.

The other matter that stood out to Randy Cable was the incessant harping on table manners. He'd never been in a "proper" household before and or experienced such rigid formality at mealtime. If Eustace ate too fast or used a utensil incorrectly, the father would come down on him with both feet for his "absurd and primitive" table manners. It made Randy nervous to pick up his fork; he never got in trouble for anything like this at home. Thirty years later, Randy is still puzzled by Mr. Conway's emphasis on mealtime etiquette. "At our dinner table," Randy recalls, "it was every guy for himself."

Yeah, well. It was something like that at Eustace's dinner table, too.

The reasoning behind a man's decision to name his firstborn son after himself has, I think, many factors. I understand that the custom is generally seen as a mere societal convention (particularly in the American

South) but it seems to me more loaded. Some interpret the custom as vanity, but I wonder whether it's vanity's opposite: insecurity. To me, it seems a touching and hopeful wish, as if the father—frightened by the importance of having created a new life, a new man, a new rival—utters a small prayer that in the naming of his baby there will be a kind of twinship between himself and the child. In wearing this most familiar name, the child is no longer a stranger or a possible usurper. It's as though the father can look upon his newborn son without fear and proclaim: *You are me; I am you.*

But he is not you, and you are not him. Which is why there is ultimately as much danger in this custom as there is comfort.

Mr. Conway's full name is Eustace Robinson Conway III, and he named his son Eustace Robinson Conway IV. From the beginning, the two were differentiated only by an adjective: Big vs. Little. They even looked alike, the Big and Little Eustaces, with the same wide and intelligent hooded brown eyes. At first, Big Eustace was beside himself with joy at having a Little Eustace in the house. He was wonderful with his baby, charmed by him, proud as could be, attentive, patient, affectionate, boastful. Wanted to play with him all the time. And when the baby got a little bigger, he'd take him out to the woods behind the family's house and point up into the trees and say, "Look . . ."

Little Eustace was bright and keen, and that certainly made sense, because Big Eustace was an acknowledged genius. The pride of an old, wealthy family of Southern landowners and businessmen, Big Eustace was a chemical engineer with a doctoral degree from MIT. (He had skipped grades in high school, skipped more grades in college, and had walked out of MIT with his doctorate in his early twenties.) He had a true gift for numbers and for science. More than a gift, it was a *love*. Calculus, to Big Eustace, unfolded its mysteries as easily as harmony unfolds for those who are blessed with musical instinct. As for physics? Gorgeous. Trigonometry? A pleasure. Chemistry? Why, there was nothing hidden in chemistry but ease, fascination, and excitement. He lived for puzzles and figures and tables and equations. He was, in his favorite self-description, a man whose "whole being is controlled by pure logic."

Was he vain? Perhaps. If so, only because it was logical to be vain in a world where other humans were amusingly careless creatures who made choices based on whims and emotion instead of precise reason.

Eustace Robinson Conway III was, through his twenties, on the faculty of the University of South Carolina and North Carolina State, where he taught chemical engineering to students not much younger than he was. It was good work, but he didn't like the politicized world of academia. He always had trouble working with people. Eventually he left teaching and found employment in the private sector, at a chemical plant. He did not socialize with his peers there, either, but his intellect was respected and a bit feared. A former co-worker, who remembers Big Eustace as *Dr.* Conway, recalls coming to him one day with a quick question about a specific chemical formula. Eager to give the answer with explicit thoroughness, Dr. Conway started writing an equation on a blackboard, and kept writing and adding more data until the equation snaked across the whole blackboard, expanding into new chemical concepts, until, giddy with excitement, he ran out of blackboard to write on. By which point, of course, he had long since lost the comprehension of his co-worker.

Frankly, he was in love with his brain, so he must have delighted in watching the evolution of his son's brain. Surely it was exciting for him to see his namesake cleverly solving all those wonderful dilemmas encountered in human infant development. See how he learns to tell sunlight from shadow? See how he learns to identify faces and objects? See how he pulls himself up to stand? How he tries to make sentences? How you can show him the shape of a leaf and he'll tell you the name of the tree? What a genius! Any minute now, he should be ready to solve calculus problems for fun!

And then Little Eustace turned two.

At breakfast on the birthday morning, Big Eustace gave a present to his son, who was still in the highchair. Big Eustace was eager to see his boy play with the gift before he left for work. It was a jigsaw puzzle. But it was far too sophisticated for a two-year-old, and Little Eustace, frustrated after a few attempts to put it together, quickly lost interest. As Mrs. Conway remembers, her husband went crazy on the kid. "He started screaming at him and saying terrible things." The child, horrified and confused, was howling at the top of his voice, and when Mrs. Conway tried to intervene, her husband screamed at her, too, for spoiling the baby and encouraging him to be a quitter and an imbecile. Jesus Christ! The puzzle was simple! It was obvious! What kind of mentally retarded child can't put together a simple jigsaw puzzle?

As perhaps goes without saying, things didn't get better as time passed. Only horribly worse. Mr. Conway decided that his son was goading him by acting stupid out of "stubbornness," and that what the boy needed, therefore, was more discipline. So it is that Eustace remembers—and his mother and siblings confirm—an upbringing that was more like a stint in a POW camp than a real childhood. If Little Eustace so much as touched a hammer from Big Eustace's toolshed without asking permission, he would be sent to his room and forced to stay there for hours without food or water. If Little Eustace didn't finish every morsel on his plate in proper time, Big Eustace would force him to sit at the dinner table all night, even if it meant the child had to sleep upright in his chair. If Little Eustace, in his play, accidentally kicked up a divot of grass from his father's lawn, he would be beaten with a wooden paddle. If Little Eustace, in doing his chores, dared to mow the grass in a counterclockwise pattern instead of the clockwise pattern his father had commanded, there would be a huge scene and hell to pay.

Looking back on it now—and he is surprisingly willing to do so—Mr. Conway concedes that mistakes may have been made. Maybe he was a little hard on the boy. But his interest was only in producing a perfect child, and his anger was the result of the keen disappointments he suffered through his son's unanticipated shortfalls.

"It is very human," he told me, "to think that you can control your children, but now I realize it's an impossible proposition. The best plan is to have no plan at all; just let them go and become the people they were meant to be. But I didn't realize that when I was a young parent. I was excited to have a son, and I figured I could manipulate Eustace to be the way I wanted him to be. But he turned out to have all these personality problems. I wanted him to be just like me!"

"How so?" I asked.

"I expected him to be a good student, at the very least, as I had been. I certainly thought that a son of mine would be able to count! I used to work with him for hours, trying to teach him how to count a stack of pennies, but he was incapable of learning. He was the antithesis of what I'd expected. I wanted to work on projects with him, but he was impossible to work with. Always a problem child. I don't understand him at all. We cannot understand each other."

On another occasion, I asked Mr. Conway, "Do you ever wish that things were different between you and Eustace?"

He answered immediately, as though he had been waiting for this very question.

"It has been a true disappointment for me to have this flawed relationship with Eustace. It is the greatest disappointment of my life. And I don't know what to do about it. I don't think there's any hope of my having a good relationship with him."

"No hope? No hope whatsoever?"

"I hesitate to subscribe to the theory that I did not love my son enough. Perhaps people will say this is true. I don't know. But I believe that I loved my son very much. I was excited to have a son. Did I tell you that? I could not *wait* for him to be born."

Eustace Conway, it must be said, also remembers those stacks of pennies. Night after night, on the living room floor, hour after hour, his father would amass and divide piles of pennies and demand of Eustace the answers to division and addition and multiplication problems. He remembers the horrifying blankness that his mind would retreat to, and his father's refusal to allow him to go to bed until he got it right, forcing him to stay up past midnight with those frightful stacks of pennies. Then his own weeping and his father's screaming. The humiliation and the endless ridicule.

There was something both extreme and personal about Mr. Conway's reactions to his oldest son. It was as if he had early made a decision to refuse to validate this child, to the point of flat-out bizarreness. When Eustace's picture began to appear in the newspaper for successes in competition with his Indian dance troupe, his father wouldn't read the articles. ("Ridiculous, in my opinion," he would say, "but nobody's listening to me.") When Eustace was presented with a national youth achievement award from the Smithsonian Institution, his father did not attend the ceremony.

At Christmas one year Little Eustace, having saved all his money, bought his father peanuts and chewing gum as a gift because he knew his father loved peanuts and chewing gum. On Christmas morning, he nervously presented his father with the gift. Big Eustace accepted the package, said "Thank you," set it aside, but never unwrapped it.

To make everything worse, Eustace was not a good student. He did all right in kindergarten (his report card shows that he could satisfactorily hop, tie his shoes, get along with others, obey orders cheerfully, and recite his telephone number), but by second grade he was getting straight C's, making only average progress, and needing, his teacher suggested, "a great deal more help at home with his work."

"Eustace puts forth little effort in his work," reported his third-grade teacher. "He needs to memorize his addition-number facts."

What a prescription! The seven-year-old was already locked down at the kitchen table for four hours a night with a father who would shut the doors and pull down the window shades (thus isolating both Big and Little Eustace from the rest of the family) and yell at his son over the arithmetic homework in dead privacy. More help at home? Eustace was already wound up like an eight-day clock over the whole concept of school, scared to death of homework, gripped in panic over the dreaded nightly cycle of effort and failure and punishment. It wasn't the brand of child abuse you read about in the papers; it wasn't as if Little Eustace was collecting cigarette burns on his arms. But make no mistake about it: he was utterly traumatized. He was so distressed that his fear manifested itself in a particular physical grip; he was constipated throughout his whole childhood, "too terrified to even take a shit."

"Night after night," Eustace remembers, "week after week, month after month, year after year, it was as if my father would cut my legs off. Then he'd cut off the stumps where the legs had been. Then he'd cut off my arms. Then he would run the sword through my body."

* * *

There were three other children in the house—Walton, Martha, and cute baby Judson. Their experiences were all different, which makes sense if you subscribe to the theory that every child in every family is basically raised in a different country, given how vastly events may vary over the years. When the other children came along, they never took the kind of heat from their father that Eustace suffered.

Judson, the youngest, seems to have missed out more than anyone on the hardest drama of the family, the way that the lucky and oblivious youngest child always seems to do. His father was "stubborn and self-ish," but Judson was never terrified of him. He was an adorable child, whom his father loved and called Little Bug. Anyway, by the time Judson was born, his father had essentially given up on raising perfect children, had turned them over to his wife, and, in his own words, had "abdicated down to the basement" to brood in resentful silence. So Judson never saw the worst of it.

Judson's childhood, in effect, was an endless summer camp, because he had this older brother, Eustace, who took him out into the woods and made him climb mountains and taught him cool things about nature. Judson was, from birth, Eustace's special project; Eustace was always getting him out of the house and into the woods, where things were safer. He was trying to keep Judson hidden from the radar of Big Eustace. It was a deliberate decision that Eustace clearly remembers making. He knew it was too late to save Walton and Martha (he felt they had already been "brainwashed" by their father), but when Judson was born, Eustace took one look at him and said to himself, "This one's mine. I'm going to save his life." In return, Judson worshipped Eustace, although, he admits, "I was never the achiever Eustace wanted me to be. I was lazy. He'd be, like, 'Let's make buckskin!' and I wanted to stay in my bedroom and play with my Star Wars action figures. But I'd do anything to have his company."

Martha, the only daughter, was a serious and responsible child who remembers a girlhood wholly different from those of her girlfriends—one of snakes and turtles and baby foxes that had to be fed live birds and long expeditions with Eustace ("the ringleader") out into the woods, where elaborate adventures took place. She remembers the dangers she and her brothers faced. All those afternoons spent messing around with raging rivers and poisonous spiders and homemade tree houses! Now, a highly organized and strictly protective suburban mother, she cannot even *begin* to comprehend why she and her brothers were allowed to glean such experiences unsupervised. She remembers a hard father, yes, but also an inconsistently permissive mother, and the fights that took place between the two parents over childrearing. ("Make up your minds!" Martha always wanted to yell at them.) And she remembers Eustace as a child who "brought trouble on himself" by not doing as well in school as Daddy expected and by being "stubborn."

As for Walton Conway, he can barely remember the details of his childhood. It was "a blur, some paintbrush strokes of a dark color." That, and a recurrent childhood nightmare that his father was going to take him down into the basement, tie him to a table, and saw off his limbs. That, and a specific middle-of-the-night episode where his parents were fighting and his father screamed at his mother that he was going to "drive an icepick through her heart." That, and a remembrance of seeing his father towering over his ten-year-old brother Eustace, threatening to "beat him to a bloody pulp."

But it wasn't as bad as Eustace makes out, Walton says. His father was certainly capable of tender moments, like drying the tears of a child with a skinned knee. And what about that horrible night when Walton threatened to run away from home and his father broke down the bedroom door, caught his son slipping over the windowsill to escape, and then shoved Walton out the window? Well, it wasn't really a *shove*. It wasn't as if Mr. Conway intentionally threw his young son out a second-story window; he "just kind of pushed me a little bit."

Anyhow. What Walton does not remember is the sense that his father was the prime source of the discontent and problems around the house. No, that was Eustace. Eustace was always the problem. Even as a young child, he made everything harder than it had to be. He was sullen, unhappy, and willful, and he "didn't do his homework." Daddy was moody and strict, yes, but he could be appeased with obedience. To both Walton and Martha, who were superior students and always at the top of their classes, the solution to the family's unhappiness was pretty obvious: if Eustace would excel in school, Daddy would be happy. If Eustace would stop being so stubborn, Daddy would stop yelling at Mother and everybody else.

"Why couldn't you give him any authority?" Walton would demand of Eustace, years later. "Why couldn't you bend? Why did you always have to do things your own way, even as a toddler, just to spite him? Why did you always have to stand up to him and make him so mad?"

When asked for examples, though, Walton can't remember a single specific instance of Eustace standing up to his father. Yet he feels certain that it must have happened. In fact, his image of Eustace as an aggressive challenger to his father, as an equally matched and willful adversary ("even as a toddler"), is one that Mr. Conway depicts and that the younger Conway siblings have all faithfully embraced. However, the notion of a combative Little Eustace is hardly consistent with the reports of outside adults who visited the Conway household during those years. Mr. Stout, of the Scheile Museum, remembers being invited to dinners at the Conways' home, where he watched young Eustace eat in petrified silence, submissive and nervous and careful to "never make eye contact with his father."

One of Eustace's aunts remembers Mr. Conway waking four-year-old Eustace late at night and bringing him down to meet the company, then tossing difficult math questions to the child and grilling him to perform. Each time Little Eustace answered incorrectly, he was mocked and humiliated by Big Eustace, because this verbal batting-around was supposed to be entertainment for the guests, mind you. And so it went, on and on, until the boy was in a tearful meltdown, at which point the aunt left the room, thinking she could watch no more of this, thinking it "sadistic, the worst abuse of a child" she had ever witnessed, and promising herself that she would never return to this house again.

And, like Mr. Stout, the aunt apparently does not remember Little Eustace, at any point in the evening, saying anything to his father along the lines of "Up yours, Dad."

Still, when Walton remembers hearing his father threaten to beat his brother to a bloody pulp, the question he asks is, *What did Eustace do to make Daddy so angry that time?* When Walton remembers hearing his father threaten to drive an icepick through his mother's heart, he supposes, *They must have been fighting about Eustace again.* And if Eustace had to spend hours locked in his room without food or water, *Well, the boy really must have misbehaved something fierce that time.*

Perhaps the more difficult part of this story to understand is where the mother was during all this pain. How could it be that Karen Conway— who had once been Karen Johnson, the unrepentant tomboy horse-back-champion able-bodied woodsman of a girl who sold her silver flute for passage to Alaska at the age of twenty-two—had grown into a woman who could not protect her son? Why was she never able to shield Little Eustace from Big Eustace?

She herself cannot explain it today. Such are the mysteries of a marriage, I suppose, and such are the tragedies of a family. Mrs. Conway says now that she was afraid of her husband. She was catching a lot of the same kind of abuse as her son. (Her husband seemed to love nothing more than egging his children on to make fun of their mother by calling her a "big fat hippo.") Her friends and family encouraged her to leave the marriage, but she never found the courage to go away for long. Some of this was surely due to Mrs. Conway's sincere Christianity, which had her convinced that divorce was a mortal sin. And some of it was due to . . . who knows? Who knows why women stay? What she does remember is that whenever she did try to defend her son, it only made her husband more furious and more extreme in his punishments of Little Eustace. So she decided early on that it was kinder not to step in or interfere.

Instead, she devised ways to deliver secret help to her son. As though Eustace were a jailed dissident doing time in the solitary confinement block of a totalitarian prison, she would slip clandestine encouragement to him, under the door and through the chinks in the walls. Sometimes she literally slipped him notes ("with love from the one who has faith in you and cares most about you . . ."), and she also showed him affection privately, when nobody was looking. She gave him both the skills and freedom to explore the woods, where he could not only excel, but could breathe in a sense of safety far away from the tornado alley that was home. And what she also gave her son, more vital than anything else, was the secret but persistent idea that no matter what his father might do or say, Eustace Robinson Conway IV would grow up to be a Man of Destiny.

The Man of Destiny theory wasn't Karen Conway's invention. She had absorbed it from her father, an extraordinary idealist named C. Walton Johnson. This character, Eustace's maternal grandfather, was an upright World War I veteran whom everyone called Chief. Immediately on returning home from the war, Chief Johnson founded the North Carolina branch of the Boy Scouts of America. He wanted to work with boys because of his strong idea—no, let's go ahead and call it an inflexible and didactic dogma—about the process by which weak little boys could be transformed into powerful Men of Destiny. He believed that this evolution was best accomplished in the challenges of a frontier-like environment, and, like many Americans before and after him, he was apprehensive about how the evaporation of the wilderness would affect the development of American manhood. And Chief Johnson was not about to stand back and let America's boys grow up effete, decadent, and pampered by the "softening and vision-curbing influence of the city."

No, sir. Not on his watch.

So the first Boy Scout troop in North Carolina was a good start, but Chief quickly grew disillusioned with the program, feeling that it pampered the boys. Therefore, in 1924, he founded an extremely rigorous private summer camp on 125 mountainous acres near Asheville. He named it Camp Sequoyah for Boys: Where the Weak Become Strong and the Strong Become Great. (Unfortunately, it is nowhere recorded whether the Weak ever became Great, but I'd be willing to bet they tried.) He asked of his campers and his staff only one thing: that they ceaselessly strive to achieve physical, moral, and intellectual perfection in every aspect of their lives. Then, and only then, could they become Men of Destiny.

"Every age has need for Men of Destiny," Chief wrote, in one of his many published tracts on the topic, "and in every age, some men will respond to the need, as did Aristotle, Galileo, and Wilson. . . . These men believed they were Men of Destiny, and prepared themselves for the task that lay ahead. They were gripped by a compulsion that they could not resist. No man becomes a Man of Destiny unless he believes, with great conviction, that he has a unique contribution to make to the society of his day. Conceit? No! Just a sense of mission and the courage to follow through. He who is *compelled* by an inner conviction that he has a mission which he *must* accomplish, that he was born for this purpose, that he *must* and *will* follow through; that man will be a Man of Destiny."

The best way to groom such heroic figures was to start with the young, Chief believed, and in the wild. After all, he wrote, "the real American boy has inherited too much of the pioneer spirit to feel at home in the city." So he suggested that parents remove their boys from the "emotional stress of life" and relocate them to "a Camp with a Purpose," where the "grandeur of the mountains," combined with the guidance of counselors selected by the director for their "mature, wholesome, intelligent, responsible leadership," would help the boys grow, "as nature and God intended, into the full stature of manhood."

Camp Sequoyah was no Hitler Youth Camp. Chief believed that no boy in America, no matter how weak or how flawed (or, incredibly, given the era, no matter what race or religion), should be excluded from the opportunity to become a Man of Destiny through attending Camp Sequoyah. Was your son a "regular healthy boy" already blessed with a "superb physique"? Why, he would naturally return from Sequoyah "with his splendid powers multiplied." Was your son "over-bright, sullen, and sometimes antagonistic?" Don't hesitate to enroll him in Sequoyah; the fresh air will teach him "the necessity of developing his body and keeping it on par with his mind." Was your son "timid, diffident, and slow to make friends?" Sequoyah would teach him to socialize. Was your son a bully? Sequoyah's counselors would teach him that picking on others was "cowardly and despicable." Why, even if your son was "big and fat and always being teased," Camp Sequoyah was where he should go, if not to achieve a superb physique, then at least to learn how to "take a joke and to make the best of being teased."

Eustace Conway's mother was Chief Johnson's only daughter. (There's a wonderful photograph of Sequoyah in the 1940s, with the whole camp gathered in rows according to age. It's all ramrod-straight men and earnest crewcut boys grinning at the camera, with one exception—the little blond girl in a white dress seated at the center of the throng—Chief's daughter, Eustace Conway's mother, age five.) Karen grew up at Camp Sequoyah, surrounded not only by woods and boys, but by ideals. She loved her father and, more than either of her siblings, obediently accepted his dogma. When it came time for Karen to marry, she even chose one of her father's favorite counselors as a husband. She fell in love with the brilliant young Eustace Conway III, who, with his strict personal discipline, physical grace, MIT degree, and keen love of the outdoors, must have seemed the incarnation of Chief's dearest principles.

And though her husband put aside his dreams of teaching the natural world when he entered corporate life, she never lost *her* belief in the woods. So when Karen Conway's first son was born, there was no question as to how she would raise him. Free, challenged, inspired to attempt heroic feats, and always outdoors. It was due to his mother's hand that Eustace could throw a knife accurately enough at the age of seven to nail a chipmunk to a tree. And kill a running squirrel at fifty feet with a bow and arrow by the time he was ten. And set forth into the woods, alone and empty-handed, when he was twelve, to live off the land and build his own shelter.

While Mr. Conway kept patiently explaining to young Eustace what a feeble idiot the boy was, Mrs. Conway went to the library every day and brought home bigger and bigger piles of inspiring American biographies for Eustace to read. George Washington, Davy Crockett, Daniel Boone, Abraham Lincoln, Kit Carson, John Frémont, Andrew Jackson, Geronimo, Red Cloud, Sitting Bull—bold, unironic tales of heroism and wilderness and fortitude. These were the lives to emulate, she told her son when Big Eustace wasn't listening. This is the kind of man you can be: a Man of Destiny.

Eustace Conway was a literal-minded creature even as a child (especially as a child), and he absorbed the morals of these stories as purely as though his mother were holding a funnel to his ear and pouring them straight into his brain. When he read that Indian braves tested their mental and physical endurance by running miles across the desert holding water in their mouths but not swallowing it, he tried to run miles through the forest doing the same. When he read that frontiersmen used to wear the same pair of buckskin trousers for years at a time, he resolved to make himself a pair and never wear anything else. When he read that Lewis and Clark brought as much paper and ink on their journey as food and bullets, he started keeping his diary. When he read of the Indian brave left behind enemy lines in a battle with settlers—wounded and abandoned with a bullet through his knee—who survived the entire winter by hiding in a ditch, covered by leaves, and eating the rodents who crawled over him . . . well, that scenario was impossible to follow exactly, but Eustace imitated the spirit of the story by asking the family dentist to please not use Novocain when filling his cavities. He wanted to learn how to endure physical pain.

Back when he was in grammar school, Eustace would bring about six such heroic biographies and action-adventure books into the classroom every day. He'd read a book until the teacher confiscated it, and then he'd start on another. When she snatched that one, he'd begin another and then another. When all the books were gone, he'd stare out the window and plan projects inspired by his readings. He was only in second grade, for instance, when he started building himself a five-story tree house (complete with a basement and walkways that extended into branches of the tree next door), modeled after the descriptions in *The Swiss Family Robinson.*

Naturally, the schoolteachers had no idea of what to do with this odd boy who would not pay attention in class. When he was in fifth grade, his teacher had to call Mrs. Conway in for a conference.

She said, "I don't think Eustace is capable of learning."

But it was too late; he was already learned, certainly in the skills and morals his mother had taught him. And if her ideas about raising her son conflicted with her husband's ideas, the trick was not to combine their philosophies into one childrearing doctrine, but to apply each individually—one loud and public, the other secretive and steadfast. The father's strict humiliations were applied only in the evenings and over the weekends; the mother's stirring challenges were reserved for the long and free days in the woods. The trait these parents shared was absolute emphasism. Both placed Eustace in the center of their attention, where he received either high praise or demeaning shame. Eustace's mother told him that he was a Man of Destiny and there was no achievement on this planet too lofty for him; his father told him he was useless.

Literal-minded creature that he was, the poor kid believed them both. How his head didn't explode from the contradictions, it's hard to say. But it is little wonder that Eustace spent a significant number of his youthful hours pondering the possibility that he might be the subject of a vast and sadistic science experiment. Maybe his whole life was playing out in some grand laboratory, where he was being tested, his reactions studied closely by scientists he could neither see nor understand. What other explanation could make sense of this? That one afternoon Eustace got a letter from his mother on the sly telling him he was "a handsome, bold, fearless, interesting, loving son of whom to be proud and for whom to be grateful," and yet, maybe later the same day, would report in his diary that his father had told him he was "no smarter 'than a nigger in the slums.' I felt like killing him. I wonder what is to happen to me."

He slept only a few hours every night. After the rest of the family had gone to bed, Eustace would stay up until two or three or four in the morning. He would finish his schoolwork, which was always drudgery for him except the rare circumstances when he had the opportunity to write term papers on topics like "The Teepee Then and Now." When his homework was done, he would write in his diary, cramming the pages with his deeds and observations.

"Today, I went to Robinwood Lake for the first time this year and I caught a big female painted turtle I had let go last winter for hibernating."

"Today, I finally saw all three tree frogs in my terrarium at the same time."

"Today, Randy Cable caught an albino salamander and I put it in alcohol."

"The black rat snake is happy in his new cage."

He would read over his journal, trying to record his progress in becoming a competent woodsman. Every day he set higher challenges for himself in the wilderness because, as he later said, "I grew up in a culture and a family that had no way of providing me with rites of passage into manhood, so I had to invent them for myself."

After writing in his journal, Eustace would stay up long into the night, obsessively perfecting his skills at beadwork and weaving. He'd sometimes spend months working on a single pair of buckskin moccasins, distracting his mind by sitting in low light with an old book about Plains Indian artifacts lying open across his bed, replicating the complicated beaded patterns in the pictures of antique Indian clothing.

His unhappy world of extremes had fostered in Eustace a fierce perfectionism. It was important for him to live every moment of his life completely free of mistakes, both to minimize his father's opportunities to ridicule him and to prove to his mother that her intense praise was earned. The bar he set for himself was incredibly high. (He would lament in his journals years later that he never felt the "timeless freedom of youth" but was instead haunted by the "overhanging threat of incompletion.") Even in his private moments, even in the middle of the night, when he was working secretly on his beloved projects of Indian beadwork, his efforts had to be faultlessly executed, or the work would bring him no comfort. Tearing up his stitches when they were imperfect and trying again, Eustace refined each line of beads across his moccasins until the patterns exactly matched those of the ancient Cheyenne masters. He was making art back there in his bedroom on Deerwood Drive that a child had no business even attempting.

When he was finally exhausted, he would turn off his light and consider sleep. Sometimes he'd listen to his parents arguing as he lay in the dark. Often, he would cry. Just as often, he would hold a hunting knife pressed against his throat as he was falling asleep. It was strangely consoling to feel the blade across his neck. It was somehow comforting to know that he could kill himself at a moment's notice if things got too bad. Having that option somehow always gave him the peace he needed to finally drift off.

# CHAPTER THREE

Thus situated, many hundred miles from our families in the howling wilderness, I believe few would have equally enjoyed the happiness we experienced. I often observed to my brother, you see how little nature requires to be satisfied? Felicity, the companion of content, is rather found in our breasts than in the enjoyment of external things.

—*Daniel Boone*

Davy Crockett ran away from home when he was thirteen years old, to escape an irate father. Daniel Boone's father used to beat his sons until they begged for mercy, but Daniel would never break. ("Canst thou not beg?" his father would demand.) Instead, young Daniel spent whole days alone in the woods to get away from his father's domain and, by the age of fifteen, had earned a reputation as one of the best hunters in the Pennsylvania wilderness. The explorer John Frémont was five when he lost his father. Kit Carson lost his father (who was killed by the falling limb of a burning tree and left his wife to raise eight children alone), and Kit ran away from home when he was sixteen. The mountain man Jim Bridger was on his own at fourteen.

None of this was unusual for the time. The wagon trails to the West were filled with young boys who had left home for any number of reasons—but no small number of them, we can be sure, hit the frontier because they believed that even the most dangerous unknowns in the world were more appealing than whatever business was going on back there in that small cabin in New England or Virginia or Tennessee. There is a lot of talk in our history books about what *drew* young men to the frontier, but I wouldn't be at all surprised if bad relationships with tough fathers was one of the major factors that *pushed* them out there.

And so it is that every generation finds a new wave of boys busting out of their homes, just dying to go anywhere that takes them away from Dad. It sure is a good way to populate a country pretty fast, although perhaps not ideal for the emotional lives of our families. Eustace Conway was trying to do the same—trying to escape. His adolescent years were an endless trauma, and he dreamed constantly of running away.

"Right before I went to bed," he wrote in his diary as a fourteen-year-old, "daddy came in and lectured me about how I should act toward people and about how I only care about myself. He said that nobody will like me and that I boss everybody and that I do not do anything for anybody else. Although it would be a dumb thing to run away, I think I would happier anywhere in the woods. If I do leave, I will try my best not to come back, even if I am starving. Anything is better than this."

But he didn't bolt. He stuck it out for three more years. Only when he had dutifully finished high school did Eustace Conway split. He took the teepee he'd made by hand (an older Native American woman who knew Eustace at the time described it as "the prettiest thing I've ever seen") and he took his knife and he took some books and he was gone.

"I hope that I am right," he confided to his diary when he moved out of his parents' home, "and that I am following a path that is indeed good for me."

What followed were probably the happiest years of Eustace's life. And the freest. He owned a teepee and he owned a motorcycle, and that was about it. He lived in and around the mountains near Gastonia. He rebuilt the motorcycle to learn about the workings of an engine. He sewed all his own clothes. He ate nettles and hunted small game with a Cherokee blowgun, using darts he made from sticks, thistledown, and strands of deer tendon. He carved his bowls and plates from wood polished with beaver fat. He made his water jugs out of the clay he dug from the basins of creeks, the same creeks where he bathed. He slept on the ground, on animal skins. He wove ropes out of bark and his own hair. He split white oak and wove it into baskets. He cooked and warmed himself over fire, and he did not touch a match for three years.

"My lodge looks in passable shape," he wrote in his diary, once his new home was in order. "And I hope that I grow to know it and myself better through the lifestyle that I am taking up at the present." His new life did take some getting used to ("In the middle of the night it began to rain and so I reluctantly got out of bed and closed the smoke flaps, which should have been taken care of earlier"), but Eustace Conway felt almost immediately that he was at last living on this earth as he had been meant to live. "I slept until seven in the morning," he wrote after one of his first nights in the teepee, "when the sun beaming down on the smoky canvas called my attention to the world. I got up and washed my face in spring water. Oh, how my body loves me! Happy day to all!"

His teepee was wonderful—a fort and a temple, a home so satisfyingly light and transient that it had none of the psychological impact of a house's overstability. He could put it together or break it down in a matter of minutes. He could pack it up, load it onto the top of a friend's car, drive it to an elementary school, and throw it together again on the playground for the delight of some grammar school kids he'd been hired to teach about nature that day. He could haul his teepee off to a powwow in another state for a weekend of dancing and fellowship with the Native Americans he had befriended over the years. He could pack it in storage while he went hitchhiking across the country on a whim, or he could hang out in his teepee, hidden somewhere in the woods, completely jazzed by the knowledge that nobody could find him.

He took a job after high school, but only for a little while. He headed down to Tennessee to work as a nature educator for learning-disabled and troubled kids at a place called the Bodine School. He was brilliant with the students, even though he was not much older than they were. He had terrific rapport with them, but he didn't hit it off so well with his bosses. Eustace Conway, it should be said, does not take much truck in working under the authority of other people. It rubs him wrong. He quickly got into a dispute with the principal, who had promised Eustace that he could live in his teepee on the grounds of the campus but had reneged on the promise. And Eustace Conway does not take much truck from people who renege on their promises.

So, restless and irritated, he took off to visit a woodsy young guy he knew named Frank, who was going to college in Alabama. They had a good weekend visit. Kicked around in the forest and shot at things with an old-fashioned black powder rifle and made jokes. But Eustace had a sense that his friend was bothered by something, and, indeed, it emerged in subsequent conversation that Frank had broken up with his girlfriend and was floundering wildly—had quit doing sports, quit going to school, then quit working at his job. He didn't have the first idea of what to do with himself next. When he finished telling Eustace his sad story, Eustace said ("and the words just leaped out of my mouth like a frog leaping out of a hot frying pan"), *Let's hike the Appalachian Trail.*

He couldn't even say where the idea had come from. But suddenly it was out there.

"Sure," Frank said. "Let's do it."

So Eustace called the principal of the Bodine School and quit his teaching job (no big deal; the guy was a jerk who broke his word, and who needs a damn job, anyhow?), and four days later the two young men were standing in a bus station in Montgomery, Alabama, waiting for a Greyhound to take them up to Bangor, Maine. The suddenness and brashness of the decision surprised even Eustace's mother, who could usually be counted on to encourage such adventures.

"Your phone call with news came as a big surprise," she wrote to him in a quick note, trying to catch him before he was gone. "I have mixed feelings about your planned hiking trip. I can understand why you desire to make such a trip and agree with the good aspects of it, but on the other side of the seesaw, it shows irresponsibility at keeping your word and inability to put important things first." What she then added was a little provocative (in addition to being obvious) but she probably threw it in there to punctuate her own concerns: "Your father feels that you are a playboy and will never settle down if you don't start taking life seriously and think more about preparing for your future. He thinks you should be working more and being more dependable to keep your promises of commitment. He disapproves!"

Well, tough. That's what people turn nineteen for.

Their adventure started right off with an adventure. Eustace and Frank bought their bus tickets but couldn't get on the bus until one last problem was solved. They were waiting at the station for a girl, a friend of Frank's, to show up with his sleeping bag, a vital piece of equipment. They waited and waited, but the girl never showed. They begged the Greyhound driver to stall, but he finally had to take off to keep to his schedule. Frank and Eustace were devastated. And then, only moments after the bus pulled away, the girl and sleeping bag arrived. Frank and Eustace jumped into the girl's station wagon and took off down the interstate, chasing the bus. When they caught up with it, Eustace told the girl to pull up alongside. They honked and waved, but, though the other passengers were staring, riveted, the driver pretended that they didn't exist. Eustace Conway wasn't going to be ignored and he damn sure wasn't going to miss this Greyhound to Maine. So he told the girl to pull her car—speeding away at seventy-five miles an hour—right up under the bus driver's window. Eustace rolled down his passenger-side window, pulled himself out, and stood on top of the station wagon, gripping the roof rack with one hand and clutching his and Frank's bus tickets with the other. He waved the tickets in front of the driver's face and kept hollering into the wind, "*Let us on this bus!*"

"At that point," Eustace remembers, "the driver decided maybe he'd better pull over and let us on. All the passengers were cheering, and as we walked down the aisle this one big fat lady shouted, 'Lawd! Y'all coulda been in a movie!'"

They got to Maine and hitchhiked to Bangor and found that they had arrived too early in the year. The rangers warned them not to even *think* about going over the timberline while there was so much deep snow and heavy ice on the ground. Of course, they ignored the warning and headed up the mountain before dawn the next day, and on that afternoon they saw a bald eagle careening in the cold and thin air, and they were on their way, a month ahead of other climbers.

Here's what they hadn't figured on: they never had enough to eat on that trail. Never, never, never. They were ravenous. They were hiking twenty-five and thirty miles a day on barely any food. They had some oatmeal with them, and that was about it. Each would have a cup of oatmeal every morning. Frank would gulp down his puny meal and then stare mournfully at Eustace while Eustace savored every flake as if it were a precious square of chocolate. On the first leg of the trip they found virtually no game on the trail to hunt; it was too early in the year for the animals to come up this high above the timberline, and, moreover, the ground was solid ice, with no edible plants in sight.

When they got to New Hampshire, half mad with hunger, Eustace spotted some partridges in the underbrush. He whipped out a length of string he'd been keeping in his pocket, fashioned a noose about eight inches in diameter, wrapped the string around a long stick, and sneaked up on the next partridge he spotted. He dropped that noose over the bird, tightened the string, made a grab, and ripped off its head. Frank was screaming and dancing and shouting and hugging and kissing Eustace while the still-flapping bird sprayed blood over the packed, white snow. "My God," Eustace recalls, "but we ate the hell out of that bird." They ate its meat; they ate its brains; they ate its feet; and, still famished, they ate every last one of its bones.

They were so driven by hunger that they became great hunters. Eustace taught Frank how to catch a bird with a noose (thank goodness for this skill, an old game he'd played with Randy Cable), and together they scrounged the trail as they headed south. They also took to eating crawfish and trout and berries, nettles, anything. They killed rattlesnakes and opened them up to see if there were baby rabbits or something else yummy inside the bellies; they'd eat the snake and whatever the snake had just eaten. Eustace even killed a spruce partridge one day with a rock. He saw the bird, thought to himself, *I need to eat that,* grabbed the nearest rock, chucked it, nailed the bird dead, and then ate every part of that blessed creature except the feathers.

They were determined to be hunters and gatherers. It was hard going and a weird place to try this out; the heavily traveled corridor of the Appalachian Trail was already so stripped by human beings that food was harder to find than in normal forests. And Eustace well knew it wouldn't make any environmental sense if every hiker on the A.T. further stripped the land by doing what he was doing. Conscious of all that and maybe feeling a little guilty about overtaxing some already overtaxed land, he continued the experiment. He knew that primitive people had traveled huge distances on foot in millennia past, eating only what they could find along the journey, and he was sure that he and Frank could endure it, too. But that didn't change the fact that they were starving to death.

They ate whatever they could hunt, pick, scavenge, or sometimes steal. When they hit Bear Mountain Park in New York State, they happened to swing through on the Fourth of July, when hundreds of Puerto Rican and Dominican families were picnicking and celebrating. It was a food bonanza for Eustace and Frank. They were dizzy with the discovery that every garbage can in the park was spilling over with beautiful tins of rice and beans and half-eaten chicken and popcorn and cake. The two of them were like Templeton the rat in that state fair scene from *Charlotte's Web*—a couple of omnivores in paradise, shouting at each other from distant garbage cans over the din of salsa music, "I found an entire ham! Oh, my God! Sweet potatoes!"

But they'd had their most desperate food experience back in Maine, when they climbed off the trail for a few days and stayed in a small town with a family who kept the community hog in the backyard. The way the community hog system worked was that everyone in the town fed the hog their table scraps and then, come butchering time, split the meat for the winter. Frank and Eustace learned of this interesting custom the day the lady of the house baked some apple pies and gave the boys a bucket of apple peelings to take out back for the hog to eat. Outside, Frank and Eustace looked at each other, looked at the apple peelings, and said, "Fuck that." They hid behind the barn and scarfed down the peelings. After that, they graciously offered to take over the feeding of the hog. To this day, all they will report about this experience is that the kind people of that small Maine town sure did throw away a lot of perfectly good food, and that the handsome community hog sure didn't gain any weight while Eustace Conway and Frank Chambless were around.

In every way, the journey was a triumph. Hiking, delight, revelation, challenge, and epiphany—day after day. Frank and Eustace found all this heightened communication with each other, a tight sense of kinship. They were on the same page about nature and what was wrong with America, and they were both heavily into Native American lore and teachings. Eustace could talk to Frank about problems with his father, and Frank could talk to Eustace about problems with *his* father and about his feelings for his girlfriend, Lori. There was an earnestness to these two young men, a perfect absence of the cynicism, detachment, and coolness that defined their generation as a whole. Each was shamelessly open with the other.

They weren't even embarrassed to talk about God. Both had been raised in Southern Baptist households, where devotion and fundamentalism were the default mode. Eustace's grandfather Chief Johnson had been a rock-solid Christian, a man of blindingly intense morals, and Eustace's mother had tried to pass those convictions along to her firstborn. Eustace had excelled in church as a kid. He was the early star of Sunday school—sharp, inquisitive, attentive. He was always a big fan of Jesus Christ. Eustace had a powerful response to the idea of Jesus going into the temple of money lenders and "knocking all the fucking tables over," and he particularly liked that bit where the Savior went deep into the wilderness to seek the big answers.

But as he grew older, he became disillusioned with the congregation and leadership of his church. He smelled insincerity and deceit everywhere. He would sit between his parents every Sunday as they bowed their heads and took in the pious sermon. Sunday after Sunday, Eustace became sadly aware of what an act this was, and how grave was the contrast between this public image of familial sanctity and the reality of the familial discord—a savage discord that was packed away in a hidden container every Sabbath so as not to disturb the neighbors. Soon, he took to looking around at the other holy-seeming families in their pews, all nicely dressed, with their heads bowed, and he couldn't help wondering what horrors were hidden behind their hymnals.

Increasingly, too, he began to take issue with the Christian cycle of pray-sin-repent-pray-sin-repent-pray-sin-repent. It seemed obvious to him that this was nothing more than a moral cop-out, writ large. You sin; you are immediately forgiven; you go out and sin some more, armed with the understanding that you'll be forgiven once again. He found it stupid, weak, and cheap. Why was there this assumption that people were destined to sin, anyhow? If people loved the Bible so much, Eustace wondered, why couldn't they just obey the clear instructions it offers and quit lying, cheating, stealing, murdering, and whoremongering? How many times you gotta read the friggin' Ten Commandments before you get them right? Stop sinning! Live the way you've been taught to live! Then you won't have to come to church every Sunday and kneel and weep and repent. And you'll have a lot more time to spend outside in the forest, where, as Eustace believed, "there is only truth to be found—no lies, no shams, no illusions, no hypocrisy. Just a truthful place, where all beings are governed by a set of perfect laws that have never changed and never will."

Of course, given his disposition and his personal force, it wasn't long before Eustace refused to go to church and started looking for his own answers. He spent his teen years studying every religion he could find, keeping the lessons of Christianity that he liked and adding to them some bits from other beliefs. He was inspired by the ecstatic love celebrations of the ancient Sufi mystics, while his attentive inner perfectionist instinctively responded to the central tenet of Buddhism—namely, that one will achieve enlightenment only through constant mindfulness. He liked the Taoist notion that people should try to be like water, should flow around hard surfaces, altering form to fit the shapes of nature and patiently wearing away at stone. He liked the spiritual lessons of the

Eastern martial arts, about bending before the aggression of others and letting them hurt themselves without harming you.

He found something in almost every religion to keep, and would talk to anyone (Mormons, Jehovah's Witnesses, Krishnas in the airports) about God. It was always the spirituality of Native Americans, though, that Eustace responded to most fully. He'd had exposure to it through the local Native American leaders he'd met at the Scheille Museum and through his study of anthropology. He could fully accept the idea that God—indeed, godliness—is to be found in every living being on this planet, and that every thing on this planet is a living being. Not only animals, but the trees and the air and even dense stones, all of them ancient and integral.

And this is where Eustace and his Appalachian Trail partner Frank had an intersection of belief, in their mutual conviction that God is to be found only in nature. That, of course, is why they were out there on the trail, the better to find this godliness within themselves and the larger world. Nor were they embarrassed to talk about this godliness, night after night. Or to take out their handmade Indian pipes in the evenings and smoke and pray, connected with each other through their belief that the pipe was the vehicle of prayer and the smoke only the sacred representation of what they were offering up to the cosmos. They knew that some might consider the idea of a couple of white guys praying with an Indian pipe to be foolish or even offensive, but Eustace and Frank weren't merely playing Indian—they were there on the brink of their manhood, living in the most earnest way they could, facing together every day's revelations and challenges. And it was this togetherness, more than anything, that Eustace cherished about the journey.

And then, in Pennsylvania, Eustace Conway met a girl.

Her name was Donna Henry. She was a nineteen-year-old college student from Pittsburgh, and she and Eustace ran into each other on the Pennsylvania leg of the Appalachian Trail. Donna was on a weekend hike with her aunt and her cousin, and their little journey was going like hell, because the aunt and the cousin were wholly out of shape and they'd overstuffed their backpacks with way too much food and gear. So, at the moment of the encounter, Donna Henry wasn't hiking; she was sitting on the edge of the trail, taking a break because her relatives had demanded one. There she sat, trying not to listen to her aunt and her cousin bitch about their sore feet and sore legs and sore backs, and along comes Eustace Conway.

By this point, Eustace had begun to shed whatever possessions he considered useless. As he raced farther south and closer toward Georgia, he'd become tired of carrying stuff, so—operating on the old favorite principle of "the more you know, the less you need"—he'd slowly rid himself of everything but his sleeping bag, a knife, some rope, and a small cooking pot. He even shed some of his clothing. He completed the last thousand miles of his journey wearing nothing but two bandanas knotted together to cover his private bits. He didn't keep so much as a jacket for warmth. As long as he was walking, he wasn't cold; when he wasn't walking, he was sleeping. When it rained, he wore a garbage bag. When he grew tired of his tedious pace (even the pace of a man burning through almost thirty miles a day), he sprinted along the trail at full speed.

So this was the apparition that loomed before Donna Henry that day on the trail: a lean, brown, bearded, and feral creature, stripped nearly bare, wearing sneakers, and tearing through the woods like a coyote. He was skinny, sure, but he rippled with muscle. And he had a terrific face. He stopped running when he saw Donna. She said hello. Eustace said hello. Then he let fly one of his world-class smiles, and Donna felt her aunt and her cousin and her heavy backpack disappear in the glow of that smile, all replaced by the certainty that her life was never going to be the same.

Now, I have a habit of speculating about the sex life of every single person I meet. Call it a hobby; call it a perversion—I'm not defending myself. I'm stating a fact. Still, I must confess that I spent months contemplating Eustace Conway before I gave the slightest thought to the possibility that he might actually be a carnal being. Particularly in comparison with his brother Judson, who is nothing but a carnal being, Eustace seemed somehow above such worldly and corporeal nonsense. As if he didn't need it.

The first time I saw the two brothers together, I noted that extreme contrast. There was Judson in the East Village bar, flirting and dancing with every female who moved through his line of vision, and there was Eustace, sitting upright in the corner, earnestly telling me about the pleasure of drinking water straight out of the ground, and about how the quality of sunlight filtered through Appalachian foliage changes your body's chemistry, and about how only those who live in the wilderness can recognize the central truth of existence, which is that death lives right beside us at all times, as close and as relevant as life itself, and that this reality is nothing to fear but is a sacred truth to be praised.

I am the Teacher of all the People, he seemed to say as he drifted out of his world and hovered over ours. *I am to be trusted and I am to be followed but I am not to be frenched* . . .

And he does, after all, bathe in icy streams, so the whole libido problem is a little hard to picture. Still—and this is what got me—Eustace Conway presented himself as an epic American masculine hero, and the whole notion of romantic or sexual love is something that is entirely missing from the classic American masculine epic.

As the writer Leslie Fielder pointed out in his seminal tome *Love and Death in the American Novel*, we Americans have the only major culture in the known world that never held romantic love to be a sacred precept. The rest of the world gets Don Juan; we get Paul Bunyan. There's no love story in *Moby-Dick*; Huckleberry Finn doesn't get the girl in the end; John Wayne never dreamed of giving up his horse for the constraints of a wife; and Davy Fuckin' Crockett doesn't date.

Whatever conflict and whatever evolution these men undergo, they do it in the company of their one true love, nature, and they do it by themselves or with the help of a trusted male sidekick. Women are for rescuing and also for tipping your hat to as you ride off into the sunset without them. And sometimes this leads to an odd circumstance— namely, that while the women in most of world literature are depicted as carefully protecting their sacred virginity, in American heroic stories, the men are just as often steadfastly chaste.

Consider, as a textbook example, James Fenimore Cooper's *Deer-slayer*. Handsome, wise, brave, and eligible Natty Bumppo never marries, because if he did, he would have to leave his world of perfect solitude at the edge of the frontier, where he is always free. Not only does the Deerslayer not marry; he doesn't really seem to like girls. When the drop-dead gorgeous and spirited and brave heroine, Judith Hutter, basically throws her slim, brunette, and flashing-eyed self at his feet, he politely declines her advances, even though he's been holed up in the mountains without female company for an awfully long time. True, he does proclaim that he will always respect her and will always be on call to save her life should she need him.

Judith, of course, doesn't get it. What an inscrutable man is this wild, buckskin-clad hero! So unlike the dashing city-born captains of the guard who live in the barracks nearby and who love to flirt and dance! She even offers to live in the middle of the woods with Natty forever, far away from the comforts of civilization, and he still turns her down. Has Deerslayer never known love?

"And where, then, is *your* sweetheart, Deerslayer?" Judith wants to know, trying to make sense of the situation.

"She's in the forest, Judith," Deerslayer replies (in a speech that exemplifies not only the relationship of the epic American man toward women and the environment, but also exemplifies really bad writing), "hanging from the boughs of the trees, in a soft rain—in the dew on the open grass—in clouds that float about in the blue heavens—the birds that sing in the woods—the sweet springs where I slake my thirst—and in all the other glorious gifts of God's providence!"

"You mean that, as yet, you've never loved one of my sex, but love best your haunts and your own manner of life?" Judith asks. (The women in these novels may be a little dense sometimes, but they're terribly helpful with exposition.)

"That's it—that's it," Deerslayer replies.

And thus he sends fair Judith on her way to go slake her thirst at some other guy's sweet spring.

So. I'm fairly well read and I'm extremely impressionable. Who could blame me for imagining at first glance that Eustace Conway would be the same man as Natty Bumppo, the Deerslayer? They even look alike ("about six feet in his moccasins, but his frame was comparatively light and slender, showing muscles, however, that promised unusual agility") and dress alike. And Eustace, remember, is the man who used to write me letters packed with such sexy-but-chaste news as "Daybreak found me looking down on my saddled horse from atop a tree full of ripe cherries—mouth full and hands full of them—and plenty more to pick." Yes, the wilderness must be Eustace's only love and God's providence his only need.

Well, I was mistaken.

So there's Eustace Conway on the Appalachian Trail in 1981, crossing paths with Donna Henry. Donna, healthy and friendly and cute as all get-out, caught Eustace's eye, and likewise. There was the greeting, then the smile. Donna didn't know why he was wearing those two handkerchiefs, but she offered him food right away, fascinated. Partly, her motive in feeding Eustace was to get him to stick around longer, because she was immediately attracted to him; partly, she wanted to lighten the packs of her crybaby aunt and whining cousin. Whatever food she gave Eustace, he ate. He ate bottomlessly, as if he was starved. Which he was.

When he said he had to fill his water bottle, Donna said, "Me, too!" and they hiked a mile to a nearby stream while he talked of the adventures he'd had on his hike from Maine. Engrossed, Donna Henry invited him to stay with her and her relatives that night for dinner. Again, he ate them out of pack and sack, all the while telling more about his daring escapades and his teepee and his primitive lifestyle.

Donna told Eustace he was welcome to camp with them that night, too. He accepted the invite, and when the sky was good and dark and the fire was good and low, Eustace crawled into Donna's tent and sidled his long, lean body right up to hers. And she was done for.

The next day, now officially in love, Donna sent her aunt and cousin down the trail with all their gear, and she hiked the next twenty-five miles with Eustace. She was in great shape—she had hiked the previous summer with some college friends—so she had no trouble keeping up with him. They talked and walked and ate blackberries right off the bushes, and Eustace taught her about every plant and rock and twig they passed along the way.

At the end of the hike, Donna had to get back to her real life in Pittsburgh, but she didn't want to leave. Eustace told her they were a good team, and she agreed—yes, they were! And the timing was good, too. Because, as it turns out, Eustace was about to lose his traveling partner. Frank Chambless was bowing out of the journey because he missed his girlfriend Lori so much and Frank felt he had a chance right now to make their love work, if he could just get out of the hike and dedicate his energy to reconciling with her. Eustace understood and accepted his friend's sincerest apologies for quitting. Still, he was very sorry to lose his traveling companion when there were still 1000 miles left to finish off. So—of course—seeing what a good hiker Donna was (not to mention a charming tent-companion), he had an inspiration. Eustace asked Donna if she might want to meet up with him in Virginia in a few weeks and join the hike. She was all for it. Donna Henry, at this moment, would have gladly agreed to hike to Islamabad for the chance to see Eustace Conway again.

A few weeks later, she got on a bus in the middle of the night with her backpack and sleeping bag and headed south to meet him. Her mother was so angry with her for running off on a whim with a skinny man dressed in bandanas that she wouldn't even say goodbye.

Well, tough. That's what people turn nineteen for.

Here's what Donna thought it would be like to hike the Appalachian Trail with Eustace Conway—more talking and walking and berry-picking and nature observations and romance and so on for the rest of time. And, yes, on the first day of the hike, Eustace did stay right beside her, and he taught her many things about trees and flowers. On the second morning of their journey, though, he woke up early and said, "I'm going on ahead of you today. I want to cover thirty miles. I'll meet you at our campsite for dinner." And they never hiked together again. Day after day, she didn't see him on the trail. He'd take off at dawn, and she'd follow. Their only communication was the instructive little notes he'd leave for her along the trail: "Donna—there's water 20 ft. down to the left. This is a good place to rest." Or, "I know this is a hard climb—you're doing great!"

Late each evening, she'd catch up with him at the camp he'd already set for them. They'd eat whatever scavenged or hunted or rotten food was on hand and then they'd sleep. Sometimes Eustace would stay up and talk deep into the night about his dreams of changing the world, which she loved to hear. Donna was never happier than at those moments, except maybe when Eustace told her with pride that she was his "tough little Italian."

All this nature stuff was new to Donna (she once asked Eustace, while they passed a herd of cattle in a mountain pasture, "Now, are those cows or horses?"), but she was open to it and was completely game. One day, after hiking twenty-five miles, they were eating dinner together while the sun was setting, and the sky looked pretty. Donna said, "Hey, Eustace, let's run up that mountain and watch the sun go down!" After hiking twenty-five miles! She was, as he often told her, "a solid sculpture of muscle" as well as a trouble-free traveling companion. There was nothing she wouldn't do to keep up with her man. Moreover, Donna believed in every dream Eustace Conway had and wanted to help him achieve it. She was inspired and invigorated by him. When morning came, he'd strike out ahead of her on the trails, and again she'd follow without hesitation or questions—and that, Donna says now, "was symbolic of the relationship."

"I just snapped right into it," she remembers. "I was drawn along behind him like a magnetic force, walking twenty-five, thirty miles a day. I was lean and mean and eager to show him that I could keep up. I was completely in love with this man. I'd have followed him to the ends of the earth."

When Eustace Conway casts his mind back on his trip down the Appalachian Trail, it's not Donna Henry or Frank Chambless whom he pictures. While he's quick to give his traveling companions their due for hauling ass and never complaining, what he mostly remembers about those wonderful months in the woods are images of himself, alone. At last—alone. Out of his family's house and out from under his father's thumb and finally on his own.

He remembers his feet aching so much that tears fell down his face as he hiked, but he never stopped walking, because he had taught himself as a child to endure physical pain like an Indian brave. He remembers times when he was so dehydrated, he'd see spots before his eyes. He remembers hiking into the town of Pearisburg, Virginia, which is right along the trail and has a hostel as well as a general store. He had been famished for so long that he decided—what the hell—to treat himself to a meal. A real meal, paid for with American currency, not some damn survivalist meal of half-digested baby rabbit borrowed from the stomach of a rattlesnake. Here's what he bought:

"The ripest, biggest, most beautiful cantaloupe you ever saw. I bought a flat of eggs, which is two and a half dozen. These were not small eggs. These were not medium eggs. These were not large eggs. These were *extra* large eggs. I bought a loaf of the heartiest wheat bread I could find. I bought a gallon of milk and a container of yogurt. I bought a round of margarine, a brick of cheese, and one big yellow onion. Then I went to the hostel kitchen and I sautéed the onion in the margarine and I scrambled up those eggs into a huge omelet, which I filled with half the brick of cheese. I ate that. Then I toasted every slice of the loaf of bread and shredded the remainder of the cheese on the toast. Then I drank the gallon of milk. Then I ate the yogurt. And then I ate the beautiful ripe melon. When I was finished, all the food was gone, but I wasn't stuffed. I just felt *satisfied* for the first time in months. I felt, *Yes, now I've finally had enough to eat.*"

He remembers another long day in Virginia, when he ended up hiking late at night to make his allotted daily miles, hiking along a dark country road in the most rural countryside. It was a Friday evening, so all the local rednecks were driving around in their trucks, listening to music and drinking and heading to parties. They kept stopping to see what Eustace was up to.

"You need a ride, son?" the good ol' boys asked.

"No, thanks," Eustace answered.

"Where you walkin' from?"

"Maine."

That answer didn't make much of an impression on the good ol' boys.

"Well, where you headed to?"

"Georgia," Eustace told them, and the guys positively flipped out, whoopin' in disbelief.

"This damn fool's walkin' all the way to *Georgia!*"

Clearly, they had never heard of Maine.

Then, feeling sorry for Eustace, they gave him a beer and drove off. Eustace walked along in the dark, drinking the beer and humming to himself and listening to the night insects of Virginia sing. About the time he finished the beer, along came another truckload of rednecks.

"You need a ride, son?"

And the conversation was repeated, word for word, right down to the punch line. "This damn fool's walkin' all the way to *Georgia!*"

Eustace finished hiking the trail in September 1981, right around his twentieth birthday. It had taken him four and a half months to complete the journey. He wrote himself a letter of congratulations—a dramatic letter such as a man can write only on his twentieth birthday, proud and earnest and swollen with amazement over the magnitude of what he'd just accomplished.

The sun has gone behind the ridge and the shadows are starting to play games in the forest. This is the last night on the Appalachian Trail, a "Long Journey of Always and Forever." It was so long ago I started, it seems only a foggy dream. My ways have changed. I have become a man. In the Indian way, I have taken a new name—it is Eagle Chaser. I am aspiring to the highest goals and morals of the King of the Winged Beings. Many tales I can tell. I have seen many places, I have seen many people, all different but mostly good. I have learned to pray often and have accepted many gifts from the most Holy Provider. I believe God helped plan this trip before I even knew of it . . . My reason for doing the trail started out fairly simple and grew in depth with time and experience. I originally wanted to get close to nature in a good wholesome way and, number two, to find more of myself. I believe that I have done well at both of these. I am very satisfied. I wish the light of day would give me more strength to finish these written thoughts but the night is rising and the shadows are no longer visible. The night animals are out and I must go forth into the cycle that I have chosen. Eustace R. Conway.

And, indeed, he did go forth into the cycle that he had chosen. Every other voyage and accomplishment in his life would grow out of this one. For instance, when Eustace found himself a few months later sitting on a picnic table in North Carolina, skinning a raccoon, a man came up to him and said, "You're Eustace Conway, right? The last time I saw you was on the Appalachian Trail and you were skinning a snake. I remember talking to you about wilderness adventure." The man introduced himself as Alan York, and the two talked for a while, and then Alan said, "Hey, let's hike across Alaska together." Eustace replied, "I don't think it's possible to hike across Alaska, but I'm pretty sure you can kayak it," and that's what they did. Eustace and Alan glided across the state, fighting cold and brutal surf, hovering inches over herring and salmon and kelp and whales.

After that, how hard could it be to travel into rural Mexico to study pottery and weaving? And that successful trip to Mexico gave the enterprising young man the confidence to fly to Guatemala, step off the plane, and ask, "Where are all the primitive people at?" It all started with the Appalachian Trail, though. And what Eustace particularly pictures when he thinks about being nineteen years old on the Appalachian Trail is one moment, a moment he will always hold as the happiest of his life.

He is in New Hampshire. He has made it out of Maine without starving or freezing to death. He comes over a ridge. Everywhere he looks, he sees exquisite pink morning light cast over snow and ice and granite. That's all. A typical view of the White Mountains in late winter. As the years pass by, Eustace will travel to many places more interesting than this, and he will see some of the spectacular views of the world, from Alaska to Australia to Arizona, so perhaps this is not the *most* beautiful sight he will see. Nor is it as heroic and chest-thumping a moment as he'll experience when he completes the trail months later, down in Georgia, where he can haul out the heavy-duty "many-tales-I-can-tell" rhetoric. But this is better. Because this is the backdrop for the moment when Eustace Conway first comprehends that he is free. He's a man, and he is exactly where he wants to be, accomplishing what he's always known he could accomplish if he made his own decisions. He's humbled and exalted and simplified and purified and saved by this moment, because it holds the realization that—so far up here on this handsome mountain—his father isn't anywhere in sight. His father can't reach him anymore. Nobody can reach him. Nobody can control him and nobody can ever punish him again.

Eustace stands there, paralyzed by joy, patting himself down in wonder. He feels like a man who has walked away from a firing squad whose guns have jammed, and he's checking himself for bullet holes—and there are none. The air smells sweet and he can feel his own heartbeat and he's laughing and laughing at the realization that he's intact.

It's the best moment of his life, because it's the moment when Eustace Conway first grasps the concept that he has survived.

 C H A P T E R   F O U R

We are a little wild here with numberless projects of social reform. Not a reading man but has a draft of a new community in his waistcoat pocket.

—*Ralph Waldo Emerson*

When Eustace Conway got back to North Carolina in the autumn of 1981, he started looking for a new place to set up his teepee. He knew he could find a great spot if he took the time to search. During these years of his early adulthood, whenever Eustace needed to settle down for any significant period, he found it easy to live on (and live off) the land of people who were kind enough to let him squat there.

"I am unique in that I live in an Indian teepee," Eustace wrote in an unsolicited letter, by means of introducing himself to a North Carolina landowner whose fine acreage he had just spied. "While looking for a piece of land to stay on this coming fall I came upon your place and I would like to know if you would consider letting me set up my camp beside the creek on your property. I don't have a lot of money, but would be able to pay a small rent. I could look after your property as a caretaker. I would be very respectful and understanding of your wishes. I have enclosed a self-addressed, stamped envelope for you to respond with. I have also enclosed a newspaper article for benefit of more information on my lifestyle."

It must have been quite a chore for Eustace to decide exactly which newspaper article to send the man; many had recently been written about him. He was getting lots of public attention and was the darling of the North Carolina reporters, who liked to visit this "quiet, unassuming, very modest young man" living "more severely than a Spartan, not even allowing himself the luxury of matches for his campfire."

The press loved him because he was perfect. Eloquent, intelligent, courteous, intriguing, and blessedly photogenic, young Eustace Conway in his teepee was the dream of any human-interest story editor. He lived off the land like an old-time mountain man, but he wasn't some scary supremacist refusing to pay his taxes and ranting about the imminent extinction of the white man. He was gentle and idealistic about nature, but he wasn't a wimpy hippie, encouraging people to take off their clothes and make out with trees. He was attractively isolated from society, but he was no hermit on the run, as his gracious welcome of the press always showed. Yes, he challenged his peers to question the assumptions of modern Americans, but he was polite and well-spoken, and could hold up his status as a straight-A college student to prove his respectability.

That's right—a straight-A college student. Interestingly, Eustace had decided to go to college after he finished hiking the Appalachian Trail. Strange choice for someone who'd hated school as much as Eustace had. But he'd always believed he could be a decent scholar if he could get his father's foot off his neck, and, indeed, he got perfect grades in college from the start, even in the math courses. It's probably safe to assume there were no other students at Gaston Community College quite like Eustace. He was a celebrity around campus, what with his teepee and his frontier clothing and calm voice and tales of adventures in the mountains and along the Mississippi River. From his fellow students, he began to get the kind of reaction he could expect for the rest of his life. The chicks, I don't know how else to say it, absolutely dug him; the guys wanted to be just like him. He was growing into his looks, becoming both more unusual and more cool in appearance—broad facial bones and a strong mouth, wide-set and hooded dark eyes, and a long, arched nose. His body was in superb shape—a friend who saw Eustace after he got off the Appalachian Trail said he looked like "a tall, hard rock"—and his hair was more black than brown. His skin was dark; his teeth were white. There was no ambiguity in this face; it was all slant and shadow and plane. He was a creature of striking vigor, one who looked to have been carved from hardwood. He smelled like an animal, but like a clean one. He turned heads. He was popular and interesting.

Scott Taylor, a student with Eustace during those years, remembers seeing him around campus with "that big smile and that buckskin and he seemed like the coolest guy in the world. I was dying to see his teepee, but you don't just invite yourself to a man's teepee." Over time, Scott did wrangle himself an invitation on a "beautiful, rainy fall day," and Eustace had Scott sit by the creek and cut up vegetables for stew. Scott had never done anything like this before and was electrified by it. He was a conservative suburban kid who had married young and was going to college to study chemistry, and he was shocked and awakened by everything Eustace said or did.

Scott remembers, "I was nineteen and so was my wife, and we had this little apartment we were trying to set up to look like the home of a typical middle-class American married couple. We were imitating our parents, not even thinking about our lives with any kind of depth. Then I invited Eustace Conway over one day, and he walked around quietly, looking at everything, and said, 'Man, you guys have a lot of material possessions.' I'd never once considered that there was any other way to live. Eustace said, 'Just imagine if you took all the money you've spent on these things and traveled around the world with it, instead, or bought books and read them. Think about how much you'd know about life.' I'm telling you, I'd never heard ideas like this. He loaned me books about carpentry, tanning, woodworking, to show me that I could learn skills and build things on my own. He'd say, 'You know, Scott, there are things you can do in your summers away from school besides just work in an office. You can hitchhike across America, or you can go see Europe.' Europe! Hitchhiking! These were the most exotic words I'd ever heard!"

In his two years at Gaston Community College, Eustace achieved strong grades and was able to transfer to the four-year Appalachian State University, located in the mountain town of Boone, North Carolina. He was nervous at first about how he would do at ASU, knowing that the institution would ask more of him intellectually than the community college had, and was still feeling a little hamstrung by the years of criticism from his father, and intimidated, too, by the prospect of having so many classmates.

On the first day of classes, he didn't even wear his buckskin; he was that afraid of drawing attention to himself. He dressed in street clothes, jumped on his motorcycle, and left his teepee early enough to have time to check out the campus and orient himself. As he was riding down into Boone, though, he noticed a freshly roadkilled rabbit on the side of the highway and, out of habit, stopped and picked it up. (Eustace had long since made roadkill a staple of his diet. His rule of thumb was that if the fleas were still alive and jumping on the pelt, the meat was fresh enough to eat.) He stuck the rabbit in his backpack, drove on, and was the first one to arrive in class, Archeology 101. He was the first to arrive by a whole hour actually, because he'd been so intent on having time to find his way around. With some major time to kill, and not eager to sit around doing nothing, he wondered if he should go ahead and skin the rabbit.

Then he had an inspiration! He remembered that his mother had often told him that "school is only what you make of it." So he decided to make something of it. He did some asking around, tracked down the professor whose class he was about to take, and introduced himself. He must have startled her. She was Professor Clawson, right out of Harvard University, and this was not only her first day of class, it was her first teaching gig ever, as well as her first time living in the South.

"Listen," Eustace said, "I know this is your class, but I have an idea. I thought maybe we could teach something interesting about archeology together today if I explain that I live in a primitive, traditional manner, you know? And I've got this rabbit that I just found dead on the side of the road and it needs to be skinned so that I can eat it tonight. How about you let me skin the rabbit in front of the class as a lesson? I'll use the tools that I've made out of rocks, just like the ones ancient people used. I could even make the tools right in front of the class. That would be a great archeology lesson, don't you think?"

She stared at him for a good, long time. Then she recovered herself and said, "OK. Let's do it."

They hiked down to the geology lab, found some good, flinty rocks, and headed over to the class. When the other students arrived, Professor Clawson introduced herself, handed out some paperwork, and said, "And now I'm turning the class over to one of your fellow students, who'll show you how to skin a rabbit in the primitive manner."

Eustace jumped up out of his seat, pulled the rabbit from his backpack with the polish of a practiced magician, picked up his rocks, and started talking enthusiastically as he chipped away to form the tools. "Careful you don't get any of those chips in your eyes, now, people!" he said, and explained how primitive man flint-napped rocks to achieve an edge so sharp that he could dismember and butcher an adult deer with two small stones; Eustace himself had done that many times. In fact, the Aztecs, he told his classmates, used to get their stone tools sharp and precise enough to perform brain surgery on one another—"Successful brain surgery!" For archeologists, Eustace said, the study of these stone tools is crucial not only for their own significance, but also because an animal butchered with them bears a specific pattern of marks on its bones, and that can help researchers determine whether the ancient creature had died a natural death or had been killed and eaten by humans.

Then Eustace strung up his roadkill rabbit with a tidy slipknot to one of the cords on the classroom's old beige venetian blinds. He quickly gutted it, discussing how the animal's large intestine was typically fairly clean, as it held only hard black fecal pellets, but that you had to be careful with the small intestine and stomach, since these contained the more brackish and foul fluids of digestion. If you accidentally nick those organs open, "that nasty stuff gets all over your meat, which is really gross."

As Eustace worked, he talked about the physiology of a wild rabbit, about how the skin is as delicate as crepe paper and therefore a challenge to handle without tearing. It's not like deerskin, he explained as he made a neat incision from the hind foot down to the anus and back up to the other foot. Deerskin is strong and supple and useful for dozens of purposes, Eustace said, but not rabbit. You can't get a wild rabbit's skin off in one piece and then just fold it over and make a mitten out of it. Carefully peeling away the rabbit's skin, which had the fragility of a damp paper towel, he pointed out that the trick with rabbit was to remove the skin in a single long strip, as if you're peeling an apple. That way, you can end up with an eight-foot strip of fur from a single rabbit, *just like this!*

Eustace passed the pelt around the classroom so that everyone could handle it. The students asked what one could do with such a fragile strip of fur. Naturally, he had the answer. The native people would take this strip of rabbit fur and wrap it tightly around a string of woven grass, with the skin facing in and the fur facing out. And when this dried, the grass and the flesh would have melded perfectly, and the people would end up with a long, strong rope. If you weave together a few dozen of these ropes, you can make a blanket that will be not only lightweight and soft, but exceedingly warm. And if you explore ancient cave dwellings in New Mexico, as Eustace Conway had done many times, you might find such a blanket hidden in a dark corner, preserved for over a thousand years in the arid desert climate.

After that day, Eustace Conway was famous all over again. He had his confidence back and even started wearing his buckskin around campus. That very first night, in fact, Professor Clawson had gone to Eustace's teepee and eaten a big bowl of roadkill rabbit stew with him.

"And she'd been a strict vegetarian until that moment!" Eustace recalls. "But she sure did enjoy that rabbit."

Welcome to the South, Professor.

Eustace lived in the teepee throughout his college years, becoming increasingly knowledgable about the science of outdoor living even as he became more educated in the classrooms of ASU. Most of the skills he needed to be comfortable in the wilderness he had mastered in childhood and adolescence. All those attentive hours of exploration and discovery in forests behind various Conway homes had paid off, as had his experiences on the Appalachian Trail. What Eustace himself calls his innate "vigilant, aggressive mindfulness" had already brought him expertise at an early age. He also spent a great deal of time during those years mastering his hunting skills. He became a student of deer behavior, recognizing that the more he knew about the animals, the better he'd be at finding them. Years later, having become a truly adept hunter, he would look back on those college days and realize that he must have missed dozens of deer; that he must have been within twenty feet of deer on numerous occasions and simply not noticed. Eustace had to learn not to just scan the forest looking for "a huge pair of antlers and a massive animal in a clearing with a big sign pointing to it saying THERE'S A DEER RIGHT HERE, EUSTACE!" Instead, he learned to spot deer as he had once spotted turtles—by attentively looking for tiny differences in color or movement in the underbrush. He learned how to catch the corner of a deer's ear flicking; how to notice small, pale patches of white belly highlighted against the autumn camouflage and recognize them for what they were. Like a musical mastermind who can pick out each nuance of every instrument in an orchestra, Eustace got so that he could hear a twig snap in the forest and know by the sound the diameter of that twig, which told him whether it had been stepped on by a heavy deer or a squirrel. Or was the snap merely the sound of a dry branch falling out of a tree in the morning breeze? Eustace learned to tell the difference.

During his years in the teepee, he also came to respect and appreciate every kind of weather that nature delivered to his home. If it rained for three weeks, there was no use objecting to it; obviously, that was what nature needed right then. Eustace would try to adapt himself and use the time indoors making clothing, reading, praying, or practicing his beadwork. He came to understand thoroughly how winter is as important and beautiful a season as spring; how ice storms are as relevant and necessary as summer sunshine. Eustace would hear his peers at school complain about the weather, and he'd go back to his teepee and write in his journal long entries about his discovery that "there is no such thing as a 'bad' day in nature. You can't stand in judgment of nature like that because she always does what she needs to do."

"My fire has been fed well tonight," Eustace Conway, college student, wrote in his journal on a frigid day in December, "and I am reaping a beautiful harvest of HEAT. Love it. I am living in a way that would be hard for many modern people to handle. For example, yesterday evening as darkness was falling I kindled a fire and proceeded to heat my water and cook my dinner. When the water was warm, I took off my upper body wear (in the freezing temperatures) and washed my hair and body. It would be too much for my fellow classmates to handle!"

This was probably true. Although, to be fair, there were some young modern people who could have related to the scene, no problem. Donna Henry, for one. Although her name doesn't appear often in the journals, Donna was there beside Eustace a lot of the time, right there in the teepee next to him, stripping off her upper body wear, too, and washing her hair in the same frigid temperatures.

Donna stuck around with Eustace after they had conquered the Appalachian Trail together. The following summer, the two of them had hiked the national parks of the West together, again at breakneck speed (he leading; she scrambling to follow), and she discovered, after all their time in the wilderness, that she desperately wanted to marry this guy. She was frank with him about it. She told him straight out that "we have a connection, we're soulmates, we're partners. This is a once-in-a-lifetime relationship." But Eustace felt he was far too immature to consider marriage. Second only perhaps to the possibility of moving back home with Dad, marriage was the last thing on Eustace's mind when he was twenty years old. This whole journey of schooling and traveling and living in the teepee was about the opposite of marriage for Eustace; it was about reaching perfect liberty.

Still, he loved Donna and appreciated her company, so he let her stick around. She moved into his teepee with him for some time while he attended college and she embraced his interests as her own. She learned to sew buckskin, took up the study of Native American culture, and started going to powwows with him, meeting his friends and playing teepee hostess.

Donna Henry was turning into Donna Reed. And she was lonely and confused about this. The fact is, she didn't get to see Eustace very much. He was powering up on a double major in anthropology and English, and when he wasn't in class, he was busy becoming the activist and teacher he increasingly felt ordained to be. Eustace Conway, in his early twenties, was a Man of Destiny in Training, and that didn't leave much time for a girlfriend. He'd begun to travel all over the South, teaching in the public schools, developing what he would later call his "dog and pony show"—a hands-on, interactive program of nature education and awareness. He was brilliant at this. He could move a conference of the most jaded businessmen to standing ovations. And kids? Kids loved Eustace as if he were a kind of woodsy Santa: "Mr. Conway you are a very nice man . . . Thank you for attending Heritage Day . . . I enjoyed learning about Indians. I especially enjoyed hearing about how they lived and what they ate . . . It was very interesting to see that you can sew your clothing together . . . When I grow up I might try to be like you . . . I think you taught me more in one day than I've learned in the eight years I've been going to school."

Eustace was also consumed by the effort of pulling together the details of his personal philosophy. He knew he was destined to be a teacher, but what was it precisely that he needed to teach the world? He wanted to alert people to the woeful beating that the modern consumer-driven life delivers to the earth. Teach people how to achieve freedom from what his grandfather had called the "softening and vision-curbing influence of the city." Train them to pay attention to their choices. ("Reduce, Reuse, and Recycle are good ideas," he would lecture, "but those three concepts should only be the last resort. What you really need to focus on are two other words that also begin with R—Reconsider and Refuse. Before you even acquire the disposable good, ask yourself why you need this consumer product. And then turn it down. Refuse it. You *can*.") What it came down to was the idea that people had to change. They had to get back to living eye-to-eye with nature, or else the world was finished. Eustace Conway believed he could show them how.

So he also spent his college years working away on the manuscript for a book—a how-to book, for lack of a better description—called

Walk in Beauty: Living Outside. It was a detailed policy plan for Americans to make the transition from insipid modern culture to a richer natural life, where they and their children could prosper far away from "smog, plastic, and a never-ending babble of nonsense enough to scramble brains, raise blood pressure, create ulcers, and sponsor heart disease." He understood that an abrupt move to the wilderness would be terrifying for most Americans, but he felt certain that if he could write a clear phase-by-phase guide, he could help even the most pampered families move back into the woods comfortably and safely. *Walk in Beauty* has a marvelous tone of you-can-do-it optimism. Every word shows how confident Eustace was, at the age of twenty-one, not only that he had the answers, but that he would be carefully listened to.

The book is organized into tidy topics, like Heating, Lighting, Wellness, Bedding ("Understanding the principles of insulation is a good starting point"), Cleanliness, Clothing, Tools, Cooking, Children, Water, Animals, Community, Fire, Solitude, Foraging, Spiritual and World View. His prose is clean and authoritative. His constant message is that the more educated one becomes in the wilderness, the less one is "roughing it" and therefore the more comfortable one's life can be. There is no reason, he assures the reader, to suffer in the woods once you know what you're doing.

"It can't be fun being miserable in the wilderness! To walk in beauty means to harmoniously fit yourself into the natural scene, producing happy, content, memorable times. Not memorable because you burned up your shoes by the fire and got dysentery from drinking bad water! But memorable in a sense of smoothing the wilderness over and making it nice, good, peaceful, beneficial, and snug—the way a home ought to be."

Go easy, Eustace reassures us. Take it step by step. "Use your backyard as a place to develop basic skills." When learning how to make warm bedding from natural materials, "try sleeping out on a cold night on your back porch at first, where you can retreat back to the bedroom and figure out what went wrong if you have to." Ready to start foraging for food and cooking on an open fire? Try it in a local park before you move to the Australian outback. "You can always order pizza if you burn your dinner. Or you can start over and do it right the second time, or the third time, getting better each time." Above all, no matter how small the detail may seem, "*Pay Attention!* It took me 3½ years in the woods before I realized the great difference a truly clean globe on an oil light can make. It wasn't that I didn't clean the globe before—I just didn't do a good enough job. But now that I keep it spotless, I can see a lot better at night."

All it takes, Eustace promises, is practice, common sense, and some basic American willingness to try something new. Stick to it, believe in yourself, and in no time at all you and your family can be living in a "hidden home in the forest [as] wonderfully peaceful" as Eustace Conway's home.

The tricky part was that his schooling and his activities and his writing all combined to keep this most natural of woodsmen out of the woods a lot of the time. There's only so much advocacy you can do from within a teepee. If you're hellbent on changing the world, then you've got to put yourself out there in the world. You must let no campaign opportunity slip by. Eustace saw everywhere opportunities to campaign, almost to the point of distraction. He wrote a blissful observation in his journal one January day: "I was glad to see the morning star through the smoke flaps this morning." But he was quick to add, "I am beginning to try and write a story about teepee life for a magazine."

He was collecting so many obligations and appointments that he was often away from his hidden home in the forest for days at a time. This meant leaving his girlfriend and old hiking partner Donna Henry in the teepee all by herself most of the day, day after day. She was the one sitting there observing nature while her man was busy teaching or studying or dancing at some powwow or being surrounded by admirers, and she was feeling less and less wonderfully peaceful about the whole deal. Donna (who today concedes that she has only herself to blame for not building an independent life from the man she worshipped) had little to do with her time but try to please Eustace and tend to the teepee in his absence.

And sometimes when Eustace did see Donna, he could be hard on her. His perfectionism didn't stop with himself. He might be irritated that she hadn't completed all her chores or didn't know how to make pancakes correctly over the fire or hadn't kept the globe of the oil lamp clean enough. And he was far too busy with his obligations to constantly show her how to do things right. She should be learning all this on her own. She should be taking the initiative!

As the months went by, Donna felt more and more that she was always screwing something up and that her best efforts would never be enough to please this man. She was nervous every day about what he was going to come down on her for. And then, one cold January afternoon, she finally broke. Eustace came into the teepee with some dead squirrels he'd found on the side of the road. He tossed them on the ground, and said, "Make soup out of these for dinner tonight." And he left, already late for his next appointment.

"Now, remember," says Donna today, thinking back on it. "This life was his dream, and I was following him and living in the teepee because I loved him. But I didn't know how to make squirrel soup. I mean, I'm from Pittsburgh, right? All he told me was to leave the heads on so that no meat would be wasted. So I tried to cut the meat off the bones, not knowing it would be better to boil the whole animal so that the meat would fall off the bone. Of course, hardly any meat came off with my knife. But I did the best I could, left the heads in the soup, and then buried the bones in the woods behind the teepee. When Eustace came home and looked at the soup with the heads floating around, he asked, 'Where's all the meat? And where are the rest of the bones?' I told him what I had done, and he was furious at me. So furious that he made me go out there, in the middle of January, in the middle of the night, and dig up those goddamn squirrel bones and show them to him, to prove how much meat I'd wasted. Then he made me wash the carcasses off and cook them up. Four days later, I left him."

It was six full years before Donna and Eustace spoke again. Donna buried herself in the study of Native American culture. She moved to an Indian reservation and married a Lakota Sioux, mostly because she thought he would be a substitute for Eustace. But the marriage was unhappy. For the sake of her son, named Tony, she pulled herself together and set out on her own. Eventually she married again—a good man, this time—started a successful publishing company, and had another child.

Yet twenty years later, Donna still loves Eustace. She thinks there's a level at which they were made for each other, and that he was a fool not to have married her. Despite the "significant emotional relationship" she shares with her decent second husband (who has gracefully accepted his wife's lasting feelings for this old lover as part of the Donna Henry package) and despite her fears that Eustace "doesn't know how to love, only how to command," she believes that she was put on this earth to be Eustace Conway's "most excellent partner." And that maybe their story isn't over. Someday, she thinks, she may live on that mountain with him again. In the meantime, she sends her son to Eustace's summer camp at Turtle Island every year to learn how to be a man.

"Eustace Conway is my son's hero," she says. "I don't know if Eustace will ever have any children of his own, but if he has any children in his heart, my Tony is one of them."

As for Eustace, he has the fondest memories of Donna, who was "the most extraordinary natural athlete I've ever met—such a strong and willing partner." She was great, he says, and probably would have made a terrific wife, but he was too young for marriage. When I asked if he remembered the famous squirrel-bone incident (my exact question was, "Please tell me you didn't really do that, Eustace!"), he sighed and supposed that it was not only a true story, but exactly the kind of story that repeats itself in his life "time and again, with many different people." He sounded thoroughly remorseful about it, about the heightened expectations he has of everyone and the way his uncompromising personality sometimes fails to make good people feel good about themselves. Then we changed the subject and finished our conversation.

But when I returned home that evening, I found a message from Eustace on my answering machine. He'd been contemplating the squirrel-bone incident and "hated to think" I didn't understand the situation. He remembered it now. And he remembered that the reason he'd made Donna dig up the squirrel bones in the middle of the night was the excellent opportunity it gave him to educate her further on the proper way to handle a squirrel carcass.

"And why waste perfectly good meat?" he went on. "And the fact that it was January was really to our advantage, because the temperature was so low. This meant the meat would have been preserved nicely in the cold ground. Whereas, if it had been the middle of summer, I might have just let it go, because the meat might have been spoiling in the sun and been covered with maggots and insects. I must have taken all this into consideration and realized that the meat was still good and that it was a good teaching opportunity and then I must have decided that it would've been a waste to just throw it out, see? So when I asked her to bring the bones back, I was only being logical."

Concluding with the hope that this all made more sense to me now, Eustace wished me a pleasant evening and hung up.

"What is this modern-day Mountain Man trying to prove?" asked one of the many newspapermen who visited Eustace Conway in his teepee during those college years. Then he quoted Eustace's reply: "Nothing. Most people like to live in houses and watch television and go to movies. I like to live in my teepee and watch the rain or snow falling and listen to the language of nature. If they feel that money and materialism are the major virtues of life, how can I sit in judgment of them? All I ask in return is the same consideration for my life."

But it wasn't quite that simple. Eustace was asking for much more than the inalienable right to be left alone to live his life in peace away from society's judging eye. Being left alone can be pretty easy—don't talk to anyone, don't go out in public, don't invite newspapermen into your home, don't tell the world how quiet the sound of the rainfall is, and don't write papers informing people how to transform their lives. If you want to be left alone, move into the woods and sit there, still and quiet. That's called becoming a hermit, and until you start mailing out letter bombs, it's a highly effective means of being ignored. If that's really what you want.

But that's not what Eustace wanted. What he wanted was the opposite of what he'd told the reporter: he wanted people to sit in judgment of him, because he believed he knew of a better way of life for all Americans, one that people should judge with great care in order to see the

truth of his vision. He wanted the people who wa
to see how he lived, to ask questions about his life,
and healthy he was, give his ideas serious contempl
He wanted to reach out to them—to all of them.

Because that's what Men of Destiny do, and Ei
had his eye on that Man of Destiny title. As did his   ....ι. vvhen he
graduated from college in 1984, with honors, Mrs. Conway wrote her
son to congratulate him on his achievement and to remind him that the
pressure was not off yet.

"You have reached a new milestone in your journey—one of out-
standing accomplishment from long and hard work," she wrote. "As one
who best understands and appreciates the circumstances under which
you attained a college degree with two major studies, I applaud and
congratulate you with great pride and awe! But remember, education
should be an ongoing process until you die. You have just done a great
piece of groundwork—may you also seek wisdom which is greater than
knowledge. I pray for God's guidance, protection, and blessings on you
as you continue your journey on this good earth. Your proud and devoted Mother."

Not that Eustace needed to be reminded. He was already impatient.
"I want to do something great, to feel that I've *made it,* that I've *arrived,*" he wrote in his journal.

And he was becoming more troubled by what he saw. There was a
particularly sad incident one night when a gang of local rednecks came
down to his teepee to ask if they could borrow some .22 shells to finish
off a big raccoon they'd treed up on the ridge behind where Eustace was
living. Seemed they'd been out drinking and hunting and having themselves a ball. But they were such incompetent hunters, they admitted to
Eustace, that they'd fired at the raccoon more than twenty times without killing it and getting it out of that tree. Surely the stubborn bugger
was wounded up there. Could Eustace give them the ammo to help
them finish off the sumbitch once and for all?

Eustace hated everything about this scene—the dogs baying, the
cacophony of gunfire ("It sounded like a war up there," he mourned
later in his journal), the ineptitude of the men, and their total disregard

animal's spirit. How could they fire away at a living creature as if
ere a plastic target in a carnival game and then leave it to suffer
while they dicked around for an hour looking for more ammo? And
what kind of sloppy bungling jackasses could miss their shot *twenty*
times? And, by the way, why should he have to deal with these idiots
invading his privacy in the middle of the night, when he was trying to
live far away from human society?

Silent on all these concerns, Eustace got up, got dressed. He didn't
have any .22 shells, but he took his black powder rifle and followed the
dogs and men and the moonlit forest path to the tree. One shot from
his antique gun, and the raccoon was cleanly finished.

"It wasn't until I skinned him," he wrote, "that I realized mine was
the only hole in the skin."

The rednecks had never even grazed the animal. Not once in twenty
shots. Not that the good ol' boys cared. All they wanted was the pelt,
which Eustace skinned for them and handed over so that they could sell
it. He almost wept as he skinned the animal, and he kept the meat to eat
later, solemnly thanking the raccoon for giving over its life. These rednecks weren't about to eat no damn raccoon meat.

The whole incident depressed him. The disregard for nature. The
greed. The stupidity. The waste. The disregard for another being's spirit,
the lack of reverence for nature's laws—it all sickened Eustace, whose mission on earth was to uphold the ancient ideas about life's inherent sacredness. But where do you start with people so callow and oblivious? People
who shoot at animals for drunken sport and don't even want the meat?

"Hell damn fire," he wrote in his journal. "What am I to do? They
would just write me off as a Grizzly Adams nature freak if I tried to explain it to them."

And that was another thing bugging Eustace. He was getting a little
tired of being seen as an eccentric, some Grizzly Adams nature freak,
when he had so much more to offer the world. He was becoming more
contemplative and agitated and he was no longer gaining satisfaction
by making his own clothes or shooting his game with a blowgun. He
was ready for something bigger, something bolder.

"I need something new, fresh, alive, stimulating," he wrote in his journal. "I need life, close-up, tooth and claw. Alive, real, power, exertion. There are more real, fulfilling, and satisfying things to do than sitting around talking to a bunch of good old boys about the same old things, year after year. I don't want to *talk* about doing things, I want to *be* doing things, and I want to know the realities and limits of life by their measure! I don't want my life to be nothing, to not make a difference. And people tell me all the time how I *am* doing so much, but I don't feel I'm even scratching the surface. Hell no, I'm not! And life is so short, I could be gone tomorrow. Vision, concentration, center . . . what? How to do it? What to do? Can I? Where do I go? Escape isn't the answer. There is only one way—destiny, destiny. To trust destiny."

It wasn't enough for him, in other words, to sit around his teepee working on moccasins and listening to the rainfall. And, speaking of his teepee, he didn't want to spend the rest of his life moving it from one piece of someone's land to another piece of someone else's land. Every place he had ever set up camp got sold out from under him and developed into neighborhoods right before his eyes. It was dreadful, having this happen. It was like standing on a sand bar and watching the tide lift. Where could he go that would be invulnerable to commercial development? And he wanted to keep teaching, but on his own terms and not necessarily for the forty-five minutes allotted to him by the principal of whatever public school he was visiting that day. He needed more challenges, more power, more people to reach. He needed more *land*.

Years later, when people would ask Eustace Conway why he lived up at Turtle Island and spent so much energy conserving his thousand acres, he would deliver his speech of explanation. It eventually became one of the most powerful segments of his public presentations.

"There is a book I used to love as a child," he would begin, "called *Return to Shady Grove*. It's about these animals who live in a wonderful forest. Life is perfect and happy and safe for them, until one day the bulldozers come and tear up their home to build a road for humans. They have nowhere to go, and their homes have been destroyed. But then one day the animals get on the boxcar of a train and head West. When they get there, they find a new forest, just like the home they lost, and everyone lives happily ever after.

"I could always relate to that book, because everywhere I ever lived has been destroyed. When I was a small child, I lived in Columbia, South Carolina, near the wilds and the woods and the swamps. Then the developers came and raped the land and destroyed it. So my family moved to Gastonia, North Carolina, where they bought a house bordering on hundreds of acres of land, divided by a clean and beautiful stream. I fell in love with that forest. I knew that forest better than I have ever known any place, because I spent every day there, playing and exploring. I enjoyed that land during my whole young life. I built forts, developed trails, trained myself to run at breakneck speed through the woods and to roll if I fell and jump up and run some more. I climbed through the underbrush and swung from tree to tree, like Tarzan. I knew the textures of the leaves and the warmth of the soil. I knew the sounds, color, and sensations of the forest.

"And then one day the surveyor's stakes started to appear all through the forest. I didn't know what the stakes were for, but I knew they were bad. I knew it was a violation of nature, and I tried to pull up the stakes wherever they appeared. But I was a child—how could I stop it? The developers tore out my forest and built hundreds and hundreds of homes slowly over the whole area until the land I loved was leveled and the stream was just polluted water. They named the development Gardner Woods, but it was a lie. There were no more woods. Gardner Woods had been decimated. The only thing left of the woods was the name.

"Then I moved into a teepee on a piece of land owned by some friends near the hardwood forest of Allen's Knob, and I lived there until the developers cleared away the forest for homes. Then I found an old mountain man in Boone named Jay Miller, and he let me put my teepee up on his beautiful Appalachian land. I loved it there. I lived on the side of Howard's Knob, a forest filled with bears, turkeys, and ginseng root. There was a natural spring just outside my teepee where I would drink every morning. And it was wonderful there until the day old Jay Miller decided to chase the mighty dollar, and he sold his land for lumber. And the timber company came and set up their sawmill right near me—a mill that got closer and closer as they dropped to the ground every last tree that stood between me and them. I was finishing my senior year of college at the time, and I literally had to wear earplugs in order to study for my exams, the saw was so loud. By the time I left, the forest I had loved, where I had gotten my life and food and clothing, was nothing but a vast field of stumps. And the beautiful spring where I used to drink was spoiled and silted.

"So what was I to do? That's when I realized that the moral of *Return to Shady Grove* was a lie. It's a bald-faced lie invented to reassure children that there is always another forest for another home somewhere out there in the West, just over the hill somewhere. It's a lie that says it's OK that the bulldozers keep coming. But it's not OK, and we need to teach people that it's a lie, because the bulldozers will keep coming until every tree is gone. There is no place that is safe. And when I realized that? Well, that's when I decided to get a forest of my own and fight to the death anyone who ever tried to destroy it. That was the only answer and the most important thing I could do with my life on this earth."

It was time to find Turtle Island.

"The land," he wrote in his diary throughout the early 1980s, as though he had to be reminded. "I need to get the land. The land! I dream it. I want it. I will sacrifice for it."

CHAPTER FIVE

This is the place!

—*Brigham Young, on first seeing the valley
of Great Salt Lake*

America has always lent herself generously—lent both her body and her capacious character—to the visions of utopians. It could be argued that anyone who ever came to America of free will has been a junior utopian, an individual with a personal idea about creating a measure of paradise in this New World, no matter how modest that idea might be. Of course, it could also be argued that this country had been a utopia for millennia before the Europeans arrived and started wrecking everything to suit their rigid plans for the space. But consider how the country must have looked to those early Europeans—free, endless, empty. Surely it was tempting to think about the kind of a society one could create here.

Of course Americans didn't originate the idea of a utopia. As usual, that would be the Greeks. And Europeans were scheming of perfect societies since before the Renaissance. Sir Thomas More, Tommaso Campanella, and Francis Bacon had their visions, as, later, did Rabelais, Montaigne, Hobbes. But what these men didn't do was turn their blueprints into reality. They were thinkers and writers, not charismatic leaders. Besides, there was no place on the battle-weary map of the Old World where one could try to found an actual utopia. Politically, geographically, and socially, it was an impossibility. So these were men who designed ships when they'd never seen an ocean. They could imagine their dream vessels to be of any size or shape they wanted; the things would never have to set sail.

But when America was discovered—or, rather, when the concept of America was invented—that's when thinkers and writers and charismatic leaders alike started to get themselves in trouble. Because this was the place to do it. If you could get yourself some land and talk enough people into joining you, you could establish your paradise. And so, in addition to the grand utopian schemes of men like Jefferson (schemes that ultimately became known as "government"), we got dozens of smaller and weirder utopian schemes scattered over the land.

Between 1800 and 1900, more than a hundred such communities rose in waves of enthusiasm across America. The Inspirationist Society of Amana was first envisioned in Germany by a stocking-weaver, a carpenter, and an illiterate serving maid. But their dream became reality only when the Amanists came to the United States, in 1842, and bought five thousand acres outside Buffalo. This strict, mostly silent, highly skilled, sober, and well-organized population thrived, and eventually sold their land at a profit and moved to Iowa, where they prospered until 1932. The Shakers also flourished, longer than anyone might have expected of a celibate community. And the industrious Rappites of Harmony impressively constructed, in their first year in Pennsylvania's Conoquenessing Valley, fifty log houses, a church, a school, a gristmill, and a barn, in addition to clearing 150 acres of land.

But most of America's model communities didn't do so well. Generally, they crumbled under the decidedly nonutopian realities of bankruptcy, internal power struggles, irresoluble philosophical disagreements, and basic human misery. New Harmony was founded in Indiana around 1825 by Robert Owen, who called his project "a new empire of goodwill," which would spread "from Community to Community, from State to State, from Continent to Continent, finally overshadowing the whole earth, shedding light, fragrance and abundance, intelligence and happiness, upon the sons of man." Hundreds upon hundreds of devotees followed Owen, but he had no sound economic plan for his community, and he quickly slunk back to England when things started falling apart. His followers went through five constitutions in a single year, split into four rival communities, and finally imploded under the pressure of a dozen lawsuits.

Bishop Hill was founded by Eric Janson, a Swede, who brought his eight hundred followers to America in 1846 to form a theoretical socialist community. The believers spent their first winter in caves in Illinois, where 144 of them died of cholera in a single fortnight, while Janson watched over them, cheerfully saying, "Go, die in peace" as his flock keeled over, one after another. The Mountain Cove Community of Spiritualists set up their perfect society in rural Virginia, exactly on the spot, they calculated, where the Garden of Eden had once stood. Like Adam and Eve, however, the Spiritualists were cast out of Eden before they knew what hit them; their experiment lasted only two years. The carefree Fruitlanders were founded by Bronson Alcott, a charming believer in "deep discussion," who thought that work should be done only when the "spirit dictates." The Fruitlanders may have set a national utopia-dismantling record; their project lasted over the summer of 1843, until everyone went home when it started getting cold.

The Icarians hurried over here from France. Their leader, Étienne Cabet, sent them off with this proclamation: "The third of February, 1848, will be an epoch-making date, for on that day, one of the grandest acts in the history of the human race was accomplished—the advance guard, departing on the ship *Rome* has left for Icaria . . . May the winds and waves be propitious to you, soldiers of humanity!" Maybe no soldiers of humanity ever suffered quite so as hard as the Icarians, who ended up on 100,000 acres of hot swampland outside New Orleans, decimated by malaria, fatigue, starvation, desertion, and death by lightning.

Still, everyone's favorite utopian has to be Charles Fourier. Fourier had it all figured out, as he explained in several enormous books. His followers sprang up everywhere across the United States in the mid-nineteenth century, especially in New England, where a severe economic crisis had put hordes of men out of work. Of the forty separate Fourierist societies formed in America, though, only three lasted for more than two years. Looking back on the phenomenon, it's hard to imagine that Fourier's ideas could have spread anywhere beyond the recesses of his own beautifully insane head. Yet there must have been something in the alluring orderliness of his vision that reassured Americans when they needed it most, when people were seeking tidy answers.

The only hope for mankind, Charles Fourier had proclaimed quite clearly, lay in a highly organized social structure—almost insect-like in its detail and hierarchy—of human associations. The smallest association, called a Group, would comprise seven people, two of whom would hover at each wing to represent "ascending" and "descending" extremes of taste, while the other three would stay in the middle to maintain equilibrium. In the ideal society, there would be a Group for every occupation (raising children, tending poultry, growing roses, etc.). Five Groups of seven made a Series, each of which, again, would have a center and two wings. And a Phalanx—the ultimate in human organization—was to be constructed of several Series joined together to create battalions of between 1620 and 1800 individuals. Each Phalanx would cover three square acres of gardens and orchards, and the members of each Phalanx would reside in a splendid Phalanstery, consisting of bedrooms, ballrooms, council chambers, libraries, and nurseries.

In Fourier's perfect society, work would be valued according to its usefulness. Therefore, the most unpleasant and necessary work (sewage maintenance, grave digging) would earn the highest pay and the highest esteem. People would work according to their natural affinities. Since children, for example, have a natural affinity for digging around in dirt and filth, they would become special garbage-scavenging groups called the Little Hordes, and they would earn high pay, as well as taking their place at the heads of every parade, where they would regularly be honored by the other citizens with the venerable "Salute of Esteem."

Fourier went so far as to claim that he had the entire workings of the universe figured out, in addition to merely understanding the workings of the perfect human society. Every planet, he said, lasted for

80,000 years, and these epochs were naturally divided into stages. When the Earth entered its eighth stage, he speculated that men would grow tails equipped with eyes, that dead bodies would be transformed into "aromatic airs," that the polar icecaps would emit perfumed dew, that six new moons would form, and that unpleasant beasts would be replaced by their harmless opposites (called "anti-sharks," for instance, or "anti-fleas"). And it would be during this episode—the glorious eighth stage of Earth—that the Fourier Phalanxes would at last spread over the entire planet, until there were exactly 2,985,984 of them, united in one brotherhood and one language.

So. As you see, one can take one's utopian ideals absolutely as far as one wants.

Still, there seems to have been a time for this kind of dreaming, and that time was the nineteenth century. By 1900, not only had most of America's idealistic communities vanished, but nobody was talking anymore about buying up land in the middle of nowhere and creating a model society with a handful of believers. As with the decline of so much else in this country, the industrial age was probably to blame. The mass production of goods, the move from an agrarian to an urban economy, the decline of individual craftsmanship—all were eroding away Americans' idea of self-sufficiency. It was getting harder to believe that one person (or one congregation, or one Phalanx) could break off from the big machine of America. The grid had begun to emerge. Or the noose had begun to tighten, if you prefer to feel that way about it. By the turn of the century, American culture—loud, strong, established, uniform, ubiquitous—hardly seemed worth trying to alter. It would not be until the 1960s, in fact, that Americans would again summon the energy (or the madness) to attempt once more the mass formation of utopian societies.

The 1960s, of course, really began in the 1950s. It all started with the rise of the Beat movement, which brought a change in music, a questioning of society, a serious interest in experimentation with drugs and sex, and a general attitude of resistance to conventionality. By the middle of the 1950s, those old romantic nineteenth-century American ideas about separating oneself from the corruptions of larger society were starting to look good again. Poets like Allen Ginsberg (heir to Walt Whitman) and writers like Jack Kerouac (who called himself an "urban Thoreau") set forth to redefine and rediscover ways to live in America without slogging through what Kerouac called the endless system of "work, produce, consume, work, produce, consume . . ."

The Beats are often associated with city life, particularly with San Francisco. But in the classic nineteenth-century style of Teddy Roosevelt, the Beat poets dutifully turned their backs on the sissifying influence of cities to seek more rugged experiences and make real men of themselves. The poet Lew Welch quit a solid copy-editing job in Chicago in the early 1960s and became a hermit in the foothills of the Sierra Mountains. The young Jack Kerouac found work in the National Forest Service, manning a fire lookout in the Cascade Mountains. (He also worked on a merchant marine ship and was a brakeman on the Southern Pacific Railroad.) Allen Ginsberg and the poet Gary Snyder took jobs on ships in the 1940s and 1950s. ("I've held employment on all levels of society," boasted Snyder. "I can pride myself on the fact that I worked nine months on a tanker at sea and nobody once ever guessed I had been to college.")

The Beats were frustrated by the numbing consumer values of contemporary America and found the wilderness and manual labor to be fine ways to, as Kerouac said, "work the blood clots right out of existence." It was back to the frontier for cleansing all over again. By the middle of the 1960s, these ideas were spreading among a wider and wider range of American youth. Kerouac's novels alone sent no end of young men scrambling across the country to find their destinies, but *Walden*—a long-neglected work celebrating both nature and nonconformity—was also rediscovered around this time, as were the essays of the great nineteenth-century naturalist John Muir. A counterculture revolution was brewing once more, and on the heels of that resistance came, almost inevitably, the new utopias.

From 1965 to 1975, tens of thousands of young Americans tried their hands at idealistic communal-living experiments. The communes were more colorful and outlandish than their nineteenth-century counterparts had been. Most failed quickly, often comically, although it's hard to not feel affection for their high idealistic notions.

There was the famous Drop City of Colorado, founded by some wild poverty-loving hippie artists, who built structures out of bottle caps and tarp (I'm not kidding) and whose short-lived utopia was filled with "all kinds of drum music and bell ringing, jingling, jangling, and chanting." Drop City's founders so loathed rules and judgments that they insisted on accepting anybody and everybody into their utopia. Which is why the place eventually burned itself out as a crash pad for drug addicts and scary biker gangs. The same fate struck the good-hearted Californians of Gorda Mountain, who founded a wide-open community in 1962, anticipating that their welcoming policy would at-tract lots of artists and dreamers. Instead, the commune had to close in 1968 after being overrun by junkies, derelicts, runaways, and criminals.

The great LSD guru Ken Kesey and his Merry Pranksters founded a casual, miniature utopia in his California home (although Kesey even-tually grew so tired of his community, calling it nothing more than "a communal lie," that he put the whole crowd on buses to Woodstock in 1969, with strict orders to never come back). Timothy Leary founded a more elaborate psychedelic utopia. His was on a lush estate in Mill-brook, New York, which had once belonged to Andrew Mellon's family. Leary's experiment was described as "a school, a commune, and a house party of unparalleled dimensions," and—while serious academics did come to Millbrook to discuss culture and poetry—nobody did the chores, and the dream disintegrated by 1965.

Other 1960s communes were defined by a similar lack of internal structure. Black Bear Ranch, initially founded on the notion of no rules whatsoever, finally caved in and created two very strict rules: (1) no sit-ting on the kitchen counters, and (2) no turning the handle on the cream separator, because, as one old hippie recalled, "it used to drive people crazy when people would sit on the kitchen counter and play with the handle on the cream separator." Other than that, you could pretty much do what you wanted at Black Bear Ranch.

It was not easy going, keeping these utopias running. The kids who founded them were just that—kids. White, middle-class, college-educated kids, most of whom had no practical farm skills. Their communes folded left and right, assaulted from the inside by drug abuse, disorganization, apathy, resentment, and bankruptcy, and attacked from the outside by mainstream America's values and laws. Morning Star Ranch in California, for example, had no end of trouble from the local sheriff, who, in 1967, arrested the commune's leader, Lou Gottlieb, for the crime of "running an organized camp in violation of state sanitary regulations." Gottlieb—who was a fantastic wiseass, in addition to being a utopian idealist—quipped at the time of his arrest, "If they can find any evidence of organization here, I wish they would show it to me."

Yes, officer, it would have been difficult to find any evidence of organization in most of these 1960s utopias. It's all too easy now to look back at them as nothing more than a spastic side effect of a feral youth movement that was really only seeking new and creative ways to avoid adult responsibility. Although, on closer examination, it must be said that not every American commune of the 1960s was a madcap carnival. Some communes were founded on serious religious principles; some had intense political agendas; some were blessed with members who soberly and conscientiously tried to lead the good and simple life. And a few hippie communes did hammer out enough management skills to ensure their long-term survival.

The simply named Farm has been communally productive in Tennessee since 1971, after some major adjustments in its original policy of total anarchy. Over the years more traditional rules and restrictions have been introduced, and more realistic ideas about maintaining the rights of the individual within the larger framework of utopian communal living have kept its members sane and relatively free of bitterness and resentment. As with any communal experiment that lasts more than a year, the Farm had to trade in much of its early romanticism for a more pragmatic organizational principle. Still, the Farm's long-running and successful social projects (several environmental teaching programs; a public advocacy law firm) reflect the original founders' idealistic dreams.

Indeed, that sense of thriving idealism seems to be as critical a factor in keeping a commune alive over the years as good bookkeeping practices and strict visitors' policies—just as, in a good marriage, a couple will more easily endure the hardships of decades if an original spark of their youthful romance can survive. As one long-term member of the Farm explained, "We've been through some pretty hard times together. There's a certain amount of sentimentality toward seeing it succeed."

On such lines, consider the famous Hog Farm of California. Hog Farm is still thriving some twenty-five years after its founding, an endurance largely credited to the charismatic guidance of its great hippie visionary leader, Hugh Romney, AKA Wavy Gravy (proudly the only American utopian ever to have had a Ben and Jerry's ice cream flavor named in his honor). Wavy Gravy has stubbornly refused over the years to compromise his free-for-all, do-gooder 1960s values, and his dream utopia thrives as a monument to the power of pure idealism. Hog Farm's summer camp (Camp Winnarainbow) is a flourishing California institution, as is the charitable-works arm of the commune, which has been successfully fighting blindness in Third World countries for years.

All those who live at Hog Farm today still follow both their charming leader and their serious political agenda steadfastly and with good humor. Their enduring success defies those who insist that conformity to society's norms is the only way to survive in modern America. For all the concessions and disappointments they may have experienced over the decades, the Hog Farmers still fight the good fight together, insistently holding true to the original irreverent notion of themselves as "an extended family, a mobile hallucination, an army of clowns."

Eustace Conway was born at the beginning of the 1960s. He passed his formative years right in the middle of this major counterculture revolution, but the freewheeling values of the time seem to have had little effect on his ideas. Modern-day hippie types respond to Eustace positively because they think he's one of them. He does seem to be a hippie at first glance, what with his long hair and his thick beard and his back-to-nature ethic and the friendly bumper sticker on his truck that reads "Friends Come in All Colors." That said, Eustace is actually quite conservative. He loathes drugs and drug-users, has no patience with sexual swingers, and has sometimes been accused of cherishing discipline over freedom. If you wanted to take his gun from him, for instance, you'd probably find yourself prying it out of his cold, dead fingers. So, no, our Eustace Conway is not exactly a mobile hallucination or a tripped-out foot soldier from some army of clowns.

But what Eustace does share with the hippie utopian dreamers of the 1960s (as well as with their romantic utopian ancestors of the 1860s) is this most American of ideals: that society is both capable of transforming and willing to transform. If you can get yourself a piece of land and some serious motivation, you can start a small project that will grow and inspire a massive change across an entire country. Eustace Conway, like any good utopian, was not afraid to try this. He was not afraid to claim that he had all the answers. He was not afraid to formulate an entirely new world view.

What he wanted Turtle Island to be was more than just a nature preserve. More than what his grandfather had made of Sequoyah. This land was not to be a summer camp where children could temporarily escape the evils of the city and grow into strong citizens. No, Eustace wanted Turtle Island to be the setting of a colossal utopian experiment in which he would try to do nothing less than change and save America. It was to be the very blueprint for the future. Time and again, he had heard that old touchy-feely adage, "If you touch only one life, then you've had an effect on the world."

Well, frankly, Eustace Conway thought that was bullshit. No reason to think so small, people! Why be content to touch only one life? Why not save the whole planet? Certainly this must be his destiny.

"God only made one person in the world like you," wrote Eustace's mother, who was always right there on the scene to remind her son of his singular calling. "And He has a special job for you to do, to use the talents He gave you."

Eustace couldn't have agreed more, and by the time he was in his mid-twenties, he was on fire with the desire to found his own utopia. The will was there; all he needed was the land.

He never expected to find his beloved Turtle Island in North

Carolina, where real estate was already getting expensive and overpopulation already a problem. But, as it turned out, hidden up in the mountains behind the college and resort town of Boone were all kinds of shady little hollers where life had not altered in decades. Property was cheap, and people were quiet up there in the hills, so Eustace asked around to see if anyone had a big tract of land for sale. When he heard "the old Alley Church place" was available, he took a ride up there with a former college professor of his who knew a lot about buying land and reading tax maps—two skills Eustace did not have at the time but would soon acquire.

What they found up at the end of that rugged dirt road was perfection. It was 107 acres of what Eustace describes now as "a classic Southern Appalachian reclaimed hardwood forest," and it was mindalteringly beautiful. It had everything Eustace was looking for—fresh spring water, good solar exposure, attractive ridge-to-ridge property lines, level ground for farming, plenty of timber for constructing buildings, and an excitingly diverse ecosystem. It was a mixed woodland landscape, dominated by locust, birch, and sourwood. The air was wet and heavy, and the understory was fern-laden and lush. It was a wonderful climate for poison ivy and also for copperheads, although there were mild species thriving here, too—trout, woodpecker, pink and yellow ladyslipper, ginseng, orchid, bloodroot, rhododendron. . . .

The soil below his feet was vigorous and black and damp. Like most woodland on the East Coast of America, this was not original-growth forest. It was a second-growth forest that was healing itself, forest that had taken over once again after having been cleared more than a century ago, farmed steadily, and then abandoned for decades (in this case, when the local hillbillies were lured down to the town below to work in factories). Wild animals had made a healthy comeback, as had the trees. There were plenty of squirrels and every sign of an increasing deer population. The density of the birds was extraordinary, and, in the damp air of early morning, it sounded to Eustace like a jungle-worthy outcry of life. He suspected that there were mountain lions nearby, too. And bears.

It was the winter of 1986 when Eustace inspected the land for the first time. The instant he pulled his truck off the main highway, he found himself in serious Appalachia, all of which became more apparent as he climbed higher and higher into the Blue Ridge Mountains. The few people who did live back here *were* first-growth. Authentic, old-timey, genuine hillbillies. Their homes were tin-roof shacks barely adhering to the walls of these steep mountain hollers. Their yards were full of fossilized appliances and prehistoric cars, and the people kept livestock like rabbits and chickens up on their roofs, up away from the foxes. The word "hardscrabble" doesn't begin to describe how hard and how scrabbled these lives appeared.

The roads were winding and unmarked, and Eustace wasn't sure whether he was in the right location, so he pulled his truck into the yard of one of these beat-down shacks and knocked on the door to ask where the old Alley Church place was. A pale, lightweight woman in a calico apron came to the door and stared at Eustace in pure terror from behind the screen. She had probably never seen a man at her door who wasn't a family member.

"She'd been making biscuit dough," he remembers, "and her hands were covered with flour, but her face was as white as the flour on her hands, and she was shaking with fear at the sight of me. When she finally spoke, her voice was so faint and breathless, I was afraid she might pass out. It was like talking to somebody who's sick in the hospital but who's still trying to speak. You want to say, 'Save your strength! Don't try to talk!' That's how shy she was."

The woman at the door was Susie Barlow, a member of the interconnected network of Appalachian families who were soon to become Eustace's neighbors. The Barlow clan, Carlton clan, and the (quite literally named) Hicks clan had all lived in this craggy mountain holler for as long as remembered history. They were kind, reclusive people, who still yanked their teeth out with homemade iron pliers when the need arose. They raised hogs and made the most magnificent fifty-pound salt-cured hams. They bred hound dogs for hunting and for sale. They kept their dog litters in their living rooms, the pups staggering about blindly in a big wooden crate, peeing all over a faded handmade patch-work quilt, which could have surely fetched several hundred dollars at auction in New York City. The Carltons and Hickses and Barlows were poor but deeply religious people who honored the Sabbath with rever-ence and handled the Bible with humility.

"I'll tell you this much," Eustace says. "You know that I have issues with Christianity, right? But when I go visit my Appalachian neighbors and they say, 'Will you pray with us, brother Eustace?' I hit that floor and I *pray*. I get down there on my knees in their kitchens, down on that worn linoleum, and I take their hard-working hands, and I pray my heart out, because these are the truest believers I have ever known."

They were perfect neighbors. It was a perfect piece of land. Eustace was ready to begin his utopian journey. But he didn't want to do it alone.

For all that he was the American romantic archetype of the solo man in the wilderness, Eustace still desperately craved a female partner to share his dream. Just as he was imagining his ideal utopian home, he was also designing (in equally precise and fantastic detail) his ideal utopian bride. He knew exactly who she would be, how she would look, what she would bring to his life.

She would be beautiful, brilliant, strong, loving, capable, and his faithful partner, the gentle touch that would humanize his brilliantly executed life plan and support his vision. She showed up in his dreams often as a young Native American beauty, quiet and loving and peace-ful. She was the Eve who would help Eustace build his Eden. She was the same dream girl, by the way, that Henry David Thoreau used to fan-tasize about back when he was holed up alone at Walden Pond—a faultless child of nature, a paragon modeled after the mythical Greek demigoddess "Hebe, cup-bearer to Jupiter, who was the daughter of Juno and wild lettuce, and who had the power of restoring gods and men to the vigor of their youth . . . probably the only thoroughly sound-conditioned, healthy and robust young lady that ever walked the globe, and wherever she came it was spring."

This was the woman of Eustace's dreams, the very picture of lushness and fertility and grace. But he wasn't having an easy time finding her. Not that he had trouble meeting women. He met loads of women; it was just hard to find the right one.

His relationship with a woman named Belinda, for instance, typified his experience with the opposite sex. Belinda, who lived in Arizona, had seen Eustace Conway talking about his life in the woods on a national television program called "PM Magazine." She immediately fell in love with him, transported by the romantic notion of this wild and articulate mountain man, and she tracked him down through the mail. They wrote passionate letters to each other, and Eustace went to stay with her briefly out West, but it never turned into something real. Belinda had a child already, which was only one of the reasons they ultimately split. Eustace was never entirely sure whether Belinda loved him as a person or as a notion.

Then there was Frances "the strong girl from England," and Eustace fell in love with her, too.

"She seems to have the wisdom, strength, and tenacity that would make a good partner," Eustace wrote of Frances in his journal. "I need the love and companionship that I have gotten so little of. I know I'm a romantic. Sometimes I think and feel that I am so logical and in ways cool-hearted and methodical, yet I can also be so young, naïve, and unrealistic."

But Frances was soon gone, and then came Bitsy, with whom Eustace fell overpoweringly in love. Bitsy was a beautiful and mysterious Apache doctor. Not just any Apache, but a descendant of Geromino's band, and she had everything Eustace always fell for: the wide smile, the long hair, the dark skin, the athletic body, the "eyes that would melt you," the confidence, the grace. But things didn't work out with Bitsy, either.

"I desire you still," she wrote, in a letter finally severing the relationship. "Yet I have been unable to come to you. You are a charmer. But I feel you want me for your needs. I do not desire to be saved or taught or led in any direction but my own at this time. You are a giver, a teacher.

This is good, for some. But I feel you want me as a glorification for you. Forgive me if this seems harsh. I do not mean it in that way. Your needs shadow mine."

He didn't take the breakup well.

"OH! GOD DAMN! BITSY!" he exploded in his journal in February of 1986. "I am crying, hitting the floor, shouting out in pain. Oh, damn, there is no release. I am not getting over it! You! I need to see you. You are the only key . . . my heart is bleeding for you. I love you like life itself, the whole universe! I am dreadful sick in love with you! What can I do? Nothing I can do. Nothing nothing nothing NOTHING NOTHING. Oh, how can I bear to lose you? I want you for a wife, a partner, to share the adventures of life. I will never find another like you . . . what does fate, God, the flowing energy of the universe have to say about *this*?"

Then, from Eustace Conway's journal, February 1987: "Valarie Spratlin. Love. New Love. Where did you come from? Did God send you? Are you real? Are you really mine? Do I love you as much as I think I do, or do I just love the love you give me? I would love to think you are the answer to prayers I have been sending. Are you the next step in my moving, educating, predestined life? Is fate that strong a ruler and are we planned for soul mates?"

Valarie Spratlin, an attractive and energetic woman ten years Eustace's senior, was working in 1987 with the Department of Natural Resources in Georgia. She was in charge of one-fifth of the state's parks. She had heard about Eustace Conway and his "dog and pony show" from a friend in North Carolina, so she invited him to Georgia to conduct some workshops in her park system. They fell in love fast. She was intrigued by his life, by his magnetism, and by his bold plans for rescuing the world. She wrote him letters addressed to "My Primitive Savage Pagan." She was into the whole iconographic picture of him—the buckskin, the teepee, the works. Her previous boyfriend had been a musician with the Allman Brothers, and she'd spent the last ten years of her life traveling around the country with the band, so she had already established herself as someone who was up for adventure.

"I know we just met a mere two weeks ago," Valarie wrote Eustace in a spontaneous little poem, "but my feelings for you continue to grow."

Soon after they met, Eustace asked Valarie to join him on a three-week tour of the Southwest, down to Mesa Verde and all the old Indian sites. "Heck, yeah," she said, and they packed up her little Toyota and headed out. She remembers that he never once let them buy any food; they had to scrounge for meals or else dine three times a day on oatmeal and raisins. "Damn," she recalls, "but he was the penny-pinchingest man I ever saw." He took her hiking down in the Grand Canyon—"not for a nice little stroll, but for the entire day, with nothing to eat again but freakin' oatmeal and raisins"—and the next day headed into Bryce Canyon for three more days of nonstop hiking. These were Eustace-style hikes: twenty-five miles at a stretch and no breaks.

"Eustace Conway," she finally said, when he insisted one evening that they climb yet another ridge to see yet another sunset, "you are pushing me *too hard.*"

He looked at her, incredulous. "But, Valarie, you may never be here again. I can't believe you'd give up the chance to see such a beautiful view."

"I'll make you a deal," she told him. "I'll climb that last goddamn mountain with you if you promise me that when we get out of here, you'll take me to a real restaurant and buy me a hamburger and french fries and a Coke *immediately.*"

He laughed and agreed, and she made the climb. She was romantic and smitten, but she was no pushover. She was cool and spunky. She knew how to draw a line with Eustace where others found it impossible to stand up to him. And she was crazy about him. She was an environmentalist by disposition and an educator by training, and here was this guy who took every belief she had about the world and multiplied it by fifty. She was behind him on all his plans, and there soon came about a subtle pronoun shift in discussions of the future. Eustace no longer talked of "my need to find good land," but "our need to find good land." This woman seemed in every way to be what he had always hoped to find: a true partner. Together, Eustace and Valarie looked all over the South for a spot that would work for his—for their—utopia.

And so it came to pass that, in the late winter of 1986, Eustace Conway drove Valarie Spratlin up into the mountains behind Boone to show her the place he was interested in buying. It was nighttime. It was freezing rain. They drove in a dilapidated old van Eustace had recently purchased, with holes in the floorboards where exhaust kept pouring in. The road up the mountain was more like a dry creek bed of boulders and ditches than anything designed for a car's passage. They finally stepped out of the van, and Eustace, delighted, shouted to Valarie, "We're here! This is it!"

It was freezing. It was dark. The wind was howling. Valarie could see nothing. She ducked under a big hemlock to get out of the weather, but some wild chickens roosting in the tree started squawking around, and their movements dumped more icy water down her back.

"I don't like it here, Eustace," she said.

"You'll like it in the morning," he promised.

There wasn't a single structure on the land. They slept under a tarp that night, and it started to snow. Around midnight, Eustace climbed alone to the highest point of the property and smoked a pipe in a prayer of thanksgiving for having found his destiny. Valarie, shivering under the tarp, was thinking, "It's snowing and I don't know where the hell I am and I'm freezing to death and that goddamn man just left me to go smoke a pipe?"

In the morning, though, when Eustace took her for a walk around the whole property, she began to see what he loved about the place. It was nothing but dense forest, yet Eustace was already mapping out the 107 acres of his personal world—bridges to go here; a teepee camp to fit there; this would make wonderful pasture; here's where the barn could go; here's where we can build cabins for guests; someday I'll buy the land on the other side of the ridge, and we'll plant buckwheat over here . . .

He could see it all. And the way he explained it so clearly? Why, she could see it, too.

The land was going to cost him nearly $80,000.

Eustace had saved some money, but not that kind of money. And there was no banker in the world who'd give a second glance to a kid in buckskin who lived in a teepee. So where can a modern mountain man get $80,000 when he needs it fast? The only person Eustace Conway knew for sure had that kind of money was his father.

Eustace didn't feel remotely comfortable hitting the old man up for money. He didn't feel comfortable around the old man at all. His father had still never said a kind word to him. Had never acknowledged that his "idiot" son had graduated with honors from college. Had never gone to hear Eustace speak before auditoriums full of captivated audiences; listened to a single story or looked at a single photograph from any of Eustace's adventures; read any of the newspaper and magazine articles written about his son. (Mrs. Conway would cut them out and leave them on the coffee table for her husband to see, but he wouldn't touch them; he'd just set his *Wall Street Journal* or his glass of water down on them, as if they were invisible.) In every way, Big Eustace was more detached from his children now that they were out of his house.

"I wish Dad would write to you," Eustace's mother wrote to her son when he was away in college, "but he seems to have a lot of hang-ups. Martha received her first letter *ever* from him on her birthday, and it was so shocking that she said she bawled while reading it."

Eustace was amazed to realize that even now, when he was in his early twenties, he was still haunted by the pain of his childhood. He had thought this would all go away once he got older, once his physical body had left the environment of home. Why was it that his father could still make him cry? Why was he still having dreams that woke him at four o'clock in the morning, "rooting up old memories of grief and pain"? Eustace was shocked to discover, during one Christmas visit to Gastonia, that his dad remained "the rudest man I have ever met, the most judgmental man I have ever met, the most critical man I have ever met."

It's not that Eustace hadn't tried to reconcile with the old man. As far back as his adolescence, he'd tried. His mother was always encouraging Little Eustace to "bend over backward" to improve his relationship with Big Eustace.

"I hope and pray so much that everything will go better for you and all of us at home next year," she had written to Eustace before his senior year of high school. "Just as you so greatly want Dad's love and respect, so does he want your love, respect and obedience. Which a child owes his parents. I feel sure one of the big reasons why Dad has always been hard for you to get along with is because he has always been 'second fiddle' all through your life, since you gave *me* most of your attention, time and dependence for all the things you need, and for affection. It started from way back when you were a little boy and, due to the fact that I gave you too much time and attention, it snowballed into a very unhappy relationship. At this point, there is still a possibility for a new happy relationship to develop between you and your Dad, but it is up to you to bring it about. In youth you are more able to be flexible in changing your behavior patterns and attitudes. *Swallow all your pride* to humble yourself before Dad and admit that you have done and said things in the past which have displeased him, but that you are willing now to try to please him to the best of your ability."

So Eustace, from the time he was twelve, wrote letters to his father. He knew that his father thought himself a gifted communicator, and he hoped that he could improve their relationship if he expressed himself properly. He would work on those letters for weeks, trying to find the most mature and respectful way to approach Big Eustace. He would write that he believed they had a difficult relationship and would like to work on healing it. He would suggest that perhaps someone could help them talk to each other. He would tell his father he was sorry to have disappointed him, and maybe if they discussed their problems without anybody yelling, he could change his behavior to make his father happier.

His father never responded to any of the letters, although occasionally he read one aloud in a mocking fashion, to entertain Eustace's siblings. There was so much to make fun of: Eustace's spelling, grammar, his audacity in speaking as an equal—that kind of thing. Big Eustace was particularly entertained by a letter Little Eustace wrote back in high school, in which he suggested that his brother Walton, who had a brilliant mind and a sensitive nature, might thrive at a private school, where he would not be bullied by the redneck kids of Gastonia High.

What a laugh! Big Eustace read that one over and over to the other kids, and everyone, even Walton, was encouraged to mock Little Eustace for presuming to tell his father what might be best for the family.

Yet, when he reached adulthood, Eustace often found himself trying again.

"I do not write to bring you pain or discouragement," he wrote once, man to man. "On the contrary. I apologize for bringing pain or anything but goodness into your life. I always have wanted to be good. Good for you, good for Mom, good for everyone. I have an overwhelming need to be accepted by you, to be appreciated, acknowledged, recognized for something better than trash (stupid, ignorant, wrong, worthless). I have a great void where I look for love. All I have ever wanted is your love. I feel like a moth near a candle. Perhaps I should accept defeat and stay away from you. But denial and distance do not satisfy the need for your acceptance."

Again, no response.

So, no, the relationship was hardly prospering, but Eustace needed to borrow a lot of money, and his father, frugal and shrewd, had it. Eustace had never asked his father for a dime; it had been a point of pride. When Mr. Conway once told young Eustace they should discuss the terms of an allowance, Eustace said, "I don't think I deserve an allowance," and that was the end of that. Eustace never asked his father for help with college tuition, although Mr. Conway happily paid the college fees for his younger children. How, then, was Eustace Conway to come to his dad in 1987 as an adult and ask for a loan? A pretty big loan.

The conversation, as we can imagine, was not genteel. Eustace got an earful from the old man: he was destined to fail in this venture; he should expect no mercy from his father when the sheriff came calling with bankruptcy papers; and who did he think he was, anyhow, to believe he could handle the responsibilities of caring for 107 acres and running a business?

"You're wrong to think you can succeed at this," his father said, over and over again.

Eustace sat like a rock in a stream, letting the cold deluge rush right by him, keeping his mouth shut and his face blank, repeating to himself the comforting chant *I know I'm right, I know I'm right, I know I'm right* . . . And, in the end, his father lent him the money.

At a competitive interest rate, of course.

On October 15, 1987, Eustace Conway bought his first piece of Turtle Island. And immediately set to work trying to pay his father back. Within one year, they were square again. He made that enormous sum of money in so short a time by driving himself through an insane deluge of work, traveling all over the South on a physically and emotionally punishing speaking tour, to teach, preach, and reach. Valarie used her connections with the Park Service to get him gigs in schools and nature centers, and Eustace turned into a driven self-promoter.

"It was an exciting time," Valarie remembers now, "those first two years up at Turtle Island. Eustace lived with me in my nice suburban house in Georgia for a while, getting his speaking arrangements together and trying to pay his father back. I acted as his agent, getting him booked all over the state. And eventually I quit my good job and sold my good house and moved up to Turtle Island. I was following my bliss. That's where I wanted to be. We worked hard to get the place going. I helped him with the first building up there, a toolshed, because the most important thing for Eustace was a place where he could gather the tools he'd need to create the rest of his vision. We lived in a teepee, and I cooked our meals on an old woodstove every day, but I was happy to be living this way because I wanted to learn those skills. I believed in what we were doing. I believed in what we were teaching. I was on a spiritual mission of my own, and mine paralleled his."

The way they lived was a nightmare and a comedy. Eustace was on the road so much of the time, he'd have to carry every piece of paper, every check, calendar, and pile of mail in an old leather satchel. They kept files of school addresses and fliers in boxes in the teepee, which would get soaked in the rain and then eaten by mice, mold, and grubs. They had no phone. One time, Eustace walked down the holler to ask one of his neighbors, old Lonnie Carlton, if he could borrow his phone to make some long-distance business calls and pay him back later. For an old Appalachian farmer like Lonnie, a long-distance phone call was maybe a once-a-year event, probably having to do with a death in the family and certainly never lasting more than two minutes. Well, Eustace got on that phone and talked to school principals and Boy Scout leaders and newspaper reporters all over the South for six straight hours. Old Lonnie just sat there watching him the entire time, slack-jawed.

When it became obvious that he'd need a phone of his own, Eustace ran a phone line from a neighbor's house up into a nearby cave, which became his office. He would hike down the mountain and climb into that cave at night during the winter and do what he remembers as "some pretty slick little business deals," networking and taking notes and lighting his work all the while with a crackling fire. Later, he got permission to run a phone line into a pole barn that belonged to his neighbor Will Hicks. Valarie put the phone in a Styrofoam cooler so that it wouldn't rust out from moisture. She remembers making business calls and negotiating hard-line fees for speaking engagements up there in the hayloft while the cows were mooing below her.

"Guys on the other end would ask, 'What's that noise I keep hearing?' and I'd say, 'Oh, it's just the television going in the other room.' I'm telling you, it was a real 'Green Acres' arrangement we had going there. Then the phone got wet and ruined. I tried to dry it out by putting it in the warm woodstove. Of course, it melted all over the place, like some kind of Salvador Dali deal. That's the way we lived."

Something was going to have to change. One night Eustace took Valarie out for a nice dinner down in Boone at the Red Onion Café, to treat her for all the work she'd been doing. And over dinner he sketched out designs on napkins for the office building he had decided they needed. Recognizing that he had a forty-day break—a rare repose—from speaking engagements, he figured over dinner that he'd build the office during that little window of time. Otherwise, it would never happen. So the next morning, before daylight, Eustace started working on it.

The building would be passive solar, twenty square feet, and made of cinderblock, glass, and rough-hewn lumber. Eustace didn't know exactly how to erect a solar building and had never built anything more sophisticated than a toolshed, but he was damn sure he could do this. He selected a good sunny spot close to the entrance of Turtle Island so that the office could serve as a welcome station and be far away from the more primitive center of camp, which was to be deeper into the woods. He dug three sides of the building down into the earth, to help contain the heat, and Valarie helped him lay a brick floor to absorb energy from the sun. The entrance was a set of handsome French doors Eustace had picked up at a flea market for five dollars. The door handles, he rebuilt from deer antlers. He placed large windows in the front of the office and set skylights, all salvaged from junkyards, into the roof for light and heat.

The front of the roof, which people can see, is covered in hand-split shingles, for aesthetic value. But the back of the roof is practical and tin. The interior walls are paneled with two-foot-wide planks of weathered white pine, which Eustace rescued from an abandoned old barn, and which give the room warmth and depth. He built two large desks from the rest of the barn planks and also built sturdy bookshelves that function as a wall, dividing the office into two separate and sunny workspaces. On the floor is an antique rug he found at a Navajo auction. High shelves along the tops of the walls hold rare baskets and pottery, including one ancient pueblo pot Eustace had noticed on the porch of an old house in Raleigh one afternoon. Immediately recognizing its worth, he offered the owner of the home twenty dollars for the piece. "Sure," the lady of the house said. "Take it. I get tired of sweeping around that old thing." Later, Eustace sent a photograph of the pot to an expert at Sotheby's, who estimated its value at several thousand dollars.

It's a lovely building, the Turtle Island office. Beautiful art and books are everywhere inside, and all around the outside grow Eustace's wildflowers—iris, Indian paintbrush, and ladyslipper. It's a warm, organic, welcoming, fully efficient passive solar structure, with its own telephone and answering machine. And Eustace designed, built, decorated, and landscaped the entire thing in forty days.

By now, Eustace was getting a reputation across the mountain range for being quite a little busybody. For instance, he bought his lumber from an old Appalachian mountain man named Taft Broyhill, who owned a sawmill. Eustace would work all day on the building and then work into the night, too, by the headlights of his truck. When he needed more lumber, he'd drive over to the next mountain and visit Taft Broyhill's mill around midnight, wake the old farmer up, and deal with him right there in the wee hours, so as not to waste perfectly good daylight time conducting commerce. Then he'd head back to Turtle Island, sleep for three or four hours, and start working on the building again long before dawn.

One night when he drove over to Taft Broyhill's place around midnight, he was accompanied by a friend who had come to help Eustace out for a few days. While the old man was piling up the lumber, Eustace noticed in a heap of scrap wood a gorgeous hickory log, far too nice a piece of wood to saw into lumber. He asked if he could buy that hunk of hickory, and would Mr. Broyhill mind sawing it down to some manageable lengths for him.

"Well, what do you want it for?" the old man asked.

"Why, sir," Eustace explained, "I was just thinking to myself how nice it would be to use that solid hickory for carving tool handles and such."

The old man obligingly started up his chain saw and, in the headlights of Eustace's truck at midnight in the falling snow, began cutting up the hickory log. Suddenly he stopped, turned off his chain saw, and stood up. He stared for a while at Eustace and his friend. Eustace, wondering what was wrong, waited for Taft Broyhill to speak.

"You know," the old man finally drawled, "I was just wonderin'—what do you boys do in your *spare* time?"

Eustace was killing himself with work. The minute the office was finished he was back on the road, making money by preaching about the bliss of primitive living and the wisdom of the Native Americans and the comforts of "the simple life." He was bolting in a frenzy from state to state, trying to convince people to give up the rat race and bask in warm communion with nature. It was a brutal existence. One friend even bought him a radar detector so that he'd stop getting speeding tickets on his endless driving sprints to shows. And by February of 1988, Eustace seemed to be looking over the precipice into a chasm of madness when he wrote:

"Long run, the big trip, this endeavor to accomplish what I am doing now, a poor boy paying for a large tract of land. So much goes into it, every day I work, trying so hard, and even today—a day without a class or lecture—I spent 12 hours doing paperwork, responding and soliciting and getting more work, more more more MORE piled on. I can take it, like an enthusiastic weightlifter in hot adrenaline—I am working even in my sleep—work-sleep, I call it—giving up time for love with Valarie, giving up time to pick the flowers . . . Atlanta, then Augusta, working in Toccoa and then Clarksville—prostitution of my time to hundreds of people—day after day pounding on stage, on stage, on stage YEELLLLING!

"I live on stage power and energy flowing, pulling it together . . . sleep 7 minutes, then get up—drive—be great. You are the best! They are on your strings like a puppet to be worked, controlled, listened to, and told—back and forth . . . ah, but the lack of understanding! Don't you know I need rest? Don't you know I need air? I need to breathe, damn it! Leave me alone, you stupid bastards! Can't you see? You stupid people, can't you understand? *That is the best program I have ever seen, you really did good!* I have heard it so many times, it's like subsisting on cardboard. What the hell. I get my land. I have a quiet nature preserve to sleep in someday at the end of a long tunnel—what a dichotomy . . . How much will I let others in? Oh, my good people of the world, I LOVE YOU—give me strength, Lord, to do my trek. Someday I will find the soft ferns and sunshine to lie down in and rest. Peace."

And at the end of a similar rant in his journal a few weeks later, Eustace added, "Not to mention trying to figure out if I want Valarie to be my mate for life."

In the summer of 1989, Eustace had his first campers at Turtle Island.

Turtle Island was no longer an idea—it was an institution. Eustace had got himself brochures, business cards, insurance plans, first-aid kits, not-for-profit status. It was real. And the kids loved it, every year. Instead of having parents drive the campers up the mountain to the makeshift parking lot, Eustace had his staff meet the families down on the road and then hike in to Turtle Island. If the parents couldn't make the hike? Well, too bad. *Say your goodbyes down here, folks.* This way, the kids would come into the fertile valley of Turtle Island through the woods, on foot, entering the kingdom as though through a sacred and secret door. The woods would finally open into the sunny meadows of the camp, and there would be this marvelous new-old world, different from anything these kids had ever known. No electricity, no running water, no traffic, no *commerce.*

And when they arrived, Eustace Conway was there to meet them, wearing his buckskin and his calmest smile. Over the course of the summer, he taught the children to eat foods they had never known, to sharpen and use knives, to carve their own spoons, to make knots and play Indian games and—every time they cut a branch off a living tree— to cut away a small lock of their own hair, to leave as an offering of thanks. He taught them to be respectful of one another and of nature. He worked to heal what he considered the spiritual damage inflicted on them by modern American culture. He'd be walking in the woods with a group of kids, for instance, and come on a patch of sweet briar. He'd no sooner tell the children how delicious the leaves tasted than they'd swarm on the plant like locusts, ripping off handfuls of branches.

"No," Eustace would say. "Don't destroy the entire plant! Be considerate of limited resources. Take one leaf, nibble a little bit of it, pass it around. Remember that the whole world isn't here for you to consume and destroy. Remember that you aren't the last person who will walk through these woods. Or the last person who will live on this planet. You've got to leave something behind."

He even taught them how to pray. After the campers woke at dawn, Eustace would lead them up to the very same hill where he had prayed with his pipe the first winter he'd slept at Turtle Island. They called the place "sunrise hill," and they would sit in silence, watching the sun come up, all of them meditating on the day. He took them on hikes to waterfalls and to ponds, and he bought an old horse for them to ride around. He taught them how to catch and eat crawdads from the stream and how to set traps for small game.

If a child said, "I don't want to kill a defenseless animal," Eustace would smile and explain, "I'll tell you a little secret, my friend. You'll never find in all of nature such a thing as a 'defenseless' animal. Except maybe some human beings I've known."

He finally had his place, a place where he could teach in an interactive and twenty-four-hour environment, with no distractions and no limits on his time or resources. Everything he wanted to show his students was right on hand. It was as if they were living inside an encyclopedia.

On a nature walk he might say, "That mushroom right there is lacteria. You have to be very careful with this species, though, because there are four mushrooms in the world that look just like that. Two of them are poisonous and two of them aren't. So don't make any hasty decisions about which ones to eat! The only way you can tell the difference is to break the mushroom open and put your tongue to the milky substance right here inside. See that? If it tastes bitter, it's poison, so stay away from it."

Or he might tell them how primitive people took care of their health with witch hazel. "It's growing right there, and it's good for all kinds of wounds."

Or he'd say, "That's black birch. Why don't you chew on that? It tastes good, right? The inner bark is the most valuable part. It's what the old-time Appalachian people used to make birch beer out of. Maybe we should do that later."

He was in bliss over the success of what he had created. There seemed no limit to what he could teach up here. The campers would return home to their suburban lives, and their parents would write letters to Eustace: "What did you do to my son, that he's so much more mature now? What did you teach him that has made him so interested in his world?"

Eustace also held week-long seminars for adults. When he took one such group out for a hike through the forest, they were walking along a river, and one of the women, who had never been in the woods before, started to scream. She saw a snake swimming against the current. Eustace was wearing only a breechcloth, so he dove into the water and caught the snake with his hands and quietly explained its physiology to the woman from the city. He had her touch it and look inside its mouth. Eventually she held the snake in her hands while her friends took photographs.

On another occasion, Eustace took a small group of kindergarteners for a walk in the woods. He pointed up at the dense overhang of foliage and told them about the different kinds of trees. He let them drink from a spring, to show them that water comes out of the ground, not just out of faucets. He let them chew on sourwood, and they were amazed that he was right, that it did taste like tart candy. As they walked through the forest, he explained how the forest floor works, its circularity. The leaves fall from the trees and crumble and decompose and turn into soil. He explained how water seeps into the ground and feeds the roots of the trees; how the insects and animals live on the forest floor, eating each other and all the organic material they can find, keeping the cycle going.

"The woods are alive," he said, but he could see that the children didn't quite get it. Then, he asked a question. "Who wants to be my helper?" When a small boy stepped forward, Eustace—with the help of the children—dug two long shallow trenches in the forest floor. And he and the little boy lay down in the trenches and the other children buried them so that only their faces were sticking out of the ground, looking straight up.

"Now, *we* are the forest floor," Eustace said. "And let's tell the others what we see and feel. Let's explain what's happening to us."

They lay there for some time in the soft forest duff, Eustace and a five-year-old child, and described what they saw and felt. How the sun hit their faces for a little while and then shade came with the waving of branches above them. They described dead pine needles falling on them and the drops of moisture from past rainfall landing on their cheeks and the insects and spiders marching over their faces. It was amazing. The children were mesmerized. And then, of course, they all wanted to be buried. So Eustace took turns burying each of them, transforming each child for a short while into the forest floor and smiling encouragingly as their sharp voices of comprehension filled the damp, clean air.

"It *is* alive!" they kept saying. "It *is* alive!"

They could scarcely believe it.

CHAPTER SIX

My public engagements consume all my time . . . I was much gratified to
hear that the first editions of my book were entirely sold out . . . I wish
to know if you have an agent in New Orleans and in the towns on the
Mississippi, there it will sell better than other places . . . send me 10
copies as I wish that number for distribution among my immediate
friends. I also wish you to understand that the Hon. Thos. Chilton of
Kentucky is entitled to one equl half of the 62½ percent of the entire
profits of the work as by the agreement between you and myself . . .

*—From a business letter written by Davy Crockett
to the publisher of his memoirs*

In May of 2000, I sat across a desk from Eustace Conway in his sunny
office. Between us was a large cardboard box that had once contained—
if its original label was to be believed—*Stilh Chain Saw Bar and Chain
Lubricant.* This is the box where Eustace stores the information about
all his land parcels, which now add up to over a thousand acres. The
box is full of manila envelopes marked, in no particular order, "Blank
Land Deeds," "Johnson Maps," "Land Tax Bills," "Cabell Gragg's Land,"
"Right-of-Way Information," "Forest Management," and a particularly
thick envelope labeled "People Who Want Land and Land For Sale."

A few months earlier, Eustace and I had ridden horses together through a foot-deep cover of crisp snow and circled the perimeter of Turtle Island. The ride took us several hours, and at some points we'd get off our horses to make it up or down the almost sheer sides of hills, but Eustace didn't once stop talking during the whole tour. He pointed out each tree and stone that marked his property line and told me who currently owned the property on the other side of the line, what those people were doing with their land, and how much he might be willing to pay for it someday. Having seen Turtle Island in the raw, I now wanted to understand it on a map.

So Eustace pulled out a huge map and unfolded it before him, as if he were a pirate. His land was blocked out in small and large connected parcels, and he told me how he'd acquired each piece over the years. What emerged was a portrait of genius. Eustace had put the thing together like a chess master. He first bought the 107 acres that made up the valley of Turtle Island, and then, as he earned money over the years, he slowly bought the peaks of each hill that surrounded the valley. The peaks of a hill are the most valuable real estate to developers, after all, since everyone wants a home right on top of a mountain. By securing these peaks, then, Eustace had made the hills below them much less attractive to any roving land speculator and therefore much less likely to be sold to someone else before he could afford to grab it.

"I wanted the crests of every ridge around me," Eustace said. "I wanted to be able to look up from my valley and see no light pollution, no homes, no erosion to destroy the forest, and I wanted to hear no sounds except nature. The crests of the ridges were key, also, because ridges are where developers build roads, and once a road has been stuck through a forest, you're finished. Roads bring people and people bring destruction, and I needed to prevent that. So I bought up all the crests. If I hadn't done that, there'd be a road running past here right now, I can promise you."

Once he owned the crests, he filled in the gaps, buying the slopes that connected his valley to the surrounding mountaintops. In this way, he guarded his watershed. What he was doing, actually, was transforming his holdings from a small, flat, low-lying basin into a large teacup—

a perfect valley—which would be protected by mountains on every side. He bought up a crucial 114 acres called the Johnson Land. ("Dick Johnson owned 40,000 acres next to me, and he put it up for sale. Obviously, I couldn't afford to buy it all, but I had to secure this one small piece right on the perimeter of Turtle Island, to keep a buffer between my nature preserve and whatever some developers might do on the other side." The Johnson Land was an emergency buy; Eustace had to come up with the cash for it in two days, and he did.) Then he bought another small chunk of land he calls the Whale's Tail, because of its shape. ("It's a beautiful acreage, with a big drop-off vista, and I knew someday somebody was going to take a look at it and think what a nice place it would be for a house, so I had to secure it.") Then he bought his most expensive and tiny piece of land, a mere five acres, for which he paid an arm and a leg. ("I realized that if I bought it, I'd control the access to the huge property on the other side of me, since this tiny spot is the only place where you can put a road. I couldn't afford to buy the big property, but I could afford to quietly buy this little roadblock here. It was just a security measure. And maybe someday I can buy up the remainder without any serious competition.")

But the most critical portion of Turtle Island was a 156.16-acre lot called the Cabell Gragg Land. Cabell Gragg was a sly old Appalachian farmer who owned this small spit of land right behind Turtle Island. It was the last piece Eustace needed to complete the watershed that would make his valley inviolable. From the first time Eustace had seen these woods, he knew this to be the place where he would someday build his home. It wasn't the most alluring 156.16 acres in the world, but if someone else got hold of it, stripped it, polluted it, or developed it, Turtle Island would be poisoned through proximity. The piece was critical. It was Eustace's Achilles' heel.

"If I couldn't nail that Cabell Gragg Land," Eustace said, "my dream was over. If someone else bought the property, that would've been it for me. I would've turned around the next day and sold all my land and walked away from this whole vision, because it would've been ruined. I'd just have to start all over again somewhere else. So here I was, waking up every day of my life for almost ten years and working my brains out to make this place successful—putting up buildings and clearing pastures and constructing bridges—knowing all the while that if I couldn't buy the Cabell Gragg Land, all that work would be for nothing."

From 1987 until 1997, Eustace tried hard to get his hands on those 156.16 acres. You can't read ten consecutive pages of his journals from that decade without hitting at least one reference to the Cabell Gragg Land. Eustace wrote Cabell Gragg countless letters, took him on tours of Turtle Island, sent him gifts, and even, as the years went on, visited him in his nursing home to negotiate terms. A dozen times Eustace thought he had a deal, and then old Cabell Gragg would back out or double the price or say he'd found a better offer. It was maddening. Eustace had a bottle of champagne he was keeping to drink in celebration of buying that land, and after ten years, the bottle had accumulated (as he puts it in his typically Eustacian precise manner) "$\frac{1}{16}^{th}$ of an inch of dust on its surface." He was willing to put together any crazy proposal to secure the property. At one point, when Gragg expressed an interest in a fancy Victorian house down in Boone, Eustace came close to buying it in order to trade it with Cabell for the land, but the deal fell through.

In the end, Eustace got his precious Cabell Gragg Land. But at a huge personal price and in the most daring and dangerous of ways.

He got it by sleeping with the devil.

There's a mountain right next to the mountains where Eustace lives, and for years and years it was nothing but forest. Tens of thousands of acres of this mountain bumped plumb up against Eustace's land, and he had a dream from the first time he saw Turtle Island to buy it all up and multiply his holdings immensely. He didn't know how he was going to do this, but he had every intention of figuring out a way. Every time he drove up to Turtle Island on the road from Boone, he passed a particular lookout point where he could pull his truck over and stand for a while and see over the ravine and valleys to a perfect view of both his property and the beautiful and enormous and forested mountain right beside it. He could think, *Someday . . . somehow . . .*

And then, one afternoon in 1994, while driving his truck from

Boone to Turtle Island, he saw a Cadillac parked at his favorite lookout point. Four men in suits were standing outside the car, looking through binoculars across the ravine to that beautiful and enormous and forested mountain. Eustace felt his heart stop. He knew right then that his dream of owning the mountain was, as of this moment, officially over. He didn't know who the men were, but he knew damn sure *what* they were, and he knew what they'd come for. It was the moral of *Return to Shady Grove* repeating itself. There's no reason on earth that men in suits scrutinize forests with binoculars clutched to their faces in this distant corner of Appalachia unless they mean to buy something. Eustace pulled his truck up right behind the Cadillac and got out. Startled, the suits turned. They lowered their binoculars and looked at him. Standing with his hands on his hips, Eustace stared them down. One of the men flushed nervously, another coughed. It was as though they'd been caught stealing something or having sex.

"Can I help you with anything, gentlemen?" Eustace asked, grimly. But it was too late; they were already helping themselves.

They didn't say a word to Eustace that day, but the truth came out over the next months. A guy named David Kaplan had come to town looking to buy up all available land in the area in order to build an expensive and exclusive resort called Heavenly Mountain, where well-heeled believers could come and practice transcendental meditation in the lap of luxury. Heavenly Mountain would need roads and a helicopter pad and a golf course and a tennis court and lots of property for buildings.

David Kaplan was smart and ambitious and seemed to have all the money in the world. Acre by acre, he acquired the land he needed. Old farms and lost ravines and clean rivers and pastures and rocky valleys— he bought them all. The joke around the hollers was that David Kaplan's land deals went this way: he'd pull up in his Jaguar at some run-down old shack and say to some run-down old hillbilly at the door, "Hi. I'm David Kaplan. Money is no object. How do you do?"

Well, look. What's done is done. Spilled milk is exactly that. Eustace put Heavenly Mountain out of his head as far as he could. He even made jokes about it. When the trees came down and the palatial meditation center went up, Eustace started calling the land Less-Heavenly Mountain, as in "Doesn't it look a lot less heavenly now?" He'd also poke fun at his new neighbors by doing a spot-on impression of the children's TV host Mr. Rogers, droning, in that unmistakable patter, "Heavenly Mountain is our neighbor. Can you say '*neigh*-bor,' children? Heavenly Mountain builds roads that are hard on our environment. Can you say '*hard*-on,' children?"

Anyway, he told himself, a transcendental meditation center wouldn't be the worst neighbor; that was definitely better than thousands of acres of one-family homes. The transcendentalists were coming to Heavenly Mountain to commune with nature, after all, and, what with their Vedic architecture and vegetarian lives, they were sincerely seeking a more harmonious relationship with the universe (even if they were building 4,000-square-foot homes in which to seek that harmony). And David Kaplan would be developing only 10 percent of his land, saving the rest of the forest from logging, hunting, and road construction. And since the resort was a place for people to come to seek peace, there would be a built-in interest in keeping the nearby property wooded and quiet, and that served Eustace's interests, too. So the arrival of David Kaplan wasn't the worst possible event in Eustace's life.

He came to see it this way: OK, so David Kaplan wanted all the property in the world. Fine; Eustace couldn't blame him for wanting it. What Eustace had to concentrate on, instead, was protecting what he already owned. Which meant that David Kaplan was welcome to buy every inch of North Carolina except the 156.16 acres of the Cabell Gragg Land.

But then Cabell Gragg started getting cute. When Eustace went to discuss the property, Cabell now started saying, "Well, you know, those transcendental meditation folks are interested in buying it." Eustace couldn't imagine this to be true; the land had no value to anyone but himself. But then he realized what was happening. As Cabell Gragg watched his neighbors get rich by selling off their valuable farms to David Kaplan, with his slick Jaguar, Cabell decided never to sell to Eustace Conway, with his beat-up 1974 pickup. Cabell wanted the satisfaction of feeling that he was in on this real estate boom, too. He was holding out for the richer man's offer.

Thereupon, Eustace called a summit meeting with David Kaplan. Now, it's not that David Kaplan and Eustace Conway were exactly in love with each other. They were direct competitors—the new-age mountain man verses the new-age real estate developer—and they were probably the two sharpest guys in the county. They'd already had some unpleasant little run-ins. David Kaplan had built himself a big fancy house on Heavenly Mountain, and his porch steps were merely four feet away from Eustace's property line. Eustace thought that was pretty rude, and said so. Moreover, one of the Heavenly Mountain Resort helicopters kept buzzing low over Eustace's nature preserve, day after day, kicking up wind and noise. Christ, how Eustace hated that! How can you keep the sanctuary of Turtle Island with a helicopter flying low overhead? But no matter how many angry phone calls Eustace made, it never stopped. He finally got so fed up that he went after the helicopter one day with a shotgun, put the pilot's face right in his sights, and shouted, *"Get the fuck off my fucking head!"*

Which David Kaplan thought was pretty rude.

So for Eustace to request a favor of David Kaplan was quite an event. It wasn't just a favor; it was a plea. Eustace, recognizing that he had no other choice, just rolled over and showed his neck to his adversary. He told David Kaplan all about the Cabell Gragg Land. He told him exactly how much acreage there was and how much it cost and how many years he had wanted it and why he needed it and what he'd do if he didn't get it. He gave this information, remember, to a man who was openly trying to obtain every inch of land he could get. Then Eustace asked David Kaplan to please buy the Cabell Gragg Land. After which, Eustace would buy the land from David Kaplan. Cabell would have the satisfaction of selling to a rich developer; Eustace would have the land he needed to preserve his dream; and David Kaplan would have . . . ? Well, there wasn't anything in this deal for David Kaplan at all, but it sure would be nice of him to do it.

David Kaplan agreed. The two men didn't sign a single piece of paper; they shook hands on the deal. "If you screw me," Eustace explained politely, "I'm finished." And he walked away, knowing that his life was in the hands of his biggest rival. It was a trapeze act. It was Russian roulette. It was like betting the farm on a pair of deuces. But it was this risk or no chance. Anyhow, he secretly suspected that David Kaplan was a decent man. Not only decent, but surely smart enough to know better than to make a lifelong enemy of a guy like Eustace Conway.

In the end, the gamble worked. David made his offer to Cabell Gragg—the same offer Eustace had been making for years—and Cabell took the bait. David Kaplan bought that crucial piece of land and two days later turned around and sold it with complete honor to Eustace.

Whose empire was now safe.

Granted, Eustace Conway may not be very current. He may not read the newspapers or listen to the radio, and it is true that he did once reply, when asked by a schoolchild in 1995 whether he knew who Bill Clinton was, "I believe Bill Clinton is an American political figure, but I'm not certain." So he's not up to the minute on the latest information, but that doesn't mean he's not as adept a businessman as any guy in a suit with a subscription to the *Economist*. Eustace is a shrewd, keen, and potentially ruthless operator—in the best sense of that word.

Still, this business side is an aspect of Eustace that people generally do not see, not unless they happen to be the people who draw the tax maps down in the Town Hall of Boone, North Carolina. People don't see that calculating side of Eustace Conway because he doesn't talk about it as much as he talks about listening to the sound of the drizzling rain and how to start a fire without a match. Hey, that's not what he's getting paid to talk about. But that's not the only reason people don't see it. For the most part, people don't see that hard business edge of Eustace because they don't want to see it. Because they're afraid that if they look too closely at that side of him, it might spoil the nice image of the buckskin, the teepee, the single shot with the antique musket, the hand-carved wooden bowl, and the wide-open and peaceful smile. That's the image they need today, the image they've always needed.

"Chivalrous in the manners and free as the winds," as the British travel writer Isabel Lucy Bird described the men of the nineteenth-century American West.

"My Primitive Pagan Savage," as Valarie Spratlin said, back when she was first falling in love with Eustace.

It's what we all think to ourselves, back when we're first falling in love with Eustace. Those of us who do, anyway. And we are legion. I know the feeling. I too had that moment of thinking this was the first truly authentic man I'd ever met, the kind of person I'd traveled to Wyoming as a twenty-two-year-old to find (indeed, to *become*)—a genuine soul uncontaminated by modern rust. What makes Eustace seem, on first encounter, like the last of some noble species is that there is nothing "virtual" about his reality. This is a guy who lives, quite literally, the life that, for the rest of the country, has largely become a metaphor.

Think of the many articles one can find every year in the *Wall Street Journal* describing some entrepreneur or businessman as being a "pioneer" or a "maverick" or a "cowboy." Think of the many times these ambitious modern men are described as "staking their claim" or boldly pushing themselves "beyond the frontier" or even "riding into the sunset." We still use this nineteenth-century lexicon to describe our boldest citizens, but it's really a code now, because these guys aren't actually pioneers; they are talented computer programmers, biogenetic researchers, politicians, or media moguls making a big splash in a fast modern economy.

But when Eustace Conway talks about staking a claim, the guy is literally staking a goddamn claim. Other frontier expressions that the rest of us use as metaphors, Eustace uses literally. He *does* sit tall in the saddle; he *does* keep his powder dry; he *is* carving out a homestead. When he talks about reining in horses or calling off the dogs or mending fences, you can be sure that there are real horses, real dogs, or real fences in the picture. And when Eustace goes in for the kill, he's not talking about a hostile takeover of a rival company; he's talking about really killing something.

I remember one time when I was at Turtle Island helping Eustace with some blacksmithing. Eustace's little blacksmith shop is always in action. He's a competent smith in the old-style farm manner, which is to say that he's not crafting fine iron filigree; he's repairing his farm equipment and fitting shoes to his horses. On this day, Eustace was heating iron rods to fix a broken piece on his antique mower. He had a number of irons cooking in his forge at the same time and, distracted by trying to teach me the basics of blacksmithing, he allowed several of them to get too hot, to the point of compromising the strength of the metal. When he saw this, he said, "Damn! I have too many irons in the fire."

Which was the first time I had ever heard that expression used in its proper context. But such is the satisfaction of being around Eustace; everything suddenly seems to be in its proper context. He makes true a notion of frontier identity that has long since passed most men of his generation, most of whom are left with nothing but the vocabulary. And the frontier vocabulary has outlived our actual frontier, because we've based our American masculine identity on that brief age of exploration and romantic independence and westward settlement. We hold on to that identity, long after it has any actual relevance, because we like the idea so much. That's why, I believe, so many men in this country carry a residual notion of themselves as pioneers.

I think particularly of my Uncle Terry, who was born on a farm in Minnesota and raised by the children of American pioneers. Terry, a sensitive and intelligent baby boomer, couldn't get off that homestead fast enough. He came East, started his own business, and now spends his days working as a computer expert. Several years ago Terry got into the computer game called Oregon Trail. The idea of the game was that you, the player, are a nineteenth-century American pioneer, heading West on a wagon trail with your family. To win the game, you have to make it to the Pacific, surviving a large number of virtual hardships, including disease, unexpected snowstorms, attacks by Indians, and starvation across rugged mountain passes. The better prepared you are—in terms of having packed the correct supplies and having selected the safest route—the better your chance of survival.

Uncle Terry loved this game and spent hours at the computer struggling to virtually head westward, much as his grandparents had struggled to literally head in the same direction a century earlier. But there was one thing that frustrated Terry about the game: the computer program didn't allow him to improvise in the face of disaster. He'd suddenly get a message on the screen telling him that the axle on his wagon had broken and that he was going to die because he couldn't proceed. The computer had proclaimed this virtual pioneer a failure. Game over, Terry would stand up from his desk and head to the refrigerator, cursing in annoyance. He'd fetch himself another beer and disparage the game's designers, comically offended.

"If I were really out there on the Oregon Trail, I know I could solve this!" he'd say. "I could figure out how to fix a damn axle. I'm not an idiot! I'd cut down a tree, rig something up!"

He probably could. Not only was Terry raised on a farm; he spent his idealistic youth tramping through the wilderness of America seeking his own kind of independence. Faced with the trials of the Oregon Trail, Terry probably would survive. But he's not out there proving this all day long. On the other hand, Eustace Conway is. Eustace *does* take his animals across the continent, *does* endure all manner of hardship, *does* figure out how to rig something up when the axle snaps.

Where it gets tricky is our deciding what we want Eustace Conway to be, in order to fulfill our notions of him, and then ignoring what doesn't fit into our first-impression romantic image. My initial reaction on witnessing Eustace Conway's life was relief. When I first heard of his life and his adventures, all I could think was *Thank God*. Thank God somebody in America was still living this way. Thank God there was at least one genuine mountain man, frontiersman, pioneer, maverick out there. Thank God there was one truly resourceful and independent wild soul left in this country. Because, at some deep emotional level, Eustace's existence signified to me that somehow it's still true, that we Americans are, against all other available evidence, a nation where people grow free and wild and strong and brave and willful, instead of lazy and fat and boring and unmotivated.

Or that's how I felt when I first met Eustace, and that's how I've since witnessed dozens of other people react when they first meet him. The initial reaction of many Americans, particularly men, when they catch a glimpse of Eustace Conway's life is: "I want to do what you're doing." In fact, on closer examination, they probably don't. While they're a little embarrassed by the ease and convenience of their modern lives, chances are they're not that ready to walk away from it all. *Not so fast, buddy . . .*

Most Americans probably don't want to live off the land in any way that would involve real discomfort, but they still catch a thrill from Eustace's continual assurance that "You can!" Because that's what most of us want to hear. We don't want to be out there in a snowstorm on the Oregon Trail, fixing the broken axle of a covered wagon; we want to feel as though we *could* do it if we had to. And Eustace lives as he does in order to provide us with that comforting proof.

"You can!" he keeps telling us.

And we keep believing him, because *he does!*

He is our mythical inner self, made flesh, which is why it's comforting to meet him. Like seeing a bald eagle. (As long as there's one left, we think, maybe things aren't so bad, after all.) Of course, embodying the mythical hopes of an entire society is a pretty big job for one man, but Eustace has always been up for it. And people also sense *that* in him; they sense his self-assurance of being large enough to serve as a living metaphor, of being strong enough to carry all our desires on his back. So it's safe to idolize him, which is an exciting experience in this callow, disillusioned age when it's not safe to idolize anybody. And people get a little dizzy with that excitement, a little irrational. I know, because I've been there.

One of my favorite pastimes is to go back and reread the entry in my own journal from about the time Eustace and Judson Conway came to visit me in New York City. I especially like the part where I first meet Eustace and describe him as "Judson's charming and wild and completely guileless older brother."

Charming? No doubt.

Wild? Absolutely.

Guileless? Guess again, sister.

There is nothing remotely guileless about this guy, and nowhere is that more evident than in his land deals. People who go up the mountain to see Eustace Conway and his land seldom ask themselves where that land came from. Turtle Island matches Eustace so completely that people believe it grew out of him or he grew out of it. Like everything Eustace represents to the public, his land seems detached from the corruptive processes of our degraded modern society. Against all reason, people find Turtle Island to be a tiny last parcel of the American frontier. And Eustace certainly couldn't have done anything as crass as buying the place; he must have just claimed it.

We can see Eustace through the eyes of Domingo Faustino Sarmiento, a nineteenth-century Argentine intellectual who once visited America long enough to see how "this independent farmer looks for fertile lands, a picturesque spot, something beside a navigable river; and when he has made up his mind, as in the most primitive times in the world's history, he says, 'This is mine!' and without further ado takes possession of the land in the name of the Kings of the World: Work and Good Will." We love this idea so much that thinking any differently about Eustace or about how he nailed his domain would ruin our marvelous and reassuring vision of him as the Last American Man. But the story of Eustace Conway *is* the story of American manhood. Shrewd, ambitious, energetic, aggressive, expansive—he stands at the end of a long and illustrious line of the same.

There's nothing anachronistic about his savvy ways. We want Eustace to be Davy Fuckin' Crockett? Well, fine. Who exactly do we think Davy Crockett was? He was a congressman, that's who. He was from the backwoods, sure, and he was a gifted hunter who had killed a bear with a knife (although probably not when he was a toddler), but he was also slick as all hell and he knew how to exploit his backwoods charisma for political advantage. In a debate with an aristocratic political opponent, the Tennessee woodsman was asked whether he agreed that there should be a radical change "in the judiciary at the next session of legislature." Crockett (dressed in rugged buckskin) won over the local crowd by drawling innocently that he had no idea there was such a thing as a creature called "a judiciary." Which was charming and funny, sure, although probably not true, since Crockett had been working in and around the judiciary for years—as a justice of the peace, a court referee, a town commissioner, and now as a member of the state legislature.

Crockett was a brilliant self-promoter who could always be counted on to give a reporter a witty, hillbilly sound bite or a dramatic tall tale about an encounter with some wild and dangerous "varmut." He was cunning enough to carefully time the release of his heroic memoirs, *The Life and Adventures of Colonel David Crockett of West Tennessee,* to coincide with his 1833 congressional election campaign. "What a miserable place a city is," moaned Crockett. And then went to live in Washington, D.C., anyhow, where he willingly got in bed with his Northeastern Whig rivals in order to see that, appropriately enough, his beloved land bill was passed.

In fact, these famous backwoods American guys all got to be famous backwoods American guys through their intelligence and ambition and carefully styled self-representations. Daniel Boone, the very model of a free-living frontiersman, was a real estate speculator (indeed, a developer) of the highest order. He founded the Kentucky town of Boonesborough and subsequently filed over twenty-nine legal claims to land, eventually owning thousands of acres. He embroiled himself in litigation over border disputes, including one nasty case that he fought through the colonial court system for more than twenty-three years. (Even in the eighteenth century, even for Daniel Boone, the process of landownership was more bureaucratically complicated than the statement "This is mine!" Boone knew how the world worked. As he wrote to one fellow settler, "No Dout you are Desireous your Land Bisness Should be Dunn, but that is a thing impossible without money.")

There happen to be a lot of heroic moments in American history that would have been impossible without money. The reason Daniel Boone became famous was that he entered into a business deal with a schoolteacher from Pennsylvania named John Filson, whose family also owned a lot of land in Kentucky and who was looking for a way to publicize the state and thus increase the value of his property. Filson ended up writing a thrilling book, *The Adventures of Colonel Daniel Boone,* which became a best seller and, as intended, a lure for settlers to come down to Kentucky and buy up all that good Boone-and-Filson-owned land. It was a vastly profitable and clever venture on Boone's part, and it also made him an icon in his own lifetime.

Both Boone and Crockett were much sharper businessmen than

you might have guessed by watching their TV shows in the 1950s. (*"The rippin'est, roarin'est, fightin'est man the frontier ever knew!"*) And they weren't the only clever ones. Kit Carson had dozens of adventure novels written about him and published in New York City while he was still alive (*Kit Carson: Knight of the Plains; Kit Carson: The Prince of the Goldhunters,* among others). And Carson's old boss, the explorer John Frémont, was smart enough to add a little romantic dash to his congressionally commissioned exploration reports to make them national best-sellers. Even Lewis and Clark knew how to sell it. When they were returning from their famous expedition, they outfitted themselves all rugged and cool when they sailed up the river into St. Louis to be welcomed by a thousand cheering residents and no small number of newspaper reporters, one of whom wrote, with admiration, "They really did have the appearance of Robinson Crusoes—dressed entirely in buckskin."

So when Eustace Conway hustles himself "a slick little business deal" or when he trades land for land or when he writes in his journal, "I just put together a big packet of news articles for publicity; there are probably 35 major news articles done on me over the years—this will be an impressive packet for selling myself," or when he exploits his mountain man persona to get himself an audience, he is not betraying his frontier American forefathers in any way; he's *honoring* them. They would recognize immediately what he's up to, and they would admire it, because running that kind of savvy operation is what success has always been about on this continent.

"Working seven days a week, all hours of the day for a year now," Eustace wrote in his journal after Turtle Island had been open a few years. "I guess I am a good example of striving for a high goal, dependent not on immediate returns but on the vision of the future, totally a part of my social and philosophical upbringing. My granddad set an example in many ways with Sequoyah. Even now, a horned owl calls, reminding me of him as the warmth of the fire lives with me."

He didn't owe his father money anymore ("and it is truly a happy day to be releasing this burden"), but there was no end of other challenges facing him. It was an effort of organization to get Boys' Camp and Girls' Camp running at Turtle Island every summer. And there were the realities of dealing with the kids themselves. Someone would cut his hand on sharp obsidian and need stitches; someone would get poison ivy; someone would get caught smoking pot and have to be sent home because of Eustace's lifelong straight-edge intolerance for drugs.

Not to mention the issues of staffing. His personal standards of excellence being what they were, Eustace soon realized it was going to be one difficult task to find solid workers whom he could trust. For a while, his brothers, Judson and Walton, worked for Eustace as counselors. They were great, but they had their own lives going and couldn't be relied on to teach at Turtle Island forever. Walton had finished college and was heading to Europe, where he would live for several years. Judson was already yearning to spend his summers in the West and would soon take off on his own adventures, riding boxcars and hitchhiking. ("I was recently backpacking in the Wind River Range of Wyoming," Judson wrote to Eustace in a typically exuberant postcard. "I fought an early blizzard for 15 miles above the timberline—12,000 feet. It came close to taking my life. It was great fun. I hope camp is going good. Oh, by the way, I'm a cowboy now.")

Aside from his brothers, it was extremely tough for Eustace to find people who would work as hard (or nearly as hard) as he did and still give him the respect he felt he deserved. For a man who often said that he found the idea of a mere eight-hour workday "disgusting," Eustace was rarely satisfied with his employees' efforts. They would come to Turtle Island "awed, amazed, and in love with this place" (as one ex-employee wrote) and then seem shocked that they had to work so hard. Again and again, he lost his team, either by their deserting or by his firing them.

He wished he could magically have the staunch staff his grandfather had worked with at Camp Sequoyah back in the 1930s, instead of these petulant modern kids with all their *feelings* and *needs*. His grandfather had demanded purity and perfection, and, by and large, he got it. If Chief so much as heard a rumor that a counselor had been seen smoking a cigarette in town on his day off, that counselor would come back to camp and find his bags packed for him. Chief never concerned himself with trampling on people's feelings or being labeled as "unfair." He had ultimate authority, which was all Eustace was asking for. That, and a commitment from people to try to work as hard as he did. Which was a tall order.

I've worked with Eustace Conway. Nobody gets to visit Turtle Island without working. I spent a week up there one autumn helping Eustace build a cabin. There were three of us on the job—Eustace, myself, and a quiet and steadfast young apprentice named Christian Kaltrider. We worked twelve hours each day, and I don't recall lunch breaks. Silent, steady work. The way Eustace works, it's like a march—numbing and constant. You get the feeling you're in a platoon. You stop thinking and just give in to the pace. Eustace is the only one who speaks at all when it's work time, and that's to issue commands, which he does with unassailable authority, although every command is polite. There was only one moment in the process where he stopped working. Eustace asked me to please go to his pile of tools and fetch him an adz.

"I'm sorry," I said, "I don't know what that is."

He described the adz for me—a tool that resembles an ax, but with a curved blade set at a right angle to the handle, used for dressing wood. I found the tool and was walking back toward the cabin to return it, when Eustace suddenly put down his hammer, stood up, wiped his forehead, and said, "I'm pretty sure I've seen the word 'adz' used in literature. Wasn't it Hemingway who wrote about the sound of the adz coming from a front yard where someone was building a coffin?"

I slapped a horsefly on my neck and offered, "Are you possibly thinking of Faulkner? I think there's a scene in *As I Lay Dying* where Faulkner describes the sound of someone building a coffin in a front yard."

"Yes, of course," Eustace said. "Faulkner."

And he returned to work. Left me standing there with an adz in my hand, staring at him. *Yes, of course. Faulkner.* Now, back to work everybody.

Eustace wanted to finish the floor of the cabin by sundown that day, so we were working fast. He was so eager to get the job done that he used a chain saw to cut up the bigger logs. Eustace was sawing through a log when the chain saw hit a knot, kicked back, and jumped up toward his face. He deflected it with his left hand, sawing into two of his fingers.

He made one quick sound like "Rah!" and pulled back his hand. The blood started pumping out. Christian and I froze, silent. Eustace shook his hand once, sending out a shower of blood, and then recommenced sawing. We waited for him to say something or try to stop the bleeding, which was fairly prolific, but he didn't. So we both kept at our work. He continued bleeding and sawing and hammering and bleeding and sawing more. By the end of the day, Eustace's entire arm, the logs, the tools, both of my hands, and both of Christian's hands were covered with blood.

And I thought, *Ah, so this is what's expected of us.*

We worked until dusk and headed back to base camp. I walked next to Eustace, and his arm hung down, dripping. We passed a flowering bush and, always the teacher, he said, "Now, that's an interesting sight. You don't usually see jewelweed with both orange and yellow blossoms on one plant. You can make an ointment out of the stem, you know, to relieve the itching of poison ivy."

"Very interesting," I said.

Only after dinner did Eustace bandage his savaged hand. He mentioned the incident just once, saying, "I'm lucky I didn't saw my fingers off."

Later that night I asked Eustace what his most serious injury had been, and he said he'd never been seriously injured. One time he did slice open his thumb in a careless moment while dressing a deer carcass. It was a deep, long cut "with the meat hanging out and everything," and it clearly needed stitches. So Eustace stitched it, using a needle and thread and the stitch he knows well from sewing buckskin. Healed just fine.

"I don't think I could sew up my own skin," I said.

"You can do anything you believe you can do."

"I don't believe I could sew up my own skin."

Eustace laughed and conceded, "Then you probably couldn't."

* * *

"People have such a hard time getting things done out here," Eustace complained in his journal in 1992. "The environment is so new. It really isn't a problem for them. It is *my* stress over their slow, ignorant pace that bothers me. *They're* blissfully enjoying every minute."

Challenges were coming at Eustace from every direction. A friend pointed out that it was a mistake for Eustace not to carry personal health insurance. "But I'm healthy!" he protested. So his friend explained that if Eustace were to be seriously injured in an accident and needed intensive care, the hospital could raid all his assets, including the value of his land, to cover the expense. Jesus Christ! Eustace had never thought of such a thing before. Plus he had no end of taxes to manage and surveying to pay for. Plus he had to deal with poachers on his land. He ran down on foot some dumb young kid who dropped a buck out of season with an illegal gun just a few hundred feet from Eustace's kitchen. Even more horrifying, he himself had been accused of poaching.

He was teaching a class of eighty young students one afternoon when four government cars and eight lawmen pulled up and arrested him for poaching deer. Tipped off by a resentful neighbor, the game warden went straight to Eustace's cache of dozens of deerskins and accused Eustace of having killed the animals without a permit. In fact, the skins had been given to Eustace by people who wanted them tanned. It was a terrifying moment.

Eustace had to spend the next month collecting letters of evidence from every person who had given him a deerskin, as well as documents from environmentalists and politicians across the South swearing that Eustace Conway was a committed naturalist who would never hunt more than was legally allowed. On the day of his trial, though, he had the balls to wear his deerskin pants to the courtroom. Why not? It's what he always wore. He strode into his trial looking like Jeremiah goddamn Johnson. Ma-Maw, the elderly Appalachian neighbor who lived down the holler and who hated the Law as much as the next hillbilly, came with Eustace to give him moral support. ("I'm afraid the judge might take these buckskin pants right off me and throw me in jail," Eustace joked to Ma-Maw, who said sternly, "Don't you worry. I have my bloomers on under this skirt. If they steal your pants, I'll just take off my bloomers and give 'em to you. You can just wear my bloomers to jail, Houston!") Ma-Maw loved all the Conway boys, but she never *could* get their names quite right . . .

When his time came to speak, Eustace gave the judge the most eloquent and impassioned earful about his life and dreams and visions of saving nature, until the judge—amazed and impressed—said, as he was signing the papers to dismiss the poaching charges, "Is there anything *I* can do to help you with Turtle Island, son?"

Eustace also had to deal with such trials as a letter that the Triangle Native American Society sent to the mayor of Garner, North Carolina. The letter expressed the society's concern over "information we have received about an individual who will be participating in an event being sponsored by your town on October 12. The person in question is Mr. Eustace Conway . . . It is our understanding that Mr. Conway presents information to the general public and special interest groups on how to survive and live off Mother Earth in as simple a way as possible. He has also been known to set up structures commonly known as tepees. Indians living in the Northeast and Southeast sections of this country never lived in tepees. North Carolina Indians lived in structures called 'long houses.' We are seriously concerned that individuals attending the special event will leave it with three very wrong impressions: (a) Mr. Conway is a Native American, (b) Mr. Conway represents and speaks for native people, and (c) North Carolina Indians lived in tepees. We humbly ask that Mr. Conway not be allowed to erect the structure commonly known as a tepee for the reasons cited above."

This was exactly the kind of shit Eustace had no time for. For the love of God, if there was anyone on the planet who knew that North Carolina Indians didn't live in teepees, it was Eustace Conway, who had studied the languages of most North Carolina Indian tribes, who could dance the most obscure dances of North Carolina Indian tribes, who regularly fed himself using the hunting techniques of North Carolina Indian tribes and who was always careful to explain to his audiences that he himself was the product of modern white American culture (in order to prove that *anyone* could live as he does) and that the teepee was a housing method of the Great Plains. Also, as he explained in his reply, "I am more than just 'an Anglo imitating the ways of the Native American,' not just a 'hobbyist.' I have a deep understanding and peace with the Indian way. . . . I guess you can't convey such feelings in a written letter . . . but in passing the pipe, living on Mother Earth, and listening to the winged ones of the air and the four-legged ones of the ground, I am honoring all the powers of the universe."

And then there were the goddamn health inspectors.

"One of the first days of camp," he wrote in his journal in July 1992, "Judson came running up to get me. I thought someone was hurt. Instead, the health inspectors in suits were coming up to inspect camp. Well, I put on a white shirt and went down to meet the demons. I kept my attitude positive—explained how this was a unique camp. I showed them all around—the camp sites, latrine, kitchen (which was very clean)—and charmed them as much as I could. They got an admiration of what we are doing. David Shelly, a young camper, gave them a knife-sharpening demonstration and lesson—impressive. They told me they would 'sleep on it' to see if they could figure out a way to accept our nonstandard situation."

His work was endless. For all his love of the winged ones of the air and the four-legged ones of the ground, he hardly had time to write his nature observations in his journals.

"I really enjoy seeing the pileated woodpecker fly over in its dipping flight," he managed to finally scribble down one morning at four A.M. when his day's work had ended. "I hear them all day long, it seems. Nice to have this treasured bird as background music. Crows aplenty and an occasional hawk. Ruby-crowned kinglets are about; one almost flew into my face when I was up on the sacred spot above the meadow-to-be. Deer tracks around, but I haven't seen any turkey this year. I enjoy the change of seasons. I look forward (and I don't say or think this enough) to the days I will be free to enjoy many of the subtle daily changes of weather and life of the Appalachian valley, here where my heart is, here where I am planting roots, here where I am fighting, here where I hope to die."

For now, though, that was a distant dream. A more typical entry was, "I called and verified several school bookings last night, always doing paperwork. I think I could do 3 hours a day and not keep caught up. I had to tell a lady last night that I couldn't do the program in the spring for her school. I had a strange feeling of pride to know I am in enough demand to have to turn work down, but I'm afraid I did not feel proper empathy for her position. I must understand the other side of the picture."

He was getting so overbooked for speaking engagements that he spent some money on producing a 45-minute video called *All My Relatives: The Circle of Life*, which he described in a letter to school principals across the South as "a classroom resource that can be used any time of the year." The video allowed Eustace to be in two places at once. "Not only for history classes, *All My Relatives* is also well suited for life sciences such as ecology and biology as well as anthropology," Eustace wrote in the covering letter. "The enclosed flier provides more information, but reading about it does not do it justice; it needs to be seen. I am very pleased with the production and happy that it can be offered to your school at such a reasonable price."

The fact is, though, that Eustace was becoming less convinced that his speaking tours were doing any good. For a man who had honestly thought he could change the world if he could borrow enough people's ears for a long enough time, the numbing routine of brief classroom visits was no longer satisfying.

"I met with a sixth-grade class today," he wrote after one unsettling encounter. "I could not believe the lack of education and inspiration I met with! They [the schoolchildren] were pitiful. . . . No motivation whatsoever. No understanding of their world. Just robots going through an established pattern of living to get by. We are truly on a survival level here—no arts or creativity. No passion. Just a slow monotone existence in oppressed ignorance. I asked if they knew what the word 'sacred' meant. They didn't know. They put money, new cars, and telephones on their lists of what was valuable to them. One out of the fifty had an idea of sacredness. The boy said, 'Life.' One small soul in the class was on the right track away from greed as a motivator, and thank goodness for him . . . I was passionately challenged by the situation and gave it a big push, trying to get them to wake up and think, but I don't feel I got very far. So here we are in the 1990s, where children are now less than human."

Only two short years after founding Turtle Island, Eustace was starting to burn out. He wrote in his journal in July 1991, "I realize that I really crave time spent alone. I don't want to be around people. The pressure of this community of folks here at Turtle Island is wearing on me. They take up my time and consume my life . . . The office—everyone wants to sit around, and I can't get any work done. Yesterday while I was trying to do paperwork, Valarie, Ayal, and Jenny came in and started having a staff discussion. What an invasion of my space! Last night someone turned off the answering machine so it wouldn't answer—after I have spent 200 hours working on the phone lines. I got ready to take a cold creek bath this morning to cool down but someone had taken my bucket from its place by the creek. I found a rotting sock in the yard. . . . The lambs were left in their pen today (not my responsibility). I let them out and thought of the day I had spent building the pen, and now nobody wants to take responsibility for the lambs.

"What am I to do? I need to figure out how to manage myself and my site so it won't be so emotionally draining. One impulse is to quit all of the activities that we do here. That would solve the problem, but that would not be good for the camp and the purpose of the center. . . . What is important? Boundaries (personal) are at stake here. Should I please others or myself? I have worked very hard to make this place what it is. What have *they* done? What investment have *they* ever made in anything that is a challenge? How am I to put up with them? Should I? Money transfers is a way that people *can* help—to give something to me that I need . . . It is shocking how this takes a toll on me. I am back now after a six-hour depressed nap in the middle of the day . . . What to do? Ideas—delegate authority—get everyone aware of my needs emotionally and give them responsibility for keeping clear. I guess I could not even be here. That's an idea. Imagine that. So many people to deal with . . . Well, good luck, Eustace."

By the next year, Eustace was feeling plumb out of luck. He was too exhausted and disillusioned even to complain in his diary. He wrote only one bleak entry for the entire year: "What I feel inspired to write today is this deep emotional dissatisfaction with the reality of our times—corruption of government—fake people—sick values and unconscious people living meaningless lives."

And, on the next page, written exactly twelve months later, this message: "Ditto, or is it spelled diddo, whatever, from last year's entry. Except worse. Maybe more cynical."

Worst of all, he was losing Valarie.

Consumed with his business and frequently on the road, Eustace was rarely with his girlfriend. She was working hard, too, and she was still in love with Eustace, but she was increasingly feeling that she had lost herself in him.

"I still love this man," Valarie told me, looking back on the relationship with fifteen years of distance. "I still have every gift he made for me, from a knife sheath decorated with beads to a little hatchet I always used up at Turtle Island to a beautiful pair of earrings. If I died tomorrow, I'd want to be buried in those earrings. I loved learning from Eustace. I loved how he always gave me do-it-yourself birthday gifts. I told him one time that I wanted a pipe of my own for ceremonies and praying, and I came home one day to find a beautiful piece of soapstone on the kitchen counter. 'What is that?' I asked. He said, 'It's your pipe, Valarie.' 'I don't get it,' I said. 'Where is it?' And he grinned that wonderful Eustace Conway grin and said, 'It's inside the stone, honey. We just have to get it out of there together.'

"I loved him, but I lost my identity in his, because he's so overwhelming and powerful. I had my own thing going in life before I met him, but I quickly became the person who was beneath him, and my world started to revolve around his. He was and is a loving but intolerant person. Someone else's opinion was never welcome. He was obsessed with making money, with buying land, with success, and he was always on the road. It got to the point where I never saw him. The only time we spoke was when he gave me orders."

Valarie and Eustace had a good mutual friend, a Native American guy named Henry, who often went to powwows with them and who taught at Turtle Island. After a few years of loneliness and dissatisfaction, after feeling more and more that she was nothing but "the First Lady of Turtle Island," Valarie had an affair with Henry. She hid the relationship from Eustace and denied that it had ever happened, even when, suspicious, he had asked her directly. Eustace, knowing something was up, took Henry off for a private evening to smoke a ceremonial pipe, and asked point blank whether he'd slept with Valarie. It is the most sacred tenet of Native American spiritually not to lie when smoking the pipe, but Henry looked Eustace in the eye and denied the affair.

Eustace was in torment. He knew in his heart that something was wrong and that he didn't have all the facts. Devastated, he broke up with Valarie because he felt he couldn't trust her. A few months after they split, Valarie came back, told him the truth, and begged for forgiveness.

But you don't lie to Eustace Conway and then get a second chance. He was too horrified to even consider taking her back or transcending the injury. It blew him apart to learn that he could not find trust in this most intimate of relationships. And after all the pain he had suffered from his father, he had promised himself to banish from his life immediately anyone who would deliberately hurt or betray him. She would have to go. Eustace meditated and anguished for a year over the question of whether he could ever trust her again, and in the end he acknowledged that he could not reach that point of forgiveness.

"Truth is sacred to me," he wrote to Valarie, telling her why they could no longer be together. "It *is* me. I live by it. I die by it. I asked you for the truth. I told you that you should always tell me the truth . . . that I did not care how much it would hurt. I begged for the truth. . . . You shit on me, you shit on our truth. What does this show about your ability to fulfill my needs? Go to hell. Goddamn! This is enough . . . How much abuse can I take? I have already witnessed my Dad's cruelty . . . I needed your support—I got a backstabbing. I love you so much. You are precious. I could just hold you and pet your sweet head forever, but my truthful self has said, enough is enough!"

And as for his friend Henry?

"To smoke the pipe with me when I was coming in need and praying and asking for the truth? And you lied like a motherfucker. You need to die. Break the pipe in half and shove the stem through your heart and you will share an inkling of the pain I know. Now the woman I wanted to marry is a whore. You don't deserve to be a human being. Fuck yourself and die."

"I do see and understand," Valarie wrote to Eustace, months after they'd separated, "how you can feel the need to avoid accepting *any* responsibility for the disintegration and ultimate failure of our relationship, because that would mean that you would have to admit that maybe, just maybe, you own a part in creating the pain which you and I now experience. To admit that might force you to take a good, hard look at yourself, and, as we both know, you don't have the time, the willingness, or even, excuse my bluntness, the humility to consider this. Believe me, I'm not trying to lessen my responsibility for what I did, but only trying to help you see the whole picture. And, yes, it's much easier to place all the blame for pain on another: 'My folks made me this way,' 'The government is screwing up the planet,' or 'Valarie broke my heart' . . . Your wanting to break up with me, because, as you said, '*I* shit on your heart,' and you can't go back on your promise to yourself not to accept anything but truth sounds great to you, I'm sure . . . But if love is real it endures all, forgives all, and even survives all. . . . In the process of going through a painful experience, you could have gained a woman who finally realized how to love and be loved, a woman who understood you, loved you, believed in you, supported you and gave up *everything* to be a part of your dream. Don't you realize that you're throwing away the greatest gift? A woman who accepts your faults, shortcomings, mental cruelties, and, yes, even your weirdness, and still loves you through it all. YOU GODDAMN STUPID CONCEITED ASSHOLE."

It was a dreadful year.

But years pass. And so do heartaches. Soon after Valarie left, along came Mandy. "Hello, Beautiful," Eustace wrote to this new love. "I appreciate getting to know you better . . . you have a lot to offer. When you can open up to this world we will be blessed for it. I feel dizzy learning you, dizzy meeting you. I do feel we were meant to come together. . . . When I am with you I feel young and innocent. I could smile into your eyes forever . . ."

Then Mandy left, and along came Marcia. "I am high from meeting Marcia. She has been a blessing to me—an inspiration and a new hope. I pray for God's guidance in all that I do."

Then along came Dale. "So kind, so supportive, she shares my vision as well as anyone."

Then there was Jenny. "A beautiful girl with black hair and a long white linen dress . . . what will become of you, of me, of desires, of dreams?"

Then there was Amy. "Beautiful long hair, innocent, radiant smile, I met her when I was teaching a workshop in a school, and she was so beautiful I could hardly concentrate on my words. I just kept staring at her and then went up to her after class and said, 'Can I spend some time with you?' "

Eustace ended up spending a good deal of time with Amy. She was a graduate student in science, brilliant and serious, and she turned out to be a great helper. He spent a week with her in her family's summer house on Cape May, New Jersey, and wrote in his journal:

"We have been housebound the week I have been here. We have gotten into paperwork for Turtle Island, with Amy typing things out on her computer and printing out master copies for me to Xerox later or mail out or whatever is appropriate . . . summer camp brochure, summer camp application, medical information and release form, lists of what should be in first-aid kits, emergency plan cards and hospital maps . . . a letter to Cabell Gragg to encourage him to sell me the land in 1994, a letter to the Turtle Island staff to thank and encourage them, list of staff members, names and phone numbers for my calendar, workshop advertisement for spring classes, list of what to bring and not to bring (revised) and orientation for campers when they come . . . confirmation contracts and more . . . Wow. Amy is very good at coming up with first-class results—a bit slow, but top-quality finished product."

Then Amy was gone, her letters filed away in an envelope that Eustace labeled: "A fantasy with Amy that was spoiled by reality—dreams turned into education. At least I lived it for what it is and learned."

Then there was Tonya, the beautiful and mysterious Aboriginal rock-climber. Eustace and Tonya went off to New Zealand and Australia for a few months and climbed every cliff and mountain they could find. She was stunning and powerful, and Eustace truly loved her, but he believed there was something hidden in her soul that held back from loving him completely, and, anyway, it was hard for Eustace to give his heart to her as much as he might have liked to because of the recent memory of the one woman who had almost broken him in half with passion and desire and misery.

That was Carla. Carla, the beautiful and mysterious Appalachian folk singer, was the massive love of Eustace Conway's life. He met her at a folk festival where he was speaking and she was singing. ("You should have seen this girl on stage playing her guitar with her long hair and miniskirts, dancing and grinding all over the place until you damn near had to mop up the whole *world*, she was that hot.") Eustace withered and melted and collapsed into love for Carla, and to this day thinks she's the closest to an ideal he's ever encountered.

"She was amazing. Here was this beautiful, modern Appalachian woman, a genuine coal miner's daughter from Kentucky who had skills from four generations back of the people I admire the most in my culture. She was like a goddess to me. She played music, wrote, danced, was the best cook I've ever met . . . was wild and free and brave and brilliant and confident and with an incredible, flexible, muscular, bronzed body. She worked with horses, could play any instrument, could cook a pie over an open fire, make medicinal herbs, make her own soap, could butcher livestock, wanted to have lots of children . . . was the most capable and generous and insatiable lover I've ever met. God, I could go on and on! . . . She was a true child of nature, and she wore sexy gingham old-timey dresses and danced through the woods like a young deer. And she was so talented it made me feel I would drop everything to help her advance her career as a musician. And she was much smarter than me! And she could sew and she could draw! And she could *spell!* She could do anything! This woman was a dream beyond even *my* capacity to dream, and I'm a goddamn dreamer!"

Almost immediately, Eustace asked Carla to marry him. And she threw back her head with laughter and said, "It would be my pleasure, Eustace."

So they got engaged, and Carla moved up to Turtle Island. Now, looking back, Carla says there were serious problems from the start. "I felt he was a kindred spirit at first. But it was no more than six weeks into the relationship that I saw things about him that frightened me. I come from an old-fashioned and rigid Appalachian patriarchy, so I was very sensitive about some of the gender roles I saw Eustace playing out. In some ways, he had a true egalitarian sense about women, but every time he got furious at me for not putting dinner on the table exactly at the right time, it made me really nervous.

"Also, my family disliked Eustace intensely. They thought he was disingenuous, a con artist. They were concerned about the power he had over me. We'd only just met when he came to my family's house, had a quick dinner with my parents, packed up my belongings, and took me away. My family is really close, and they felt like I'd been stolen. Eustace thought my family was turning me against him, so he tried to keep me isolated from them. Well, when my father and my brothers realized that, they practically loaded their guns onto their truck to come and get me back."

It wasn't long before Carla, a world-class free spirit, began to drift. Soon, she was involved with someone else. Eustace discovered her indiscretion in the strangest way. He got an enormous phone bill one month—hundreds of dollars of phone calls placed from his office in the middle of the night to the same number. Curious, Eustace dialed the number, and when a man answered, Eustace explained his situation. Then he had an inspiration.

"You don't happen to know someone named Carla, do you?" he asked.

"Sure," said the guy. "She's my girlfriend."

"No kidding," Eustace said. "And here I thought she was my fiancée."

It seems that Carla had been sneaking out of the teepee every night and hiking down to the office to call this sexy banjo player she'd been having an affair with. Another betrayal. This was not, as the old cowboy song goes, Eustace Conway's first rodeo. And, as we know, Eustace is not a man who can live with someone he perceives to be a liar and cheat. Carla had to go. It had been a marathon love affair, and now it was over. Eustace was unraveled by it. He was flattened. He was *riven*.

In December 1993, he wrote in his journal: "Fighting depression, resentment, and pain. It really hurts, the relationship with Carla, the rejection, the 'not working out.' I have never tried so hard—I gave it everything I had. I have never hurt so much."

He was thirty-two years old and was shocked to look around and suddenly notice that, while he had accomplished much through sheer force of will, he didn't have a wife and children. By this point, he should have been well into a family. Where was the beautiful woman with the loose curls and the gingham dress making buttermilk pancakes in the breaking light of dawn? Where were the strong and sturdy youngsters, playing quietly on the cabin floor and learning from their gentle father how to whittle hickory? Where had Eustace gone wrong? Why couldn't he keep these women he fell in love with? They always seemed oppressed or overwhelmed by him. And he didn't feel they understood him or supported him. Maybe he was picking the wrong kind of person. Maybe he was incapable of sustaining intimacy or was too fearful of being hurt to let a relationship take its often twisty turns. Maybe he needed to try a new approach. It was becoming clear that, in love, Eustace was failing to make this most essential connection.

He asked a friend who was a psychologist to come to Turtle Island for a walk one day. He took her in the woods and told her that he feared that there was something wrong with him emotionally, that he couldn't make his relationships with other people work. The folks he labored with at Turtle Island were always angry at him or misunderstanding him, and he wasn't as close to his brothers as he would like to be, and he was always driving women away or not getting close enough to trust people. He told her about his childhood and confessed that he still held a lot of pain about his father and wondered whether this was all connected.

"I think I need to talk to a professional," he said.

The psychologist answered, "Everything you need to make you

happy, Eustace, is right here in this forest. Modern psychology isn't for you. You're the healthiest person I know." Man, do people ever get a dream of Eustace Conway in their minds and then make it *stick*. This woman must have been so compelled by a Thoreau-inspired and idealized vision of life in the wilderness ("There can be no very black melancholy to him who lives in the midst of nature and has his senses still") that she didn't want to take a closer look at someone who was not a concept, but a real and afflicted person. Maybe it would have cost her too much to let go of her idea of Eustace. It's hard to blame her; she wouldn't have been the first woman to deny all appearances to keep this pagan savage as pure in her heart as he was the day she first met him.

Not necessarily convinced, and still deeply depressed, Eustace tried his father one more time.

"I am psychologically sick," he wrote to his dad, "beaten down by years of oppression. I am damaged. I hurt. Every day I wake up and I am in pain over this. Show this letter to a psychologist and see if they have any advice for me. Please don't misunderstand my most sincere gratitude for the help you give me with chores like money management. I do *very much* appreciate it. I hope that rather than be interpreted as an 'attack,' my emotional truths can be appreciated as fuel for growth and understanding. A healthier relationship is my goal, not a more aggravated one. Respectfully, Eustace."

Again, no response.

I know Eustace Conway's parents well. I've been a guest in their home and eaten dinner with them many times. Like everybody else, I call Mrs. Conway "Big Mom," and, like everyone else, I adore her. I love her generosity and her stories about when she lived in Alaska. I love that, whenever I come to her door, she hugs me and says, "There's our mountain girl!"

And I must admit that I enjoy being around Eustace Conway's father. I like his intelligence and his wit, and I find him to be endlessly inquisitive in the same bizarre and precise way as his son; he wants to know exactly how many hours it took me to drive from Boone to Gastonia, and when I tell him, he calculates immediately (and correctly) that I must have stopped for forty-five minutes to have a meal or I would have arrived sooner. His precision, of course, is relentless. Being a "creature of perfect logic," he doesn't yield an inch and I can see where he would be impossible to live with. His conversations with his wife are filled with such baffling exchanges:

MRS. CONWAY: There's a slight chance that Judson will come visit tomorrow.

MR. CONWAY: Why do you say that? You don't know that to be true at all. Did he call to say he was coming?

MRS. CONWAY: No, but I left a message on his machine to invite him.

MR. CONWAY: Then it's puzzling to me why you would say that there is a slight chance he's coming to visit us. Exactly what percentage of a chance do you suppose that would be, Karen, when we haven't heard from the boy at all? Obviously, we know nothing about whether he will be coming or not. To say that there is a "slight chance" is incorrect and misleading of you.

MRS. CONWAY: I'm sorry.

MR. CONWAY: But nobody listens to my opinions.

So you can imagine.

Still, I can talk to the man. When I visit the Conways, I often talk to Big Eustace about the *Wizard of Oz* books, the wonderful series of fantasy stories that L. Frank Baum wrote back at the turn of the century. It seems that Big Eustace and I were both raised reading the same beautiful hardcover editions of these books. (In Mr. Conway's childhood, he received one book a year as a Christmas present, while I inherited the entire antique set from my grandmother.) Most people don't know that there were sequels to the original Dorothy Gale story, so Big Eustace was delighted to find that I knew the stories well and could recall each lush Art Deco illustration and discuss the most obscure characters. Tik-Tok, Billina the Chicken, the Hungry Tiger, the Gnome King, the Rollers, and Polychrome (the rainbow's daughter)—I know them all, and so does he, and we can talk about that stuff for hours.

Other times, he takes me out to his yard and teaches me about the birds of North Carolina. And once we went outside at midnight to look at the stars. "Have you seen Mars lately?" Mr. Conway asked. I admitted that I had not, so he pointed it out to me. He told me that he likes to come out every night to follow that planet's orbit in order to see how close Mars is drifting toward Saturn.

"They've been getting closer and closer each day for three months," he said. "After all, remember what the word 'planet' means—wandering body."

So sometimes Big Eustace and I talk about books and sometimes we talk about opera and sometimes we talk about constellations. But mostly we talk about his son. Big Eustace always wants to know how Little Eustace is doing up there at Turtle Island. Who are his apprentices? Is he planning any big trips? Has he constructed more buildings? How does that treacherous road up the mountain look? Does he seem overworked or depressed?

I try to fill him in. And once—because I cannot stay away from the most silent intimacies of other people's private lives—I said, "He's doing well, Mr. Conway, but I believe he is desperate for your approval."

"That's nonsense."

"No, it's not nonsense. It's true."

"He doesn't ever talk to me," he answered, "so I never know what's going on with him. He wants nothing to do with me, apparently."

Indeed, the two Eustace Conways rarely talk and they see each other even less. The occasional Christmas will just about do it for the year between these two men, and Little Eustace is loath to sleep at his parents' home because he so dislikes being around his father. Still, one evening in the spring of the year 2000, Eustace returned home to Gastonia to spend the night. It was odd to the point of shocking that he would appear on their doorstep in the middle of May, when there was no big family holiday as a motivator. But Eustace had some lumber he wanted to check out near Gastonia, so he thought he'd drop by for dinner. I went with him.

We pulled up to the house, the house where Eustace had lived the worst years of his life, and found his father standing in the front yard, picking at an old lawn mower, which was small, push-style, beat-up, and fully rusted. Eustace stepped out of the truck and smiled.

"What do you have there, Dad?" he asked.

"This is a perfectly good lawn mower that I found in someone's trash last night when I was out riding my bicycle."

"No kidding? Someone threw that away?"

"Isn't that ridiculous? It's perfectly good."

"That's a nice-looking lawn mower, Dad. Real nice."

The mower actually looked as if it had been fished out of the bottom of a pond.

"Does it run?" Eustace asked.

"Naturally it runs."

"Boy, that is nice."

I had never before seen Eustace Conway and his father together. After all my years of connection to the family, this was the first face-to-face meeting I'd witnessed. I can't say what I'd expected, but not this—not Eustace leaning against his truck with a casual smile, complimenting his father's salvaged lawn mower. And not this beaming father, giddy to show off his latest find.

"You can see here, son, that there was a break in one of the handlebars, but I welded a piece of metal over it like so, and now it's perfectly operable."

"Nice."

"Do you have a use for this at Turtle Island?"

"I'll tell you what, Dad. I can find a use for that lawn mower. I could take the motor out for some other purpose, or I could disassemble it and use the parts, or I could use the mower myself or give it to one of my neighbors. That'd be great. I'd be happy to take it. I can always find a use for things; you know that."

The next minute, father and son, both grinning, were loading the mower into the back of Eustace's truck.

Lord, what a dinner it was in Gastonia that night! The two Eustaces entertained each other all evening. They had no eyes for anyone else. I had never seen Mr. Conway so animated, and Eustace, too, was in high form. I swear they were showing each other off to me. They were on fire for each other. And it was more heartbreaking for me to see these two men craving each other's approval than it would have been to watch them fight. They could not, it seemed, have been more doggedly seeking closeness.

They nudged each other to tell favorite family stories. Eustace got his dad to tell about the time he went to the emergency room with a seriously cut leg and got so irritated that the nurses ignored him that he lay down on the floor in front of the triage desk and refused to move until he was attended to. Then Mr. Conway beamed while Eustace told adventure stories about hiking the Appalachian Trail, specifically about the time he was so thirsty, he drank water from around the carcass of a raccoon he'd found rotting in a stagnant puddle "with blue ribbons of putrefied flesh waving around in the water." Mr. Conway howled, thrilled by the scene.

"I can't imagine anyone else who would do such a thing!" he exclaimed.

After dinner, Eustace and his father stepped out into the yard to discuss the health of a certain holly bush that might need to be transplanted. It was a balmy Southern evening, and the sun hung so low in the sky against feathery clouds that the air was everywhere traced with a golden haze. The men stood in the yard, hands in their pockets, talking about the holly. Then, suddenly, there was a birdsong—long and melodic. Like actors cued by the same director, father and son looked up at the same moment.

"What is that?" Eustace asked. "Is that a mockingbird?"

"I don't know . . ."

Again, the birdsong.

"Whoa," Eustace said, standing quite still.

"I've never heard a mockingbird sing like that," Mr. Conway said, in a low and intimate voice. "I think it may be a catbird."

The melody played again—sweet, extended.

"That doesn't sound like any catbird I've ever heard," Eustace said.

"I have to admit, neither have I. It sounds like a flute, doesn't it? I don't know that it could be a mockingbird. I'd swear it was a catbird, but I've never heard a catbird sound so . . . harmonic."

"I've heard birds singing like that only in rainforests," said the son.

"It almost sounds operatic," said the father.

Quietly, they stood together, heads titled back, gazing up into the dapple of lush foliage from the overgrown dogwood and magnolia. The bird sang as though reading from music, like a soprano warming up for a concert, running through scale after scale. What common North Carolina bird could possibly make such a superb song? They weighed the options. At this season, at this hour, what could it be? The men wore identical expressions of enraptured perplexity as they listened to the bird and heard out each other's intelligent speculations.

"Can you see it?" Mr. Conway asked.

"You know, Dad, I think it's coming from around the corner of the house," Eustace whispered.

"Yes! I think you're right."

"Let me go see if I can spot him, figure out what he is."

"Yes! Go!"

Eustace crept around the corner of his father's house as the bird sang on. Mr. Conway watched his son with an expression of perfect and relaxed pleasure. His face was all pride and interest. It was a lovely moment.

So I had to ask. "Mr. Conway? Do you think Eustace will find the bird?"

Mr. Conway's expression of pleasure erased itself swiftly, replaced by a hard and more familiar look—annoyance. The transformation took only an instant, but it was like watching an ugly metal garage door slam down over an attractive storefront. A most unsightly security measure. Clearly, he had forgotten I was there. Had I been eavesdropping? Had I watched the whole scene unfold? And was I now asking him to somehow validate his son?

"No," Mr. Conway said, firmly. "He won't find the bird. He's no good at such things. Now, if one of his brothers was here, he'd find it. Those men have a talent for birds. But not Eustace. He's hopeless at such things."

With that, Mr. Conway walked away and into the house. Closed the door behind him. He walked right away from the finest hour of the evening. I was staggered. Would it have been so painful for this man, who was obviously brimming with pleasure, to say a kind word about his son? After all this time? Would it have killed him to yield a single goddamn centimeter once in his life?

Apparently so.

The conclusion of this story, needless to say, is that Eustace Conway did spot that bird. Of course he did. He sneaked up under the bird because he had decided to do so, and because he can do anything he decides to do. He caught it singing and confirmed that it was a catbird, after all—but what a voice! Had ever a catbird sung a prettier song? Eustace confirmed this and then came darting around the corner of the house, bursting with excitement.

"I saw it, Dad!" Little Eustace yelled to Big Eustace, but it was too late.

He glanced around the yard for a moment.

Where was Dad?

Gone.

But why?

Who the hell will ever know?

Eustace had come running around the house with such excitement because he wanted to tell his father what he had seen and learned. He wasn't doing it for anybody else. But his father wouldn't hear it, wouldn't be present to witness it. So Eustace took a breath. Recovered himself. Then he adopted once more the voice of the world's most sober and weary teacher.

And he told *me* all about it, instead.

CHAPTER SEVEN

Before him lies a boundless continent, and he urges forward as if time pressed and he was afraid of finding no room for his exertions.

—*Alexis de Tocqueville*

Eustace owns ten horses at the moment. He's the first to admit that owning ten horses is absurd and decadent and completely unnecessary for the size of his little farm, but he can't refuse them when they're as beautiful as these.

Now, I've been around horses. I grew up with people who were magic with horses. My grandfather ran a fine stable, and I've worked on a ranch owned by a man who kept his seventy-five horses in line without the least bit of effort, but I have never seen anybody more naturally gifted with horses than Eustace. Horses listen to him. They pay attention. When Eustace walks through his pastures, the horses look up from their grazing to watch him pass, holding still, awaiting word—a devoted harem, a clutch of hopeful brides.

Which is all the more impressive considering that Eustace didn't grow up with horses and he didn't own one until ten years ago. He held off for a long time because horses are fussy and take up lots of acreage and money. When you're living off the land, it's much easier to feed yourself than it is to feed a horse. But he always knew he would get horses someday. It was part of the master plan. He bought an antique horse-drawn mowing machine, for instance, years before he had either a meadow to mow or a horse to mow it with.

When he'd finally cleared away enough trees to create suitable pastureland up at Turtle Island, he borrowed a big old Percheron mare from a local farmer and used the mare for his campers to ride and for him to practice farming with. The horse was slow and lumbering, but even being around that staid creature got Eustace's blood going. He wanted more. So he bought himself a solid young draft horse named Bonnie and, with her, learned how to anticipate a horse's anxiety and intellect, how to make split-second decisions of command, and how to be confident in his orders. Eustace found himself two human teachers, as well—an old hillbilly farmer named Hoy Moretz, who knew everything about breaking livestock in the traditional manner, and a young Mennonite named Johnny Ruhl, who had an intuition for horses that Eustace believed to be unmatched. Eustace would bring his horse over to these men for lessons and then hang around as they worked with their animals, watching and learning. Hoy and Johnny found Eustace to be an ideal student—attentive and talented, and easy to teach, because he seemed to understand intuitively the old country adage about why God gave man two ears and only one mouth: he could shut up and he could listen.

Eustace did a lot of farming and hauling with Bonnie, and she was built for that. She was an ox in horse's clothing, and he was grateful for her. But he was also fascinated with the idea of taking a horse on the road for some serious distance travel. So every so often he would saddle up his big farm mare and head off into the mountains for a few days at a time, just to get a feel for what it might be like to travel with an animal as a partner. Eustace loved the idea, but Bonnie was definitely not built for such adventures. She was too slow, too thick. Then Eustace began to crave a real riding horse. He wanted a smooth motorcycle instead of the hulking bulldozer that was Bonnie. And so, with the advice and consent of his teachers, in 1994 he bought himself a pure Morgan, a championship endurance racer named Hasty.

Hasty was every bit his name. Moreover, Hasty came to Eustace nicely trained. Where Eustace had had to teach Bonnie how to behave, Hasty now taught Eustace how to behave. Eustace paid close attention and learned quickly, until he and Hasty were equals, able to spend their days teaching each other how to be a pair. Eustace started taking long-distance journeys with Hasty, riding down from the mountains to the North Carolina coast. As he'd expected, he did indeed love the physical challenge of sustaining a fast pace over uncertain terrain with an animal partner and no guarantee of safety. What he hadn't expected, though, was the intensely heightened level of interaction he was experiencing with regular Americans as he rode through their lives on horseback. There was something about the presence and romance of a horse that drew people in.

The reaction was extraordinary and universal. One New Year's Day, when Eustace was riding Hasty toward the coast, he passed through a poverty-stricken neighborhood in rural North Carolina. It was all grim run-down shacks and trailers and yards full of rusted cars. As he rode past one ramshackle home, he noticed a huge commotion in the backyard. Maybe a hundred people, all black and all poor, had gathered for a massive family reunion and feast. The smells of barbecuing meat hovered in the cold January air. The entire humble property was rocking and humming with the buzz of celebration. When the people spotted Eustace—this shady and bearded mountain man, this white dude on a horse with a shotgun across his saddle—they laughed and applauded and called out, "Ride on in!" So Eustace swung his horse right into the yard, right into the center of this big family reunion. Just like that, he was family. He was embraced and welcomed and celebrated like any distant cousin. The family crowded around and took turns asking for horseback rides. They had a million questions. They wanted to know everything about Eustace and his utopian message and his destination. They fed him until he could hardly move, stuffed him to the brim with good ham and pies and collard greens and corn bread and beer, and then let him go on his way, with a cheering delegation running behind, blessing him, then thinning out, then vanishing.

To Eustace, who had spent the better part of his life devising ways to break down walls and enter the consciousness of every kind of American, this was a revelation. It was a spontaneous and satisfying encounter, and he well knew that he would never have been welcomed to such a gathering without the horse as an icebreaker. Eustace had traveled all over America—on foot, by hitchhiking, in boxcars, and on long drives—but nothing had prepared him for the intimacy with the nation that a horse could give him. It was the answer.

Clearly, it was time to plan a horse trip across the continent.

Eustace wanted to ride across America and he wanted to bring his younger brother Judson along. Judson Conway was excellent company, the dream traveling companion for a trip like this. But beyond that, Eustace felt that he and Judson, as brothers, needed some epic sharing experience. He recognized that he still thought of Judson as a little boy, as some soft kid hiding in the bedroom with Star Wars action figures, and he wanted to erase that image. Judson was a man now. Judson was a hunter and a horseman and a seasoned traveler and a working cowboy. Eustace wanted to witness him in all these shapes, while also experiencing a marathon of adventures that would surely draw the two brothers together as equals.

Judson, needless to say, was all over this. Did he want to drop out of modern society and cross America on horseback like an authentic heroic Hollywood high plains drifter? Heck, yeah! Judson was wild for the plan, hungry for the "life on the edge, chance to live large" opportunity. He threw himself into the idea with a swan dive, announcing that he was game to take off at a moment's notice, hot for the chase. Just point him West and say the word—and watch his dust fly.

And so it was decided. They even agreed on a name for themselves. They'd be the Long Riders. Eustace, naturally, got right on the ball with the organizing. He figured out how many horses they'd need, how much money they should bring, what kind of guns they should take, and how much time it all would require. He collected maps and anecdotes from other long-distance horse travelers, trying to anticipate every possible contingency. Of course it was almost impossible to imagine exactly what they might face out there; the important thing was to have a smart route, good horses, and a strong beginning.

Eustace chose a southern path across the nation. The Long Riders would start out on Jekyll Island, off the coast of Georgia, and head west as fast as they could, tearing through Alabama, Mississippi, Louisiana, Texas, New Mexico, Arizona, and right into California. Eustace's general scheme was to skirt the major cities and not get arrested or hit by any trucks (his mother made him promise not to let baby Judson be killed)—and that was about as far ahead as he could reasonably plan. It was imperative to concentrate on speed. This was not to be a lazy, contemplative walkabout. He wanted to push himself and his brother and the horses to their absolute limits, to see exactly how smoothly they could consume so many miles while experiencing the harsh tutorial of physical challenge.

And then, quite suddenly, they had another partner.

Judson, in his Judsonian way, had been talking up the journey and he had caught the ear of his friend Susan Klimkowski, a native North Carolinian who had worked with Judson on that ranch in Wyoming. Unassumingly pretty, terrifically shy, and surprisingly tough, twenty-five-year-old Susan had more years of experience on horseback than Judson and Eustace combined. She was one of those people who ride before they walk. She was no thrill seeker and no show-off, and she didn't pretend to be a child of destiny, but when she heard about the trip across America, it stirred in her an intense resolve. She had to go along.

Judson had worked with Susan in the Rockies long enough to know that she could handle the physical demands of the trip, but he told her she'd have to talk it over with Eustace in person. In a gesture of perfect respect and instinct, Susan asked Eustace Conway whether she could join the Long Riders, not by calling him on the telephone and making a verbal plea, but by riding her horse up the mountain to his home and discussing the matter from the saddle. She presented herself to Eustace, in other words, as she would present herself to the entire challenge—already packed, obviously capable, and asking for nothing but the word "Yes."

Which Eustace gave her. He was impressed by her presentation and could tell that she knew her way around a horse. If she could keep up, she could come along. And the extra bonus attraction was that Susan came with a nice pickup truck and a handsome new horse trailer, which Eustace thought might be an excellent accompaniment to the journey. He knew that such a trip could be completed without a support vehicle, but he also knew that they were way over their heads already with a serious learning curve, and that a safe portable space in which to store injured horses or extra blankets might take away some of the pressure and danger. It would be a bit of a drag—Eustace and Judson and Susan would have to take turns driving the trailer up ahead on the road every day, then hitch back to the horses to begin the day's ride. They'd pound leather together to cover the miles up to where the trailer was parked and then leapfrog ahead the next morning. It would be a burden, but worth the trouble.

Fair enough. So now they were three. Three people and four horses and one truck and one trailer and a whole continent unfolding before them. On Christmas Day of 1995, they set off. They were all wearing Santa hats, laughing their heads off, energized and keen. Right off the bat, they found an unopened bottle of Bacardi on the side of the road. "Blessings from God, a gift from nature," Eustace declared, and they slammed back the rum and commenced their journey.

Eustace was riding Hasty. Susan was riding Mac, a reliable black twelve-year-old Tennessee Walker. Judson was alternating between Spur, a lovely silver Arabian he'd picked up at an auction, and Chief, a horse bought fresh for this adventure, which the Conway boys had named after their legendary grandfather, Chief Johnson.

"Poor Chief," Judson said, on the day they bought him. "He's been hanging out in a pasture his whole life and has no idea what he's about to get into. He's on his way to learning what being a horse is all about."

It wasn't as if any of them, horses or humans, had a clear idea of what they were about to get into. ("We did not know what we were doing," Eustace would say later. "And that is a fact.") Eustace was considerably more keyed up and nervous than Susan and Judson, who were still at the point of thinking that the trip would be nothing but nonstop fun. Eustace had enough sense to worry whether they'd even survive. Whatever was to happen, though, Eustace was ready to document it. He brought a small tape recorder with him and eighteen cassette tapes, and he kept an oral journal as they rode. Part of his reason for doing this was to avoid the slow process of writing down his recollections. And his steady, stream-of-consciousness ramblings on the tapes are, indeed, all the more evocative for the sounds of the birds and traffic and horses' hooves in the background.

"I'm holding the tape recorder in one hand and the pack horse in the other," he says on Day Two of the journey. "Saw some beautiful Spanish moss scenery, a little girl in a bright jacket on a huge old pine tree, molasses presses, furnaces, palmettos. Road is fairly littered with trash here, cups, beer cartons, cigarette cartons, bottles, wrappers, cans, bottles, aluminum foil. Amazing, the trash. Twenty to thirty feet away, however, it's beautiful. Backlit trees, plantation pines. Sort of a mono-culture. Very sandy soil. Right now I'm as free as anyone in America. It's so satisfying to be here, away from responsibilities, I wish more people had the simple life."

So he was documenting his experience, but there was also an ethnographer at work within him. Eustace was eager to interview the regular Americans they met along the way. He'd been thinking more and more in recent years about the disappearance of regional dialects due to the pervasive influence of mass media. He could hear it happen-ing in his holler back home, where the old Appalachian folks seemed to speak a language entirely different from their grandchildren's. The grandparents still had an Elizabethan drawl (they pronounced the word "sword" with a definitive *w*, for instance) and called tools and animals by ancient words that would soon be extinct, seeing that their younger relatives were all starting to sound like New York City disc jockeys. Eu-stace relishes authentic and distinctive dialects and is a brilliant mimic, too. He knew this would be his last chance to capture a wide representa-tion of American Southern voices, since the Long Riders often literally rode through people's backyards. They had an all-access pass and were riding a plumb line right through the center of American life—no bar-riers, no boundaries, no margins of limitation. It was almost as if they were ghosts, and every wall before them became nonexistent. They could smell and touch and reach the people as they passed through. Eustace caught on tape an old Georgia cracker asking, "What kind of farm y'all have?"

"Well, sir," Eustace began, "I have about a thousand acres in North Carolina. I guess you could say that I run a primitive and traditional farm up there, as well as a nature education center . . ."

But the cracker interrupted. No, no. He didn't want to know what kind of *farm* Eustace had; he wanted to know what kind of *fire arm* Eustace had. Then on the tape you can hear Eustace laughing and laughing and politely clarifying.

And he loved the black voices in Georgia, too, like the elderly man on the porch swing who used Eustace's tape to reminisce about growing up in a sharecropper's family:

"My daddy would pass through the rooms and say, 'Git up, boys.' We didn't have no lights. He say, 'Git up, boys!' and next time he say, 'I thought you boys were s'posed to git up' . . . Ain't no such thing as child abuse back then and you *better* get out the bed, cuz I wanna tell you something—my daddy was 275 pounds of *pure man*, and when he say, 'Git up, boy,' you *better* hit that floor."

It was easy to get people to talk. It helped, of course, that the riders were so romantically evocative. Eustace was all tall and lean in his antique U.S. Cavalry saddle, wild and bearded and often shirtless, wearing feathers in his hair and riding expertly without even a bit in Hasty's mouth. He looked like a deserter from the Texas Rangers, some unfettered Jeb who'd lost his unit and turned Injun. Judson and Susan were dressed like dusty, old-time wranglers—all chaps and spurs and beat-up cowboys hats and long duster coats and bandanas. Their look was only partly self-conscious; these are exactly the clothes to wear when you're on horseback all day, exposed to sun, rain, snow, underbrush, and dust.

To Judson's eternal credit, he was willing at times to sacrifice his authentic cowboy image for practicality. He took to wearing pastel-colored spandex leggings under his chaps, which used to freak the hell out of the macho truck drivers and ranch hands they'd meet along the way. But the slick material kept Judson from getting saddle burns, and when he got too restless from endless riding, he could pull off his boots, toss on a pair of Nikes, and jog a few miles alongside his horse, just to stay in shape and work the kinks out of his legs.

The riders themselves were plenty compelling. But it was the horses that drew people in. "Everywhere we went," Judson said, "we were a parade." Suburban children outside Atlanta came running toward them without a flinch of hesitation, just to hug their horses. It would be the same story with the poor white farming families they later met in Texas.

It would even be the same story on the Apache reservation out in Arizona. The reservation was a desolate and impoverished land they'd considered skirting, because white people for hundreds of miles had warned them against risking their lives at the hands of "those scary bad-ass motherfucker Apaches." But Eustace, who knew enough of both ancient history and current politics to respect this warning, wouldn't budge from his chosen route. As he proclaimed to his nervous partners, "We do not change our course because of goddamn racial prejudice. What have we learned so far on this journey, people? Who has not been kind to us yet? Black, white, Hispanic—everyone's been good to us. And if we start dodging people out of fear, then we've destroyed everything we supposedly stand for. You guys can take the detour, but I'm riding right across this goddamn reservation, with or without you. And I don't give a shit if I get shot in the head for it, either."

So the Long Riders did ride straight across the Apache reservation, all together. And the Apaches did turn out to be some scary bad-ass motherfuckers who took the Long Riders into their homes for the night, offering food for both the riders and their horses.

It would be the same story months down the road, when they passed through the urban squalor of the San Diego ghettos ("Don't do it!" white people warned), and the Mexican kids came streaming out of their homes to ask for rides on the horses while the parents took pictures and handed out food and blessings. All across the nation, the same welcome. Everywhere TV cameras and sheriffs' escorts would follow them from one county line to the next. They met mayors and ministers from coast to coast, who came out to speak for the people in town after town, welcoming them. It was a frenzy of hospitality and excitement.

Cars would pull over on the road, the drivers would jump out, run over to the Long Riders, ask the same questions over and over: "Who are you? Where are you going? What can we do to help you?" And always this one: "I want to do what you're doing." "You can," Eustace would reply each time. "You can!"

Their days began at four A.M., when they took care of their horses and tried to imagine where, in the next thirty to fifty miles, they were going to find food and water for themselves and their animals. Every day, someone would have to drive the trailer miles ahead and then hitch back to the camp so that they could start riding together. This took a huge amount of time; sometimes two Long Riders would be delayed whole hours while the third tried gamely to get a lift. And their days didn't end until after midnight. The pace of their riding was fierce. They were all limping and busted from riding so hard, but they never let up, never walked, only trotted.

They rode for such long stretches between vets and farriers that Eustace became adept at doctoring his own animals and caring for their hooves. He'd watched farriers put shoes on his horses so many times that he was sure he could figure out how to do it. He called Hoy Moretz, his hillbilly horse mentor back in North Carolina, and asked whether it would be advisable to do his own shoeing out here on the journey, and the man gave him a strong warning. "Don't do it. You're a smart boy, but you're not a professional. You can learn how to shoe your own horses back on your farm at home, but there's too much at stake on the road to risk injuring one of your animals through ignorance." Sane advice, and Eustace couldn't agree more, but he disregarded it in the end because we all know what necessity is the mother of. He had to learn, so he did learn. He also gave his horses shots and medicine and adjusted their feed and talked endlessly on the tapes about their physical condition.

"Hasty pissed really dark blood near the end of his stream; that has me worried . . . fell twice today, seems impossible, but it happened, hit his face right on the ground . . . I put a blindfold across his eyes and led him around to get him prepped for the bridge that's coming up. Because there's a chance if we can get one horse to cross this new kind of bridge with the metal grate that the horses can see under and are really afraid of, well, maybe they'll all pass and we'll be safe. . . . Found a little rock up in Spur's hoof that's making him hurt . . . trying to watch out for their ligaments; can't let a single sore go untreated out here."

Several times along the way Eustace realized that they needed newer or fresher horsepower, so he'd stop to buy or trade livestock. That's how they came to acquire Cajun, Fat Albert, Blackie, and Chavez. It's also how they got the immortal mule, Peter Rabbit.

Peter Rabbit came from down in Mississippi. Eustace was determined to buy the Long Riders a mule, because he wanted a strong pack animal. So he started putting out the word to everyone he met along the road that he was looking to buy. Someone had mentioned a horseman nearby with a big farm who surely had some animals he'd sell off. The farmer, Pierson Gay, was handsome, conservative, and elegant—a classic Southern Gentleman with a well-tended white mustache. The Long Riders telephoned him from the road and said what they were looking for. He agreed to put them up for the night in his stables and to discuss horse-trading. As Judson recalled it, though, "When we rode up to his farm, looking all long-haired and greasy and like a bunch of dirtbag hippies, Pierson literally had to turn his head from the sight of us. He's such a clean-cut man, I swear to God, he almost retched in disgust."

But there's a way that horse people can communicate their expertise with horses—a private code, maybe. Just as Eustace had been immediately convinced that Susan Klimkowski knew how to ride by watching her show up at his mountain home on horseback, it didn't take Pierson Gay long to notice that these kids knew what they were doing. And as far as livestock was concerned, Pierson had one animal he was willing to sell—a big, good-looking, white devil of a mule. Strong as can be. Name was Peter Rabbit. Eustace and Judson and Susan checked out Peter Rabbit and found him to be healthy and sturdy, just what they needed for their extra loads. Pierson told them he'd sell the mule for $1000. Now these Long Riders, especially Eustace, knew how to negotiate for an animal; you never accept the first price. They came back to Pierson and offered $900. At this, Mr. Pierson Gay walked away, muttering as he exited the barn, "A thousand dollars; that's the price. That's what the mule's worth to me and that's what I said he costs, so you can give me a thousand dollars or I'll leave Peter Rabbit right there in the pasture; won't hurt my feelings a bit."

They coughed up the thousand bucks.

There were some problems with Peter Rabbit, though. Pierson Gay made no attempt to hide them. There are always problems with mules. Unlike most horses, mules are brainy and often malicious. Mules can think, reason, plot, and exact vengeance. You have to keep your guard up around mules, and this one in particular was satanic. Here were the rules. You couldn't touch Peter Rabbit's ears, or he would try to kill you. That made putting a bridle on the mule a life-risking operation. You couldn't touch Peter Rabbit's belly, or he would try to kill you. That made putting a saddle on the mule a dicey bit of work, too. Other times, warned Pierson Gay (who was a competent expert with quadrupeds and had long ago given up on breaking this mule), Peter Rabbit was apt to try to kill you for no apparent reason whatsoever. And you also couldn't touch his feet. Or he'd try to kill you.

Still, he was a mighty powerful animal. So they bought him.

The Long Riders rode off the next day with Peter Rabbit all fresh and strong in their pack string. It wasn't long before the mule made his presence known. It was pouring down rain, and Judson was trying to put a plastic tarp over his horse to protect the goods. The tarp was flapping and whipping about in the wind, and Peter Rabbit didn't like that one bit. He hauled off and slammed Judson with a full-force kick that hit the cowboy right in the meatiest section of his thigh. If it had landed elsewhere, it could have been a knee-snapping, arm-breaking, hip-smashing, skull-caving, or gut-crushing blow. As it was, Peter Rabbit's hearty kick threw Judson five feet up in the air and then landed him right on the ground, where, Judson admits, he lay quietly on the damp grass, letting the rain fall on his face and thinking how pleasant it was to rest on his back and take a breather for a moment on this brutal journey.

But Eustace sprang into action. He'd been keeping his eye on Peter Rabbit, expecting a clash of wills between them, and waiting for his moment to explain to the mule who was in charge here. This was the moment. Mule and man squared off for the first of what would be dozens of physical altercations. Eustace took a swing at the mule, as if he were in a bar brawl, and shouted right up in his face, "*Don't you ever kick my brother again!*" The mule swung around to kick Eustace, who grabbed the animal's lead rope in one hand and grabbed a whip in the other and started beating the mule. Peter Rabbit kicked and dragged Eustace for a few hundred feet, but Eustace held on to that lead rope tight and fierce. Peter Rabbit slung Eustace up against trees and rocks, kicking and biting, both of them braying their lungs out. Judson and Susan ran and hid in the woods, terrified, and Judson kept shouting, "Jesus Christ, Eustace! Just quit! He's trying to kill you!" But Eustace held on and took his kicks and then worked the mule over to a set of picturesque and antique gas pumps at a run-down old gas station and tied the mule up.

Then they had a little conversation.

Eustace, reduced now (or elevated) to a purely brutish state, clamped on to Peter Rabbit's nose with his teeth and bit down, hard. Then he pried open Peter Rabbit's mouth and bellowed into it like a grizzly on attack. Then he grabbed Peter Rabbit's ears and chewed on them, too, all the while growling and howling like a wounded ogre. Then he circled the mule, beating him with his fists. Then he picked up each of the mule's feet—one at a time, to show his dominance—and yelled into each hoof as if it were some kind of bestial telephone. Cars driving by on the highway slowed down—*way* down—as they passed this scene, and pale faces peered out from the passing automobiles, riveted. Judson and Susan, in shock, huddled in the woods, watching this all unfold.

"What can I tell you?" Judson whispered to Susan, both afraid and deeply proud. "My brother's an animal."

Eustace worked Peter Rabbit over for a little while longer and then let the mule go. Peter Rabbit slunk off, surely thinking to himself, *Holy shit . . .*

A few more conversations like this occurred between Eustace Conway and Peter Rabbit along the course of the journey before the mule, who was no idiot, got the picture. He acknowledged, for the first time in his mulish life, that someone else would be making the decisions. And by the time they got to California, that mule was so polite and disciplined and well trained that the Long Riders had to let Pierson Gay know about it. They took a photograph of Peter Rabbit. In the picture, Eustace is standing in front of the mule, biting one of its ears. Susan is squatting below the mule, tickling its belly. And Judson is standing on the mule's back, arms flung wide open, grinning.

They mailed the photo to Mississippi, to Peter Rabbit's original owners. A few weeks later, Eustace called the Pierson Gay residence to see whether they'd received the photo. Mrs. Pierson Gay, a most gentle and refined Southern lady, answered the phone. Why, yes, she drawled charmingly, they had received the photograph.

"So what do you think of that old mule now?" Eustace asked.

"My *word*, honey," replied Mrs. Pierson Gay in her most feathery antebellum Southern accent, "it looks like Peter Rabbit done went and got himself a *Hah-vahd* education."

It wasn't a parade every day. They had great times on their journey, but they also rode for long and desolate episodes along desert highways where nobody drove by and the garbage blew like tumbleweeds. In rural Texas, they rode through a blinding sandstorm, surviving it only by pulling their bandanas up over their faces, a good system until a Texas state trooper stopped them and demanded that they remove their "masks" because "folks is getting nervous y'all are some kinda outlaws." At other points in the journey, they hit assassin waves of heat so oppressive that Eustace feared the horses might die and that their own lungs would combust from the scorch. Sometimes they'd stop around lunchtime and try to duck the heat under a patch of shade.

Judson would say, "How long do we have for a break?"

"Ten minutes," Eustace would answer, and Judson and Susan would lie down, cover their faces with their hats, and catch exactly ten minutes of sleep. But Eustace never slept. His energies were consumed by caring for the horses. In those ten minutes, he'd make the rounds, check the feet, test knots on the lead ropes, look into the animals' eyes, feel for saddle sores. He wasn't concerned about the heat or his own physical exhaustion; only worried about the horses.

The worst weather they hit was in Louisiana, where they rode into a crippling four-day ice storm. It came on them out of nowhere in the form of a fierce freezing rain, and soon the three riders looked as if they were encased in a quarter inch of glass. Everything was frozen—hats, stirrups, saddlebags, boots, beards. This was the only weather that ever stopped the Long Riders, and it was not because of personal discomfort; it was because Eustace refused to endanger the horses' safety on those slick roads of solid ice. Trying to find a place to hole up for the storm, they ended up taking shelter beneath the awnings of a small old-time grocery store. Eustace released Judson onto the local citizenry, telling him to use his famous charm to secure some warm beds for the riders that night and a warm barn for the horses.

"Go work the situation, little brother," said Eustace. "Do what you do best."

Judson, who does work fast, dutifully struck up a friendship with some fellers who were chewing tobacco in the general store. And within minutes the Long Riders had been invited to wait out the ice storm at a nearby compound, run by an organization of white militia rednecks representing the Patriot Movement. These militiamen were, according to Eustace Conway's description, "some people who think that the United States government has way too much control over our lives, which is basically not a bad idea and I agree with many of their points, although I wasn't impressed with their level of disorganization, and they all drank so much alcohol that they couldn't forward their message efficiently."

"Yeah, we got a place you can stay," one of the militiamen drawled. "Y'all got any guns? Well, you won't need 'em at our place! We got loads of guns."

For the next two days, the Long Riders were guests of the Patriot Movement. Trapped in the small Louisiana farmhouse by the weather, Susan and Judson spent two cozy days getting stone drunk with these staunch defenders of America's sacred Second Amendment rights and shooting guns for kicks. Meanwhile, Eustace tried to remain sober and productive, spending those forty-eight hours calling everyone he had ever met across America, trying to see if anyone knew somebody who might want to join the Long Riders and drive the truck and trailer. Eustace was fed up with all the bullshit of driving ahead and hitchhiking back. Sure enough, after about a hundred phone calls, he found his driver, a nineteen-year-old boy nicknamed Swamper, who had nothing else to do with his life at the moment but hop on a Greyhound bus back in North Carolina and join the team in Louisiana.

When the ice storm ended, the Long Riders bade farewell to their militia friends and headed west again with their new partner, young Swamper, driving the support vehicle, pushing on toward Texas.

Texas was a highlight for Eustace, because that's where he bought himself the greatest horse of his life—his beloved Hobo. Hobo was a made-for-travelin' Registered Standard Breed. Hobo would become a legend, the fastest and smartest and most loyal horse Eustace ever met. Eustace bought Hobo on the road in the middle of Texas from a farmer named Mr. Garland, and what a find that was. The farmer was leaning on his fence when the Long Riders trotted by, and they all set to talking. As Mr. Garland described this horse he was thinking of selling ("he's kind of thin and fast") Eustace's mouth almost started watering. From the brief conversation, he could fill out the whole story. This Texan had bought himself a beautiful and speedy horse because he loved the idea of it, but now he found the animal too fast to handle. Bring it on!

"You want to try him out?" the Texan asked.

Eustace got on Hobo for a test drive and said, "Come up, boy." In one dizzying nanosecond that horse went from contentedly grazing in the field to a formidable G-force gallop. Eustace's hat flew off, and he was barely hanging on by his heels.

"I don't think your brother can manage that horse," Mr. Garland said to Judson, who was watching from the fence, and Judson said, "Oh, he'll manage."

What a day! Eustace was afraid it would be rude and obscene to tell that Texan how good this horse felt between his legs on the test drive, how fine and thrilling it was when Hobo opened up and took off across the pastures "like a born challenger, like a rocket," how he couldn't help thinking that nothing in the world had felt so good between his legs except maybe Carla's body . . .

He bought Hobo right then and there and rode off with him. Eustace and this spectacular horse had the most amazing interaction, right from day one. As Eustace would say, "All I'd have to do is think, and as fast as I could articulate the thought, Hobo would respond." This was an animal that finally matched Eustace's will—a true partner, an animal that wanted to *go*. Hobo was a brilliant addition. The Long Riders needed an eager pace horse like Hobo to keep up their momentum. It was hard sometimes to stay motivated. All of them—horses and horsemen—were suffering from injuries and strain and weariness. Judson always shot off his pistol in celebration as they crossed a state border, for instance, but there was a nasty accident one day when he did this on the Arizona–New Mexico border and Eustace's horse took off in a panic and threw him. Eustace wasn't riding Hobo or Hasty that day, but was trying out a horse they'd purchased recently—Blackie, a strong and skittish mustang blend, which apparently had no liking for guns. When Judson shot off his pistol, the horse went ballistic, and Eustace landed on the top of his head on a rock and split his scalp. He was so badly hurt, he could barely see straight, and every step gave him a spasm, but he let the blood clot as a bandage and kept riding, because "What was I gonna do? *Not* continue on?"

This was no joy ride. They were not sashaying across America. They were burning up the miles, which meant they were tired all the time. They were hungry and hurting. They argued with one another. Sadly, the very opposite of what Eustace had wanted from this trip was happening. He had hoped to strengthen his relationship with Judson, but, instead, Judson was slipping farther and farther away from his hero-worshipping attitude toward his older brother. Judson wanted to have fun on this trip, and resented Eustace's unyielding fixation on speed, which never allowed them time to stop and take in the surroundings.

"What can I say about Eustace?" Judson asked later. "He's gotta be goddamn Ernest Shackleton all the time, set every world record, be the fastest this and the best that. He could never relax and have a good time. That's not why Susan and I took the trip."

The cross-country journey was turning into a vast canvas on which the differences between the Conway brothers were boldly highlighted. There was Eustace on one side—driven by his ancient mythological themes of heroes and destinies. And there beside him was Judson— driven by his desire to have a good time and armed with a thoroughly modern sensibility about the roles that people play in this world. It was this super self-conscious sensibility of Judson Conway's (a sensibility, by the way, that he shares with pretty much every modern American except his brother) that enabled him to joke, "Hey, I'm a real cowboy now!" as he fired off his six-shooter. Judson was riding his horse across America because he knew that people used to do that kind of thing and because it was cool and fun to masquerade as an icon. Eustace was riding his horse across America because he wanted the icon to *live*. For Judson it was a delicious game; for Eustace, it was an acutely serious endeavor.

"Susan and I would've been happy to go at half the pace and have more time to hang out and smell the flowers," Judson said.

"Just because I'm traveling fifty miles a day," Eustace countered, "doesn't mean I can't smell the flowers. I'm smelling the goddamn flowers as I'm speeding by! And I'm smelling fifty miles more of 'em than other people. First of all, we needed the speed on this trip because of scheduling—Judson and Susan had to get back to their jobs, so we didn't have forever to get to California. Also, I wanted to learn how much we were capable of. Both the horses and the riders. I wanted to push, to scrutinize, to challenge, to bend the realm of the possible. I wanted to put our limitations under a microscope and stare at them, understand them, and reject them. Look, it wasn't important to me to be comfortable on this trip or to even have fun. When I have a goal, when I'm in the middle of a challenge like this, I don't need the things other people need. I don't need to sleep or eat or be warm or dry. I can live on nothing when I stop eating and sleeping."

"That's called dying, Eustace," I said.

"No." He grinned. "That's called living."

It's hard to see where this urgency fits into Eustace's more Zen-like philosophies of living in perfect harmony with the gentle rhythms of nature, about "being like water." This journey was definitely not about being like water; it was about being a cross-country, cross-cutting buzzsaw. And the effect was not calming. Eustace's partners could hardly stand his unremitting determination. Judson took to drinking whiskey every night on the trip as a way to soften the impact of his brother's intensity.

"I know Eustace hated seeing me getting drunk and oblivious," he said, "but it kept me sane."

Eustace was relentless and his leadership was often oppressive, but he stands by all his decisions, even to this day. "People don't understand—Judson and Susan didn't understand—that it was no accident we covered all that distance without getting ourselves or our animals killed or seriously hurt. I know other people who've tried to ride a horse across America and got all messed up—horses injured, equipment stolen, mugged, beaten up, hit by cars. That didn't happen to us, because I was fucking vigilant. I made about a thousand private decisions every day, each one narrowing the odds of hitting trouble. If I decided to cross the road, it was for a reason. If I could shift my horse slightly so that he walked on grass instead of gravel for just four steps, I'd do that, saving his legs four steps of impact.

"At the end of every day, when we were looking for campsites, my computer brain would kick in and evaluate each possibility, taking in about three dozen contingencies nobody else would have considered. *What kind of neighborhood is this meadow near? Is there an exit route behind the meadow in case we need to make a quick move? Are there loose wires on the ground that the horses could get tangled up in? Is there fresh grass across the road that's going to lure the horses to head over the highway in the middle of the night and get hit? Will people see us from the road and stop to ask what we're up to and waste our energy when we need to be caring for the horses?* Judson and Susan never saw this process. They kept saying, 'How about this spot, Eustace? This looks like a nice place to camp.' And I'd say, 'Nope, nope, nope' and not bother to explain why."

Judson and Susan, already chafing under Eustace's command, mutinied in Arizona. They literally came to a fork in the road. Judson and Susan wanted to veer off the highway and take a wilder route for the day, heading down into a rugged canyon for a shortcut that promised some serious all-terrain adventure. Eustace balked. He wanted to stay on the highway, a duller and less scenic ride that would put more miles on the horses, but considerably less impact. The Long Riders held a group meeting.

"It's not safe," Eustace said. "You don't know what you'll encounter down there. You could run into a canyon wall or an impassable river and have to backtrack ten miles, lose the whole day. You could get killed. You don't have a map or any reliable information. You're going to encounter loose rockslides and poor trails and dangerous creeks that will beat the hell out of your horses. Your animals are already pushed to the edge; it's cruel to make this demand on them. It's too dangerous a risk."

"We're tired of riding on the highway," Judson complained. "We came on this trip because we wanted to see the country, and this is our chance to get back down into nature. We want to be more spontaneous, live closer to the edge."

They took a vote and, of course, Judson and Susan won. Eustace wouldn't budge. "I'm dead against it," he said. "You can take the canyon trail if you want to, but I'm not coming."

It was a devastating moment for Judson. They'd made a pact before setting out on the journey that democratic action would rule the day; if there was ever a dispute over the next move, majority opinion would rule. They would never split up over a disagreement, and now they were doing exactly that. On this heroic twenty-five-hundred-mile journey, there was to be one sad thirty-mile gap in the middle of the country where the inseparable partners separated because they could not reach a consensus.

"I thought we were supposed to be a team," Judson said to his brother.

And Eustace replied, "I'm happy to be on a team as long as we always do what I know is right."

Judson and Susan headed off down the canyon.

"It was the coolest day of the whole journey," Judson recalled. "Wild scenery and nature. We rode through rivers up to our horses' bellies and we rode through ancient rock spires. We loved every minute of it, laughing and singing the whole time. It was everything I'd imagined the trip could be. We felt like old-time outlaws. And Eustace missed it."

"Their horses came back limping," Eustace remembered. "They never should have been down there. They could have been killed, or they could have destroyed their animals. I was right."

From then on, Judson decided to shut his mouth and go along with Eustace's commands, because it was more peaceful to submit than to fight. But as he rode alongside his older brother, he endured the dreadful sense of knowing that they would never be the same after this.

They made it to the Pacific by Easter, as they'd planned. No desertions and no deaths. They rode through San Diego to where they could smell the ocean. When they broke over the last highway and got to the beach, Eustace rode his horse right into the surf, as though he'd like to ride Hobo all the way to China. He was in tears, still pushing.

Not so Judson and Susan. They were finished with this brutal trip. It was over, and they were thrilled. Judson went directly to where people were. He rode his horse right into a bar and sat—*on his horse!*—for several hours, spinning his six-shooter and telling stories while the customers crowded up to him and the bartender bought him round after round. As for Susan, she tied her horse outside the bar and walked into the crowd quietly, garnering no particular attention.

They spent the next week in San Diego, where their mothers came to meet them. Mrs. Conway and Mrs. Klimkowski wanted to take the kids all around the town, to show them Sea World and tour the zoo and eat at fancy restaurants. Judson and Susan were more than happy to be pampered, but Eustace stayed clear of everyone, silent and morose.

"I don't know how they could turn it off like that," Eustace said later. "I wanted to tell them, 'Hey, you guys just had this incredible experience with your horses and you can forget it? One day you're living life so intensely and the next day you can hop in the car and go get a fucking Tastee-Freez? Like it never happened?' They didn't seem to care at all."

He spent the week alone, brooding, riding his horse every day, all day long, up and down the beach. His companions would ask, "Aren't you sick of riding yet?" No. Never. Eustace rode the beach for hours, contemplating his journey, facing down the undeniable limitation of the Pacific Ocean, and dealing with the geographical reality of his personal Manifest Destiny: that there was nowhere else to *go*. The country dead-ended right here. It was over. If only another continent would appear out of the sea so that he could conquer it, too . . .

They drove the horses back to North Carolina in the trailer. Gave them a nice break. Eustace may not have needed to relax after the journey, but he was bent on letting his beloved Hobo relax for a while.

So Hobo got a nice rest in a trailer, riding all the way home to North Carolina like a celebrity. Back at Turtle Island, Eustace gave the horse several months in the pasture to unwind before they started riding together again. Of course, riding was going to be different at Turtle Island from what it had been on the road. Eustace needed Hobo now for farm work more than for speed. He needed to ride Hobo when he was out surveying property and he needed to hitch Hobo up to help drag logs and sleds filled with tools. They worked hard and well together. Hobo had a sweetness that even surpassed his speed.

And then, one day, long months after the Long Riders trip was over, Eustace decided that he and Hobo had earned an old-fashioned joy ride. So they took off from the stress and hubbub of Turtle Island and rode up into the mountains. They climbed and climbed to a high meadow, where, Eustace remembers, he let go of the reins and spread his arms wide and allowed Hobo to open up and run for the sheer delight of it in the high, bright air.

They rode back home, quiet and happy. But when they were almost in sight of the barn, Hobo tripped. He tripped on a tiny rock. You could hardly call it an accident, it was so insignificant. This beautiful horse, which had crossed the continent without injury or complaint, which could scale loose rock and sheer Appalachian slopes without a moment's hesitation and always responded with intelligence and eagerness to Eustace's faintest hints of communication, just stumbled over a common stone. Hobo took a funny little step and broke his leg, and the femur snapped nearly in half.

"No," Eustace said, leaping off his horse. "No, please, no . . ."

Hobo couldn't put any weight on the leg. He was confused and kept turning around to look at the injured limb. And at Eustace, hoping for an answer to what had gone wrong. Eustace left Hobo there alone and ran to his office, where he made desperate phone calls to his mentors, the hillbilly Hoy Moretz and the Mennonite Johnny Ruhl. He called every veterinarian he knew, and every farrier, but when he described what had happened, all they could do was confirm what he already knew: that nothing could be done. Eustace would have to shoot his friend. After all they'd been through together, to have this happen on a fine afternoon at home, when they were almost in sight of the barn . . .

Eustace got his shotgun and went back to the horse. Hobo was standing there, as before, looking at his leg and then at Eustace, trying to make sense of it. "I'm so sorry, Hobo," Eustace said, "and I love you so much." And then he shot Hobo in the head.

The horse buckled to the ground, and Eustace collapsed with him, sobbing. He clung to Hobo's neck as the horse died, telling him about all the good times they'd had together and about how brave he always was and thanking him. How could this have happened? They were only *steps* away from the barn . . .

Later in the day—and this was the hardest part—Eustace returned to cut off Hobo's mane and tail. These would mean much to him in the years to come. Maybe if Eustace ever got a horse someday who was worthy, he could take strands from the mane and tail of Hobo and weave them into a bridle for the new animal, and this would be a fine tribute. To make that first cut, though, to disturb his friend's body with a knife, was almost impossible, and Eustace cried as if the weight of his grief would fell every tree in the woods.

He left Hobo where he'd fallen. He wanted the vultures to eat him. He knew that the Native Americans believed vultures to be the sacred transport, the means by which a spirit is delivered from the earth up into the sky. So Eustace left Hobo there, where the birds could find him. Which means that, even today, whenever Eustace is working outside and sees vultures drifting in the air, he looks up and says hello, because he knows that's where Hobo lives now.

When springtime came, Eustace returned to where Hobo had fallen to look over his friend's bones. He wanted to collect the vulture feathers he found around Hobo's body and keep them in a sacred place. But his intention was not merely spiritual; Eustace also wanted to examine Hobo's broken femur, now that the meat was gone from it. He had a suspicion that the break may have been inevitable. He'd often wondered whether Hobo had once been a racehorse and sustained a career-ending injury, and that's why the farmer in Texas had ended up with him and was willing to sell him for a reasonable price. Maybe Hobo had carried this stress fracture around for years, and there had always been this weakness in the bone, and it had been only a matter of time before it broke again.

And indeed, when Eustace studied Hobo's bleached bones, he found his suspicion to be correct—the bone had always been cracked; the injury had always been there. This moment, when Eustace knelt on the ground and examined the bone with a scientific eye, is crucial, because it shows how, even in his grief, Eustace Conway always searches for logic and for answers. Life goes on, after all, and one must always seek the lesson even through the sorrow. Never remain static; never stop collecting information.

And it's this same reluctance to remain static that made Eustace Conway, only two years after the Long Riders trip had ended, attempt another insanely ambitious horse journey. Because one must always keep pushing. One must always scrutinize and challenge and put one's limitations under a microscope to examine and reject.

Of course, Eustace didn't embark on the same journey. No reason to repeat experience, after all. But a slightly different adventure this time. Having mastered transcontinental horsemanship on a saddle, Eustace decided to hitch his horses up to a lightweight buggy and take them on a lightning-fast tour of the Great Plains of North America, riding a twenty-five-hundred-mile circle across Nebraska, South Dakota, North Dakota, up into Canada, through Manitoba, Alberta, and Saskatchewan, then back down into Montana and Wyoming. He figured he could do it in under sixty days. He had a different partner now. He was riding with his new girlfriend. He had recently allowed himself to fall in love for the first time after having survived the whirling tornado of Carla. It had been a few years, but he was ready. He was excited about this new love of his, and he called me up shortly after he met the girl to tell me all about her.

"What's she like?" I asked.

"Beautiful, intelligent, kind, young. Half Mexican. The most beautiful skin you ever saw."

"What's her name?" I asked.

"Patience."

"It better be!"

Patience Harrison was a twenty-three-year-old schoolteacher. She was young, but certainly tough enough for a voyage like the one Eustace was about to take. She was a superb athlete, the former captain of the Duke field hockey team, and she was bold; she'd already traveled across Africa under much harder circumstances than she would encounter in Canada. Eustace was mad about her.

He loved Patience for her brains and for her winning personality and for her physical courage. The first time she came to visit Turtle Island, Eustace took her for a buggy ride. He asked whether she wanted to try driving the horses for a while, and she reached for the reins without a moment's hesitation, totally game. He thought, *Wow, that's the girl for me.* He was also won over by a video he saw of Patience playing collegiate field hockey. In the video, you can see her take a nasty hit by an opponent with a flying stick and then drop to the ground in pain. She had broken her wrist. Then she gets up and tries to run after her opponent, even as her arm is dangling all wrong at her side. Then she's down again on the ground in pain. Then she's up for another attempt, hauling ass down the field, teeth gritted, refusing to quit. Forget about pornography; this was the sexiest video image of a woman Eustace had ever seen.

And he loved Patience, it must be said, for her looks. She was gorgeous. Now, Eustace Conway isn't ever going to have a girlfriend who isn't gorgeous, but Patience was, as Eustace later put it, "my ideal. Can you imagine ever being with your ideal? With her Mexican background, she has that dark skin and dark eyes and white teeth that I find to be the most beautiful look in the world. I desire her so much. I'm never with her that I don't desire her. Everything about her—her hands, her body, her lips, her ears, the gloss of her hair—I worship every cell of that girl."

He declared his love to her with his typical fervor.

"With rainbows in my eyes I see your beauty," he wrote to her in an early letter. "With sunshine in my heart, I feel love for you. Guided by butterflies I flow toward freedom with you. With the fertile rains of hope I dream of our future. With more passion than you would be comfortable with, I want you."

There was certainly no contesting that last statement. Patience Harrison was plenty compelled by Eustace and fascinated by his romantic life, but from the beginning she was cool to his ardor. It took him forever to coax her into physical intimacy in private, and she wasn't physically attentive to him in public, either, not somebody who would even hold hands when people were watching. She was decidedly uncomfortable with his passion and found it difficult not to look away in embarrassment whenever he tried to gaze deep into her eyes. She disliked it immensely when he called her Baby, and grew annoyed at how fixated he was on her beauty, complaining, "Could you sometimes tell me that I'm intelligent or talented or interesting, instead of just gorgeous?"

At which Eustace would joke, "You have the most intelligent glossy black hair I've ever seen. Your smile and eyes are hauntingly talented. You have the most interesting body in the world."

It did not, to most observers, seem a perfect match. Patience was a thoroughly modern young woman who had always kept boyfriends at a distance in order to maintain her independence. (She was so standoffish, she joked, that one of her ex-boyfriends had nicknamed her "Prudence.") Eustace, who, as always, wanted a seamless union of fiery proportions, was stung by her coldness. Moreover, Patience wasn't too sure about giving up her life to go live at Turtle Island forever as the new First Lady. But her biggest reservation, she would later admit, was that she was terrified by a comment Eustace had made early on about wanting to have thirteen children with her.

That's right: thirteen.

I just had to ask Eustace about that.

Actually, my exact question was: "Please tell me you didn't really say that."

His response was, "One hundred years ago a woman wouldn't have been scared by that idea!"

Which was such a disappointing answer. Setting aside the perfectly obvious fact that it *isn't* a hundred years ago, there is so much else wrong with this statement that I'm not sure where to start dissecting it. Eustace Conway, as a true student of history and anthropology, should know better. Even a hundred years ago, the average birth rate of the American woman had dropped to a mere 3.5 children per lifetime. Women were already using birth control and had publicly begun debating how raising huge families would effect their economic and social standing. You have to look a lot farther back than a century, in other words, to find the kind of enthusiastic breeders Eustace was dreaming about.

And even then there are other considerations. Take Daniel Boone's wife, for example, the steadfast Ms. Rebecca Boone. Married at seventeen, Rebecca immediately inherited the two orphaned children of Boone's dead brother. She then had ten children (who lived) of her own out there on the frontier, adopted the six motherless children of her widowed brother, and helped care for many of the thirty-three babies spawned by her four daughters.

Rebecca Boone lived most of her adult life in a fort. She and her children starved through the winters. Her sons were wounded and killed by Indians; her daughters were merely kidnapped by them. In the middle of her marriage, Rebecca was able to move her family back to her safe and comfortable home settlement in North Carolina for two wonderful years while Daniel was out founding a new colony in Kentucky. When he came back to fetch her, she nearly revolted, almost refusing to return to the deep woods with him. He insisted; she resisted. The marriage, history suggests, came perilously close to ending. Rebecca was a loyal wife, though, and so, in the end, she followed her husband into the wilderness. But she was exhausted. A missionary who came through a Boone settlement in the 1780s remembered meeting Rebecca Boone and sitting with this "quiet soul" in front of her tiny cabin while she wept and told him of her troubles and hardships and of "the distress and fear in her heart."

So, yes, Eustace was correct in a sense. Many pioneer women had lots of children. But were they totally *into* it? Did they absolutely dig having all those babies? Was this some kind of inspired decision? Somehow I can't picture Rebecca Boone turning handsprings of joy on the day she discovered, deep in the forest and well into her forties, that she was pregnant for the tenth time. Similarly, I can't picture young Patience Harrison—recent Duke graduate and honor student and ambitious world traveler—getting all giddy with anticipation when Eustace Conway said he wanted to have thirteen kids with her.

And she didn't take comfort when Eustace assured her that thirteen kids was only his dream, that he had lots of dreams he never expected to be fulfilled, that he would even consider having no children at all if that's what she wanted, or they could adopt children, or there were any number of other options they could discuss. Furthermore, he wanted to know whether Patience had experienced a people, such as the Amish or the Maya of Guatemala, who truly cherished and valued children? Maybe her opinions would change if she could see firsthand, as Eustace had, the inspiring way those cultures fold large families into the greater society with such ease and pleasure. Still, the number echoed in Patience's head like the vibrations from a great tolling cathedral bell.

Thir-teen! Thir-teen! Thir-teen!

That wasn't the only problem between them, anyway. Patience was cautious and hesitant and remote with Eustace. But he still loved her. He attributed her hesitancy to her youth, and he hoped they would slowly come together over time to burn with a brighter passion. Maybe they could work things out on this adventure. Maybe the buggy ride would make everything better.

Eustace, even more than on the Long Riders trip, wanted to push himself and his horses to the very edge of endurance. He knew his horses could move a lot faster pulling a buggy than carrying a man, and he wanted to see how fast they could travel. The buggy was light and quick, not a heavy-duty farm rig, and the horses were fitted with slick nylon harnesses that would be more efficient than leather.

He was demonic about not making the horses carry extra weight. He had to approve of every item of clothing Patience wanted to bring to make sure that a pair of frivolous socks wouldn't add an ounce of strain to his animals. Patience once stopped at a store in North Dakota and bought a jar of pickles for snacking, and Eustace gave her hell about it. "All that glass and fluid and pickles makes a lot of extra weight for my horses to pull all day," he ranted, and didn't let up until the offending item was consumed and discarded. With his horses, particularly on a difficult journey, he was concerned, attentive, vigilant. Miles from a vet and pushing his animals to the limits of their endurance, he was zealously aware of "every step my horses took, everything they ate, everything they drank, every scab, every limp, every booger, the color of their urine every time they pissed, the frequency of their stools, every tiny flick of the ear, everything."

Eustace was even more fanatical about speed on this journey than on the Long Riders trip. He was so obsessed with not wasting a moment's time that when he saw a gate approaching, he'd hand the reins to Patience, leap off the buggy, and sprint ahead to open the gate. Then he'd slam it shut and sprint ahead to catch up with her. He wouldn't even stop the buggy to relieve himself, choosing, instead, to leap off and piss in the woods while the horses trotted on, then catch up on foot at full speed.

Eustace and Patience got so that they could change and replace their horses' shoes—over fifty such stops on the trip—quicker than an Indy 500 pit team, Patience handing Eustace the tools, Eustace fixing the shoe swiftly and flawlessly. They moved across the plains, as Eustace later reported, "faster than a cloud's shadow across the bent grass." They stopped for virtually nothing. Eustace had fliers made up with information about the trip—press releases, really—that they handed to people when the inevitable million questions came up and they had to hustle on their way. They had not a moment's leisure. When some ranchers in Canada invited them to stick around for a few days to enjoy the yearly round-up and branding, Patience wanted to stay, but Eustace said, "There will be lots of brandings and round-ups, but only one chance for us to ever set a world speed record by going twenty-five hundred miles in fifty-six days."

The trip was most certainly a success in horsemanship, organization, and safety. But the relationship, already vulnerable, was murdered by it. Eustace and Patience were getting four hours of sleep a night, careening across the prairie, freezing, miserable, intense. The weather was brutal. When it wasn't a 70 mph wind, it was freezing rain. Their hands stopped working from the cold, so they couldn't unfasten harnesses and buckles at the end of each day. They ate horrible food or didn't eat at all.

There were some unforgettable moments, of course. The scenery was extraordinary. They had a wonderful time for a few days riding through a no-man's-land—a swath of ownerless land *within* the Canadian-American border, in which they felt as if they were riding nowhere on the mapped earth. When the rain and sleet abated, they read Cormac Mc-Carthy novels to each other. That was nice. They met many generous people, and Eustace liked sitting back and letting Patience be her gracious, disarming self. He liked watching her win over strangers, who would fall in love with her and then offer them housing, food, help for the horses. And their teamwork with the animals was striking. What was most impressive, though, was that Patience—competitive athlete that she was—never once complained about the physical toll and long hours of the journey.

"That," she told me, "was the easy part."

The hard part was that they were passing whole days without speaking to each other, except about the horses. And they weren't sleeping together. No conversation, no physical contact.

"I never cried because I was tired or in pain," Patience said. "But I cried a lot toward the end about the relationship with Eustace. It sucked."

The journey itself was heroic, in other words, but the situation was unfortunately reminiscent of Ursula K. LeGuin's sharp observation that "the backside of heroism is often rather sad; women and servants know that."

Patience couldn't stand Eustace's constant dominance over her. "I used to be a tomboy," she said. "I used to intimidate men with my strength. I was a modern woman with a lot of confidence in myself before I met him. But slowly he overtook me until I had no power anymore. That's how it happens with Eustace; you get sucked into the vortex of his goals and his life, and then you're lost. I disappeared to him. Lots of times, local reporters would ask to join us for the trip, so he'd ride in the buggy with the reporter and I'd follow in the reporter's car. He'd charm each guy and talk to him all day, but the next day, when I rode beside him for twenty hours, he'd never say a word to me. All he did on that trip was boss me around and tell me what to do."

"Of course I told her what to do," Eustace agreed. "Of course I was in charge, because I knew what had to be done. I had the background and the experience to understand the animals and the realities of long-distance survival and to save her life and my life and the horses' lives on two thousand different occasions, and she didn't even notice fifteen hundred of those times. I never had her respect about that. She got more sulky and more immature when we were working together. She had no idea what it took to get us alive across that prairie. We had the goal to set a world speed record. And if I'm going to take on something like that, I'm taking it on a hundred percent, and she needs to respect my knowledge and stop having childish reactions to my leadership."

When I asked Eustace whether it would have helped to pull the buggy over for a day to sit in a meadow and talk over the problems they were having, he said, "That wasn't part of the program. That would have ruined our goal."

Patience later complained (just as Judson had complained on the Long Riders voyage) that Eustace acted like his father during this trip. Patience had spent enough time around Eustace's parents to be upset by the dominance and disdain Big Eustace showed his wife, and now she felt she was getting the same treatment from Little Eustace. The same kind of tyranny, the same level of perfectionism, the same refusal to respond to the needs of anyone else. To both Patience and Judson, Eustace came across on these horse journeys not only as impossible, but as tragic. What could be sadder than a man who literally travels to the ends of the earth but still cannot avoid becoming his father?

But I'm not convinced that Eustace was *becoming* his father on these journeys so much as *honoring* him, trying to prove again that he was worthy, brave, accomplished, and logical. Just as he had tried to prove with all his most daring adventures and mind-numbing accomplishments. As much as Eustace may have wanted to love Patience and his brother, he could not put their needs first when the stake of each of these journeys was so massive—nothing less than the prize of getting his father's attention at last. He was still concentrating on the older and sadder love story, one that was so bitterly unresolved. Big Eustace had never given his son a word or a nod of recognition despite all his achievements. What more did Eustace have to do to get the man to acknowledge that his son was not a miserable, pathetic, idiotic failure? Would an equestrian world speed record do it?

Would *two*?

One cannot level against Eustace a more hurtful charge than that he is behaving like his father. "I would be glad to put a gun in my mouth and blow my own head off," he said, "if I ever believed I treated anyone the way that man treated me." Certainly Eustace opens himself up to more self-doubt and self-criticism than his father has ever done, and he has suffered deeply (no more so than on these long horse journeys) over his troubles in relating to people. He knows of these problems; he sees the patterns; he works to correct the situations. But he does not always know what to do. He is self-aware enough to know that he is, in his word, "damaged," but he doesn't know how to repair himself. He knows that he was way over his head with Patience Harrison, that, for whatever reasons, he couldn't communicate with her on the journey in a way that gave them any chance at a relationship. Maybe it was her immaturity; maybe it was his relentless perfectionism; maybe it was a corrosive combination of their combined weaknesses. But the whole thing was a disaster.

"Maybe," he said, "we should have concentrated more on our relationship and less on our goals, but our goals sometimes felt like the only thing we had in common. I don't know what I should have done. I'm not good at this kind of thing. I just hoped we could work it out later."

There was no later. Not really. They limped along in their relationship for a year after the buggy journey, but Patience ended up taking a job down in Boone, coaching field hockey, and slowly peeled herself away from Eustace and from Turtle Island. And no number of his passionate fifteen-page letters ("I am sorry if I have not been able to articulate my self, feelings, perspective, in a way that you could understand . . . I pray someday when you are strong enough or ready you can experience this profound love I am feeling") could win her back.

Patience had run out of it.

What killed Eustace about Patience was that she didn't understand him. She didn't understand how much he loved her. She didn't understand his emotional limitations and scars. His goals. How much love he needed from her. How much love he was willing to give her. And how much he wanted to see that she trusted him. She didn't understand anything about him.

And it is exactly this perceived lack of appreciation, lack of understanding, lack of faith, that burned Eustace to an emotional crisp. After suffering under a father who told him he was crazy and worthless and a total failure, how could he now be subjected to a person (especially someone who was supposedly in love with him) who didn't trust him or believe in his expertise? Well, that was altogether too familiar. And if the woman he loved couldn't understand him, how could he expect to gain understanding from anyone else? Where could he find recognition and sympathy? In whose arms? In whose eyes? Eustace Conway was becoming more certain that nobody would ever really know him, that this intense isolation would be a permanent condition. That he was a refugee in this world by birth and by destiny.

"I feel like Ishi," he said.

The story of Ishi was one that had haunted Eustace from childhood. Ishi was an Indian of the California people, a primitive, Stone Age culture that lived for centuries in the canyons outside Los Angeles. In the late nineteenth century, Ishi's people were killed in genocidal attacks as the white man pushed farther up into the canyons looking for gold and ranch land. By the turn of the century, the understanding among anthropologists was that the California Indians were extinct. Until August 29, 1911, that is. On that day, right in the middle of an age of railroads and telephones, Ishi, a healthy native in his fifties, wandered down to a ranch valley in Oroville, California. He was naked, and his hair was burned off, to symbolize mourning. He had been hiding in the canyons since childhood with a sister and a grandmother, and now that they had both passed away, he, overcome with grief and loneliness, had taken a long journey on foot, ready to travel "into the next world." Which is where he ended up. He was a Stone Age man who had walked right into modern industrial America. It took researchers and ethnographers weeks to figure out who Ishi was, and to piece together a language by which to communicate with him. They found him, of course, to be a priceless vault of anthropological information. He taught them language, myths, and hunting techniques (including a form of archery that had previously been observed only in Mongolia). The anthropologists who studied Ishi ended up bringing him to their museum, where he worked as a janitor.

"This man," Eustace said in disbelief, "with his unbelievably articulate ability to live in the wilderness, was pushing a broom all day."

Ishi also made arrowheads for visitors, who would come to see him on display at the museum once a week. He learned to speak some English, took to wearing trousers, saw vaudeville acts, rode trains, and died of tuberculosis within the decade.

"I swear to God I feel like Ishi sometimes," Eustace said. "Completely different from everyone else in this world, the last of my kind, stranded. Just trying to communicate. Trying to teach people something. But constantly misunderstood."

Eustace had run into this understanding-deficit throughout his horse journeys. He met young people who were vegetarian environmentalists and were upset to see him dressed in animal skins or to learn that he hunted for food. He reached the point where he no longer had the energy to explain how much more destructive to the environment their synthetic-fleece clothing was, seeing that it was made of nonrenewable material produced in polluting and resource-gobbling factories. Or that they didn't know where their food came from, or how the earth suffered from its manufacture and packaging. And then there were the animal rights people, who objected to the cruelty they perceived in watching Eustace push his horses so hard.

"There were people out there who owned fat horses, horses that were nothing but pasture potatoes," Eustace observed, "and they had never seen a horse that was truly in shape before they saw mine. My horses are lean, long-muscled, skinny, capable animals that have worked and traveled their whole lives. These are athletes built for the long haul. That's what horses were made to be. Nobody takes better care of animals than I do. But I heard people say, 'You aren't feeding those ponies enough!' and it made me angry. I wanted to say, 'Listen, people. I'm feeding my horses so goddamn much food it would flat-out *kill* your lazy old horse stuck in your stupid little pasture.' But my horses were lean because they were burning it off."

The most upsetting incident occurred in Gillette, Wyoming. Eustace and Patience and their horses had just finished a 51-mile day. They hitched the buggy to the rail of a dusty saloon that looked like a movie set and went inside for a burger. On their way out of town, an old cowboy swung by and took a look at Eustace's best horse, Hasty, his trusted Morgan, who, fed and watered, was resting with his head down. The cowboy said, "That horse ain't got no heart. I've been around horses my whole life, and I can tell you that animal has one foot in the grave. You better pull him out and give him up."

Eustace didn't say a word. He didn't tell the cowboy that Hasty had traveled thousands of miles in his life. He didn't say that Hasty had once kept a 45-beat-per-minute heart rate after trotting fourteen miles—lower than the pulse rate of most horses at rest. Wasn't even breathing hard. He didn't mention that Hasty would cover nearly 450 miles in the next eight days. Or that Eustace Conway wouldn't trade that horse for a million dollars.

"Hasty was just a bay," Eustace told me. "Brown horse with a black mane and tail. He was the most common-looking horse you ever saw, but he was a hero. People had no idea what I was sitting on with that horse. That cowboy said Hasty didn't have any heart; I'm telling you this horse was nothing *but* heart. Hasty was my champion, and he loved to go. We experienced adventures together that this cowboy couldn't even have imagined, and we understood each other. We pushed each other to go as far and as fast as we could, and Hasty loved it. I'm telling you, that horse hasn't even found his limits yet. And I never met anyone who understands what that means."

There's a guy down in Kentucky who is (because somebody has to be) the world's foremost authority on the history of long-distance equestrian travel. His name is CuChullaine O'Reilly, and he owns the world's largest collection of books on equestrian adventure. He himself has ridden horses on five epic journeys across Central Asia, including one trip to the Himalayan Mountains, where one of his horses died and was eaten by the locals.

"You gotta put Eustace Conway in context," says CuChullaine O'Reilly, who actually can. "I know my stuff, and let me tell you that this guy is the real deal. Because how many people in this country keep horses? Hundreds of thousands, right? And how many of them have ridden their horses more than fifty miles away from a barn? Nobody. Because it's terrifying to put yourself and your animal out there in the world with no security. I know all about this.

"Look, the distances Eustace has traveled aren't in themselves remarkable. I know a couple who've gone over eighteen thousand miles on horseback. I know a guy from Maine who went for a fourteen-thousand-mile ride a few years ago. So crossing the country is not in itself a big deal. What's extraordinary is that Eustace did it in 103 days. Unbelievable. That's the fastest anyone has traveled long distance on horseback in at least twenty-five years, probably longer. The fact that Eustace did it without having been a real horseman before is astonishing. He used his wilderness skills and audacity and intelligence, and he made this journey virtually free of mistakes. And the buggy journey? To turn around and master buggies so fast? It's mind-boggling. There are only a few people who are Eustace's peers in horsemanship, and they are all lifelong horsemen who do nothing else. They do their research for two years before a long journey, and then they get sponsors and bring along private veterinarians and lots and lots of money. And they make lots of mistakes he didn't make."

There are three factors, according to CuChullaine O'Reilly, that a man needs in order to be a brilliant endurance rider: courage, resolve, and romance. Eustace has all these, in spades. And something else, too. He has a kind of preternatural gift. To CuChullaine O'Reilly, Eustace Conway's crossing the country in 103 days was an accomplishment as exciting as an untrained Iowa farm boy stepping up to a footrace and casually breaking a four-minute mile. You can't just *do* that. But Eustace did.

In this regard, and in terms of pure and authentic character value, CuChullaine O'Reilly finds Eustace comparable only to one other person, the Alaskan wildman Eugene Glasscock. Eugene Glasscock is a bearded and hard-boiled recluse ("Mr. Mountain," he's called at home) who got a wild hair one day back in the 1980s and decided to ride his horse from the Arctic Circle down to the Equator. Wearing, of course, handmade buckskins. The crazy freak. He barely made it alive through the Yukon and Rockies, and he was attacked by machete-wielding bandits in Mexico, and he had to swim beside his horse across some raging rivers down in Guatemala. He liked the jungle, though. That's why Mr. Mountain still lives down there in Central America, someplace totally off the map. Too bad he's difficult to get in touch with, says CuChullaine O'Reilly, because it'd sure be fun to get Eugene Glasscock and Eustace Conway together for a weekend "so that they could go off and tell stories and get drunk and eat some possums."

"Nobody can understand Eustace," he says. "Because what you get when a modern-day American encounters Eustace Conway and his horse is the twenty-first century running head-on into a six-thousand-year-old nomadic tradition that regular people cannot understand. They are so removed from that episode of their humanity that it is foreign to them. They have no idea of what trans-species communication is. They don't understand that Eustace uses his horsemanship not as a prestige gimmick or as a means of winning blue ribbons or collecting rodeo belt buckles, but as a way to become bonded to another animal so that together they pass through curtain after curtain of incomprehensible and invisible experience until they reach the indescribable other side."

But there's one other thing that the world's foremost expert on equestrian endurance travel believes about Eustace Conway. He says there's still more to come from Eustace. He thinks Eustace hasn't even begun to show us what he can do. He thinks Eustace has the capacity for "some real Jason and the Argonauts type of superhuman adventure. Maybe."

Why only *maybe*?

"Because," he explains, "I think he's reached a plateau in his life. He's pushed himself as far as he can go using his charisma and courage, and now he needs to go on a spiritual journey. He needs to do something that is private. He's postured himself in public for so many years that he doesn't know himself. There are parts of his soul he can't begin to understand, and until he learns these things about himself, he'll never be the nomad he's meant to be. He's a brave man, but he's not a spiritual pilgrim yet. Until he goes out in the world, all alone, and cuts away the ropes and publicity and ego and bullshit and does something truly heroic, he's just blowing smoke up his own ass. And I'll tell you another thing. He's no goddamn farmer, and he should quit trying to be one. That's not his nature. He needs to get away from all that. He should stop trying to save the world. Because until he stops living in his grandfather's shadow and pretending that he likes digging holes in the ground and planting vegetables on that goddamn farm, he will never be Jason of the Argonauts."

Adds CuChullaine O'Reilly, "But that's just my opinion."

CHAPTER EIGHT

I alone comprehend the true plan and the means of fulfilling it.

—*Charles Fourier, Utopian*

Eustace Conway's grandfather founded Camp Sequoyah in 1924 and ran his domain with an exacting command until the moment of his death, by heart attack, when he was eighty. He died in the harness, as they say, never slowing his stride. And he hadn't named a successor to his legacy. After his funeral, it was revealed that there was no plan for the camp to continue without him. While Chief always had a large staff working for him, he didn't trust anyone enough to turn over the management of the operation, never having found anyone he believed capable of running his beloved Sequoyah—his "Camp With a Purpose" where "the Weak Become Strong and the Strong Become Great"—up to his rigorous standards.

When campers and staff arrived at Camp Sequoyah for the summer, Chief took over every aspect of their lives. He dictated how they would dress, when they'd exercise, when they would pray, and what they would eat. One counselor remembers the day Chief Johnson took him into his office and spent a full hour delivering a lecture on how best to sweep a room. Another counselor once got a lecture on how best to use a paperclip. ("The big loop goes to the back of the document; the small loop to the front.") Naturally, Chief prohibited tobacco, cursing, and alcohol from his property. But he also strictly forbade Coca-Cola, vinegar, pepper, and denim. There was a rumor that Chief even put saltpeter in the applesauce to "curb desire" and keep his boys away from the temptations of self-abuse. ("We *did* eat an awful lot of applesauce," said one old Sequoyan when I brought it up.) Hair was not to touch ears. Campers were to wear pressed white shirts on Sundays. Camp nurses, the only females on the workforce, were to be matronly and plain so as not to cause sexual disturbance by their presence. Staff members were to be graded throughout the summer on their physical and social progress, with extra credit given for such traits as Loyalty, Readiness to Shoulder Responsibility, and Personal Magnetism.

He was uncompromising. He did not hand out praise. Nobody was ever good enough for Chief. Nobody worked harder or more efficiently than Chief. He carved that camp from virgin wilderness, creating it with his own strength and genius. He had suffered through the first winters up at Sequoyah in a log cabin, had defined every philosophical notion that made the camp unique, had built its every structure, and had kept the operation alive (and thriving) throughout the hard times of the Great Depression and World War II. So who was going to tell Chief Johnson how anything was done? Nobody. As his grandson Eustace would complain fifty years later in his journal about the lackluster employees of his own empire, Turtle Island, "I have worked hard to make this place what it is. What have *they* done? How can *they* respect it? What investment have *they* made in anything that is a serious challenge? How can I put up with them?"

Well, you can put up with them by assuming absolute power over them, body and soul. That's what Chief did. Chief had a series of "talks" he delivered to the campers at different points of their stay, based on their ages. Included were discussions of God and Nature and Honesty and Courage and How to Become a Man of Destiny, and also warnings about Masturbation and Dating. He spoke to the boys about "The

Effect of a Rational Sex Life Upon Marriage and Offspring" (Talk #5) and about "Venereal Disease" (Talk #6). When his boys left Camp Sequoyah, Chief stayed in touch with them—with the many thousands of them—sending them motivational messages every Christmas, as well as sending out his own earnest pamphlets, which he mailed off at key moments of their lives:

A Letter to Boys About to Leave Home for Preparatory School
A Letter to Young Men About to Enter College
A Letter to Young Men on the Occasion of Their Twenty-first Birthday
A Letter to Young Men About to Get Married
A Letter to Young Men Who Have Just Become Fathers

Every boy was Chief's son. And his boys went on to become doctors, judges, teachers, soldiers—the stalwart backbone of the American South for decades. Every one of their achievements was his achievement. One woman wrote Chief a letter back in the 1950s assuring him that her son, a former Sequoyan, had passed through two years of the Navy without appearing to have acquired any "of the bad habits for which sailors are sometimes known. I feel that the vision he caught at Sequoyah has been and will continue to be a shining guiding light along his way."

Every boy was Chief's son, yes. But he also had two flesh-and-blood sons of his own, Harold and Bill Johnson, the brothers of Eustace Conway's mother, Karen.

"The youth of each generation should be aware of the role some of them will be privileged to play in the progress of man toward a Higher Destiny," Chief wrote, and no youths had this responsibility thrust upon them harder than Chief's sons. And yet Harold and Bill, perhaps we should not be surprised to learn, both went completely ballistic on their dad. They were smoking and drinking by the age of fifteen. Alternatively sullen and willful. Shooting off guns and racing cars. Disobedient and indignant.

"They were just the opposite," recalled one old Sequoyan, "of what

Chief desperately wanted in a son. He had always envisioned them to be the ideal boys."

Chief could make no sense of why his sons had gone wrong. Maybe it was the mother's fault. Mrs. Chief, as she was forever known, was always confounding her husband by not being as rigorous a disciplinarian as he would have liked. But what could you expect? Mrs. Chief was not her husband's doctrinarian equal. She was a gifted pianist and a college graduate and a frustrated urban sophisticate who was emotional and unpredictable and often resentful about spending her life in the woods with thousands of boys. She had, it was always said with great delicacy, "an artistic temperament." Unlike her husband, who kept a logical hold on the more animalistic aspects of human nature, Mrs. Chief was known to sometimes scream her head off in fits of frustration and anger. She was also known to sneak away sometimes to play sexy and rollicking ragtime tunes on the piano when her husband was out of earshot. She probably liked pepper, too.

So maybe what happened to the sons was Mrs. Chief's fault. That's what Chief probably figured. Both boys busted out of that house the first chance they got. It was Harold, Chief's firstborn, who caused his father the most trouble. *Canst thou not beg?* No, Harold Johnson could not beg and could not submit to his father, not from day one. And he couldn't stand it at home. As Harold's nephew Eustace wrote in his adolescent diary decades later: "While it would be a dumb thing to run away, I think I would be happier anywhere in the woods if I could only get away. If I do leave, I will try my best not to come back, even if I am starving. Anything is better than this."

Harold ran away to Alaska when he was seventeen. Like generations of American boys before him, he headed to the frontier to get out from under the authority of the old man. He could not be in the same house with his father. They had no means of dialogue. His father would never praise Harold, never let up on him, never give him an inch of space within which to move or grow. But Harold wanted to be a big man, and it came to pass that there was not room in this town for the two of them. Harold had to go.

He'd read some Jack London and got an itch. By the time he made it to Seward, he had only fifty cents in his pocket. He was hungry, scared, and alone, but he damn sure wasn't going back to Camp Sequoyah. He found work on a road crew. Then he got himself a motorcycle and went to school to learn how to repair engines. And then, on the brink of World War II, he enlisted in the Marines (much to the horror of his father, who had been a committed pacifist ever since witnessing the carnage in the trenches in France). Harold was stationed in Hawaii, where he taught jungle survival to Air Force pilots. After the war, he refused to move back South and founded one business after another up in Alaska—an ice cream shop, a boat dealership, a mail-order color slide developing operation. Then he built and sold generator sets, a lucrative scheme in a state that still had no power grid. Then he set up a diesel engine business and became a millionaire. He was six feet five, strong, and dashing. And was always known as a charming, magnetic, big, controlling, and powerful man who worked endless hours, had a genius for self-promotion, and did not easily give praise or welcome the opinions of others.

When Chief Johnson died at the age of eighty, there was nobody to take over Camp Sequoyah. Neither of Chief's sons wanted to run the camp. Harold hated the South and had his own empire to manage up in Alaska. Bill, the younger and more troubled child, had become a real estate developer, of all heretical things. It was his wish to sell off some of the beautiful forested dynasty of Camp Sequoyah, which his father had preserved over so many decades, for housing and lumber.

Something crucial must be noted here about the Johnson family. What seems never to have been discussed was the possibility that Chief's daughter might take over the camp. Despite Karen's deep commitment to her father's vision and her competence in the wilderness, she was never considered a candidate for leadership. Not seen as strong enough, perhaps. But Karen's husband very much wanted to run that camp, was dying for the chance. And we know, of course, that her husband was Eustace Robinson Conway III.

That was Big Eustace, who had come to Camp Sequoyah after MIT to work with children and to live in nature. One of Chief's star counselors, brilliant, energetic, dedicated, and physically adept, Big Eustace loved the wilderness, held the camp's endurance hiking record, and was a gifted teacher and a patient leader of boys. He was adored at Camp Sequoyah. (I went to a Camp Sequoyah reunion once and met there a number of grown men who said, when I mentioned Eustace Conway, "Is he here? My God, I would give anything to see him again! He was the best nature educator I ever had! I worshipped him!" It took me some time to do the math and estimate the ages and realize that these old guys were talking about my Eustace's *father*.) With his calculating intellect and passion for nature, Big Eustace believed he had the brains and the spirit to take over Sequoyah one day. And, as he freely admitted to me, he married Karen Johnson "halfway because of the person that she was and halfway to get my hands on that camp of her father's."

The fact is, he would have been great at running the place. As one old Sequoyan remembered, Big Eustace was "as straight-laced, as dedicated, and as competent as Chief himself. We all assumed he'd take over the camp one day. He was the closest thing we ever saw to someone with the capacity to keep it running up to Chief's standards." But when Chief died, he left no such word in his will. And Harold and Bill declared that they would fight to the death to keep the camp out of their brother-in-law's control. They hated their sister's husband. They hated him for his intellectual arrogance and his dismissiveness of them. They thought him an opportunist and wouldn't let him near the place.

So the camp floundered through years of substandard management, run by lesser men from outside the family. As for Big Eustace, he gave up his dreams of becoming a nature educator and worked as an engineer at a chemical plant. Living in a box, working in a box, driving from box to box in a box with wheels. He never again set foot near Sequoyah. And when Little Eustace turned out to be a willful and wild boy who preferred the woods to school, Big Eustace would regularly attack him with the accusation that he was "irregular, abnormal, stubborn, and impossible, just like your Johnson uncles."

The camp finally withered to nothingness. The solid handmade log cabins lay empty. When the camp was finally abandoned in the 1970s, Little Eustace Conway was a teenager. He was already a skilled woodsman and a fierce leader, the one who had every kid in his neighborhood working on regulated shifts around the clock to tend to his extensive personal turtle collection.

"I want Camp Sequoyah," Little Eustace said. "Give it to me! Let me run it! I know I could do it!"

Of course nobody listened to him. He was just a kid.

Summer, 1999.

When Eustace Conway returned to his thousand acres of Turtle Island after his adventures crossing America on horseback and in buggies, he found his paradise to be, well, a mess.

There was a lot more to Turtle Island after years of Eustace's improvements and developments; the place was no longer a rugged nature preserve but a highly organized and highly functional primitive farm. It was dotted with buildings, all of which Eustace had built in various traditional styles. There was his private passive solar office, yes. But he'd also built several public structures, including a comfortable bunkhouse for visitors called "Everybody's," the design of which he borrowed from a neighbor's traditional barn.

He'd built a handsome toolshed, crafted perfectly in line with the buildings of Daniel Boone's era, what with its hand-split oak door and handmade hinges and chinks filled with manure and clay. He based this design on buildings he'd seen at historic sites. And a hog pen of half-dovetailed logs, notched in the traditional Appalachian style. And a chicken house with a foundation of stone sunk nine inches into the ground to keep predators from digging in and stealing eggs. And a corn crib with nice pungeon floors and, although "a hundred years from now, someone might wish I hadn't used pine, so be it. I needed to get the job done." He'd built a blacksmith shop of locust and oak, right on the site of a blacksmith shop that stood there two hundred years ago, when what is now Turtle Island was the only thoroughfare for this whole section of the Appalachian Mountains. He used the stones of the original building to make forges, where he now does all his own smithing. He'd created an outdoor kitchen. And, over the course of a summer, with a team of dozens of young people who'd never worked construction before, he'd crafted a forty-foot-tall locust and pine and poplar barn, put together without a single sawn board, containing sixty-foot-long beams and boasting a cantilevered roof, six horse stalls, and thousands of hand-split shingles.

And more, too.

In the middle of this building spree, a North Carolina anthropology professor heard about this gifted young man who lived up there in the mountains, made buildings without the use of nails, farmed with livestock, and survived off the land. Intrigued, she sent a student to Turtle Island one day to ask Eustace whether he'd consider coming down from the mountain to speak to her class and explain how he had done all this. Dutifully, Eustace considered the offer. Then he sent the student back down the mountain with a simple message for the good professor. "Tell her I did it by working my fucking ass off."

Turtle Island was by now a vast and complicated place. Aside from organizing the educational programs, the mere running of the farm was an enormous job. There were horses and cows and turkeys to tend to, barns to keep up, fences to mend, pastures to plow, gardens to cultivate, and hay to bale. It took a tremendous amount of work to keep the place running, and Eustace had left it all in the hands of his apprentices. He did so with the greatest trepidation. Before he went on his horse journeys, he gave his apprentices lists and lectures to make sure they understood exactly how to care for the property, but, in the end, he narrowed his commands down to two basic components: "Please," Eustace begged. "Just don't kill any of my animals and don't burn down any of my buildings."

Well, they hadn't killed any of his animals. They hadn't burned down any of his buildings, either. But when Eustace returned, he found Turtle Island to be in extreme disorder. Gardens were overrun by weeds; bridges needed repair; goats were in the wrong pasture; the paths were overgrown. Nobody had been handling publicity and scheduling, which meant that not one single school group was on the schedule to visit Turtle Island that fall, which, in turn, meant that money would be short throughout the winter.

Eustace's workers were willing and hard-working people, but the fact is that Eustace had never found anyone he trusted to manage Turtle Island so that the institution would thrive in his absence. Of course, it's hard to imagine that there's anyone able or willing to put in the hours that Eustace did. He'd had some apprentices who were good with people and some who were good with livestock and some who were good at manual labor and some who had a slight talent for business. But no one could do everything Eustace could, which was *everything*. And no one was willing to work all day on building a barn and then sit up all night making phone calls and writing land deeds.

What he needed was a clone.

In lieu of that, he had hired a program manager, a gifted young naturalist who could take over the duties of running the camping and educational side of Turtle Island, so that Eustace could focus on his own baby, the apprenticeship program. Eustace believed that it was through this intense tutorial program that he would have the most healthy effect. He had long ago begun to wonder whether dealing with group after group of random campers was really going to change anything about American society.

"I'm sitting under the walnut tree in the parking lot on the freshly cut grass," he had written in his journal during one such crisis of conscience, not long after Turtle Island had opened. "I need to be cooking supper for the delinquents here from the 'youth at risk' group. I don't want to face them. Let them suffer and die is the attitude I have quickly developed in the face of their disruptive disrespect. I am feeling weak . . . I don't know if I really want to make this place what I dreamed. I know I *could*. I *could* make it succeed, but do I want that?"

He had decided that the answer was to keep the camping and day programs, but put someone else in charge of them so that he could focus on the apprentices. He wanted to throw his energy and ability behind the intimate, long-term, one-on-one teaching relationships he would develop with his direct trainees. Then they would take their skills out into the world and teach others, who would teach others, and so the change would come, more slowly, perhaps, than Eustace had dreamed when he was twenty years old, but still the change would come.

He was *almost* certain of it.

* * *

There was a girl. She was a hippie. Her name was Alice. Alice loved nature more than anything, and she wanted to live in the woods and be self-sufficient, and her sister, who knew Eustace Conway, said, "Alice, this is the man for you." Alice got in touch with Eustace and told him that she wanted to live close to nature, just as he did. One afternoon, she visited Turtle Island, and Eustace gave her a tour and some of his brochures and told her to think about whether she'd like to work as an apprentice. She took one look at the babbling brooks, the swaying trees, the farm animals grazing in the fields, and the peaceful, welcoming sign at the front gate (*No Shirt, No Shoes, No Problem!*), and thought she had surely reached paradise.

Swiftly, Alice wrote to Eustace, assuring him that, "my instincts say YES! From the little I've seen and read, Turtle Island holds certain qualities that feel truest to my heart. It's like a dream come true. I'm also grateful for your open welcome and would be honored to come to live, learn, work, and play with you and the land. I remember as a young girl watching 'Little House on the Prairie,' dreaming of someday living it instead of watching it. Dedication to family, living in harmony with nature. Ah . . . sweet life."

After seven months at Turtle Island, Alice wrote Eustace a different kind of letter.

"When I first got here, I asked for a day off a week. You told me I didn't deserve it. Yet Jennie's second weekend out she got a day off. You showed her how to skin a deer, when I had to work my butt off for you to even recognize me as a student . . . you make me work so hard . . . make me feel unworthy . . . I feel unappreciated and unwanted . . . you say the more you get to know me the more disappointed you are in me . . . you've been working me ten to twelve hours a day . . . maybe I shouldn't be here."

And then Alice was gone. Fired. Dismissed.

What was the problem? What happened in the seven months between "sweet life" and "maybe I shouldn't be here"?

Well, according to Eustace, the problem was that Alice was a hippie, a dreamer, and a lounge-about. She'd done a whole lot of drugs in her life, and maybe that was why her brain worked slowly and she was absent-minded and she had trouble learning how to do things right. She didn't work quickly or efficiently. She couldn't absorb skills, no matter how many times she was shown the correct procedure. And she took up too much of Eustace's emotional energy, always wanting to sit in his office and talk about nature and her feelings and the dream she had last night and the poem she'd just written.

And Eustace was afraid that Alice might accidentally kill somebody or herself. Alice routinely pulled cockamamie stunts like leaving candles burning unattended on the windowsills of wooden buildings. Several times she wandered, daydreaming, into the path of falling timber as Eustace was clearing away pastureland. Worst of all, one day when Alice was working with Eustace as he was getting into his buggy to train a young horse, she released the animal from its tether before handing Eustace his reins. The horse, young and skittish, took off on a wild ride, and Eustace was stuck in the buggy, empty-handed, powerless to control the animal. The horse tore through the woods while Eustace held on for his life, trying to think of the softest place to bail out and save himself. He ended up taking a header right into a bush at twenty-five miles an hour, landing right on his face and hurting himself seriously. The horse wrecked the buggy into the side of the blacksmith shop and sustained injuries of its own.

"I had been rebuilding that buggy, which was a Mennonite antique, for months," Eustace recalled, "and it was completely destroyed. That cost me $2000. And I wouldn't take $10,000 for the psychological damage it did to the horse to be in a bad wreck like that at such a young age. It took me nearly a year to get that horse to a place where he could relax pulling a buggy again. And it was all because of Alice's carelessness."

Two weeks later, she made the same mistake again. That's when Eustace told her she had to go. She was too senseless and dangerous to keep around, lost as she always seemed to be in her "Little House on the Prairie" fantasyland.

Dismissing apprentices is never easy, particularly since it's a point of pride for Eustace Conway to claim that anyone can learn to live this primitive life and that he is that man who can teach anybody. It's a failure of the dream to have to tell somebody, "You must leave here because you are incapable of learning." Or, "You must leave here because you are impossible to have around." It's a terrible moment when Eustace Conway's refrain turns from "You *can!*" to "You *can't!*"

I once asked Eustace what percentage of the apprentices had left Turtle Island under angry or bitter circumstances. Without hesitating, he said, "Eighty-five percent. Although my program manager would probably say it was closer to ninety-five."

OK, let's round that off to 90 percent. It's hard to look at such an attrition rate without pinning the label of bad leadership on Eustace. Turtle Island is his world, after all, and he is accountable for what happens in his world. If he can't keep his world populated, then something is clearly wrong with the scheme. If I were a stockholder in a company where 90 percent of the employees were quitting or being fired each year, I might consider asking the CEO some hard questions about his management policies.

On the other hand, maybe the number makes perfect sense. Maybe it shouldn't be easy to stay on Turtle Island. Maybe only 10 percent of the population are able to cut it. What if the comparison model was the Navy SEAL training program? How many of those guys do they lose each year? And who's left after everybody else quits? The strongest, right? The people who are going up to Turtle Island, though, are not necessarily the people most suited for the place.

"Again and again," Eustace said, "I attract people who have dreams of nature but no experience with nature at all. They come up here, and the only comparison they make is 'Wow, it looks just like the Nature Channel.'"

One of my favorite Turtle Island apprentices was an intelligent and soft-spoken young guy named Jason. He hailed from a well-to-do suburban family, had been raised in comfort, and been carefully educated in expensive private schools. When I asked Jason why he wanted to commit the next two years of his life to studying under Eustace Conway, he said, "Because I've been unhappy, and I didn't know where else to go to get happy."

Saddened by the unexpected death of his beloved father, angry at his mother for her "narrow-minded Christianity," annoyed by his "useless professors," disgusted with his peers, "who ignorantly refuse to listen to my songs and their warnings about environmental destruction," Jason had recently dropped out of college. When he heard about Eustace, he thought that a stay at Turtle Island would provide the enlightenment he sought. He saw Eustace as a larger-than-life hero who "goes out in the world and meets his destiny without fear of obstacles, and who can make things work where most people are satisfied to see something stay broken and die."

In a dramatic gesture, Jason decided to walk to Turtle Island all the way from Charlotte during Christmas vacation, but he got only about five miles down the road. It was freezing rain and he was overpacked and couldn't figure out where he was going to camp that night or how to stay dry. Demoralized and hungry, he called his girlfriend from a gas station, and she drove him the rest of the way to Turtle Island.

Jason's dream was to achieve perfect self-sufficiency. He didn't want to deal with phony Americans and their materialistic stupidity. He planned on moving to Alaska and homesteading up there in the last frontier. He wanted to live off the land, and he hoped that Eustace would teach him how to do it. He dreamed that life would be better in Alaska, where "a man can still hunt for food to feed his family without going through the bureaucracy of getting a hunting license."

"Have you ever *been* hunting?" I asked Jason.

"Well, not yet," Jason said, grinning sheepishly.

Jason was the very model of the young guy who typically comes to Eustace Conway for guidance. He was trying to discover how to be a man in a society that no longer had a clear path for him. Just as Eustace Conway had struggled as a teenager to find rituals to lead *him* into manhood, Jason was struggling to find some ceremony or meaning that would help define his own ascension. But he had no role models, his culture had no satisfying coming-of-age ritual for him, and his background had provided him with none of the manly skills that were so attractive to him. He was, by his own admission, lost.

This is the same disturbing cultural question that Joseph Campbell spent years asking. What happens to young people in a society that has lost all trace of ritual? Because adolescence is a transitional period, it is an inherently perilous journey. But culture and ritual are supposed to protect us through the transitions of life, holding us in safety during danger and answering confusing questions about identity and change, in order to keep us from getting separated from the community during our hardest personal journeys.

In more primitive societies, a boy might go through an entire year of initiation rites to usher him into manhood. He might endure ritual scarification or rigorous tests of endurance, or he might be sent away from the community for a period of meditation and solitude, after which he would return to the fold and be seen by all as a changed being. He will have moved safely from boyhood into manhood, and he will know exactly when that happened and what is now expected of him, because his role is so clearly codified. But how is a modern American boy supposed to know when he has reached manhood? When he gets his driver's license? When he smokes pot for the first time? When he experiences unprotected sex with a young girl who herself has no idea whether she's a woman now or not?

Jason didn't know. All he knew was that he ached for some sort of confirmation of his adulthood, and college life wasn't giving it to him. He had no idea where to find what he sought, but he was compelled by the idea that Eustace might help. Jason did have a beautiful girlfriend, and he maintained the romantic idea that the two of them would homestead in Alaska together someday, but she apparently had her own ideas. She was young, affluent, a brilliant student, as reflexively feminist as most of her generation, and she had an itch to see the world. She had limitless possibilities before her. Jason hoped she would "settle down" eventually with him, but that struck me as doubtful, and, indeed, after the next few months she left him. And that hardly made Jason feel better about himself as a man in the making.

Jason's discomfort in his own skin seemed to me typical of many young American men, who see their female peers soar into a new world and often have trouble catching up. When Jason looks out into American society, after all, what does he see? Aside from the environmental and consumer crisis that so offends his sensibilities, he is facing a world undergoing a total cultural and gender upheaval. Men are still largely in charge, mind you, but they are slipping fast. Modern America is a society where college-educated men have seen their incomes drop 20 percent over the last twenty-five years. A society where women complete high school and college at significantly higher rates than men, and have new doors of opportunity opened to them every day. A society where a third of all wives make more money than their husbands. A society where women are increasingly in control of their biological and economic destinies, often choosing to raise their children alone or not to have children at all or to leave an identifiable man out of the reproductive picture entirely, through the miracles of the sperm bank. A society, in other words, where a man is not necessary in the way he was customarily needed—to protect, to provide, to procreate.

I was at a women's professional basketball game in New York recently. As a girl I had been a serious basketball player, but there was no such thing as the WNBA back then, so I've watched this league grow in recent years with the greatest interest. I love going to the games and seeing talented female athletes compete for decent salaries. Mostly, though, I love watching the spectators, who tend to be enthusiastic and athletic preteen girls. On this night at a New York Liberty game, I saw something amazing. A handful of twelve-year-old girls ran to the railing in front of their seats and unfurled a sheet on which they'd written:

W.N.B.A. = WHO NEEDS BOYS, ANYHOW?

As cheers rose throughout the entire arena, all I could think was that Eustace Conway's grandfather must be whirling in his grave.

So, given the current culture, it's no wonder that a guy like Jason would want to move to Alaska and reclaim some noble and antique ideal of manhood. But he had an immense distance to travel—not geographic—before he could consider being a pioneer, before he could correctly learn what he was "for." Jason was keen and, heaven knows, sincere. He had a terrific smile, and Eustace enjoyed his company and his songs warning of environmental destruction. But Jason had an ego as soft and vulnerable as a fresh bruise, and he comported himself with a certain compensatory arrogance that made him difficult to teach. And, given his protected suburban upbringing, he had a big, fat, gaping lack of common sense. Shortly after arriving at Turtle Island, he borrowed one of Eustace's work trucks for a trip down to South Carolina and accidentally drove the entire trip at seventy-five miles an hour with the vehicle locked in four-wheel drive.

As Eustace said later in wonder, "I can't believe my truck even existed that distance in such a condition."

Indeed, by the time Jason arrived at his destination, the engine was ruined.

"Didn't you notice anything strange about the way the truck was running?" Eustace asked Jason, when he called to report that the truck's engine block had "suddenly" cracked.

"It *was* making a lot of noise," Jason admitted. "It did seem kind of weird. The engine was roaring and grinding so loud, I had to turn the music all the way up to drown out the noise."

It cost Eustace thousands of dollars to get his best truck running again.

Over the next nine months of Jason's apprenticeship (he would quit long before his two-year commitment was up, having grown unhappy with Eustace's leadership), he acquired impressive proficiency in primitive farming and other rugged skills, but he also wrecked two more of Eustace's vehicles. And when Eustace asked Jason to consider paying him back for some of the damage, Jason became deeply offended. How dare this so-called natural man show an attachment to material possessions! What a hypocrite Eustace was!

"Don't put your shit on me, Eustace," Jason wrote soon after leaving Turtle Island. "I don't need to feel this way. I need relationships that enrich my life, not ones that bring me down. I feel your truck is more important to you than I am . . . To borrow words from Lester, the father in *American Beauty*, 'It's just a fucking couch!' "

Again and again this shift takes place in Eustace's life. He is worshipped, and then his worshippers are horrified to find that he is not their godlike ideal. By and large, the people who come to Eustace are seekers, and when they meet this charismatic icon, they are certain that their search is over, that all their questions will be answered, which is why they so quickly and unconditionally hand their lives over to him. And it's not only young men who fall into this pattern.

"For five days I was in infinity," wrote one typically amazed young woman, after a short visit to Turtle Island. "Tiny pieces of my breath were everywhere in the white pines and the sassafras. Thank you, Creator! Thank you, Eustace! It has influenced me forever. It is the one place I know I want to be. If you ever need another hand, I'll give you both of mine!"

After such a glorified introduction, it can be mortifying to learn that life at Turtle Island is grueling and that Eustace is another flawed human being, with his own teeming brew of unanswered questions. Not many seekers survive this shock, a shock I've come to refer to as the Eustace Conway Whiplash Effect. (Eustace, by the way, has since co-opted the phrase, going so far as to wonder whether he should perhaps distribute neck braces to all apprentices as a preventive measure to help them survive the inevitable trauma of disenchantment. He jokes, "People will ask, 'Why do I need to wear this neck brace, Eustace?' and I'll nod wisely and say, 'Oh, you'll see.' ")

This is the same reason that it's challenging for Eustace to maintain lasting friendships. There are hundreds, perhaps thousands of people intimately connected to his life, but many of them seem to fall into one of two categories: enchanted disciples or disillusioned heretics. Most people find it impossible to drop their notions of Eustace as an icon long enough to befriend him as a person. He could probably count on one hand the number of people he considers close friends, and even those relationships are often strained, both by Eustace's lifelong fear of betrayal (which has kept him from pursuing full intimacy in friendships) and by his insistence that he cannot be truly understood by anyone (which doesn't help, either). Eustace doesn't believe that even the man he would call his best friend—a sensitive, kind, skilled woodsman named Preston Roberts, whom he met in college—completely understands him.

Preston and Eustace used to dream, back in college, that they would form a nature preserve together and raise their families side by side, along with their buddy Frank Chambless, who had hiked the Appalachian Trail with Eustace. But when the time came to buy Turtle Island, Preston and Frank were only marginally involved in the operation. Frank bought a small piece of land near the preserve but sold it years later, to Eustace's chagrin, to raise money. After that sale, Frank virtually disappeared from Eustace's life, and Eustace never understood why.

Preston Roberts bought land near Turtle Island and kept it. He has labored on many of the Turtle Island buildings and has taught at summer camp over the years. He and Eustace take off every now and again for a horse journey or a hiking adventure, where they can bask in each other's company and in the splendor of nature. Preston admires Eustace immensely and would gladly take a bullet for him. But despite Eustace's repeated invitations, he has not yet elected to move his family to Turtle Island permanently. As Preston's wife explained, "My husband has always been a little afraid that he'd lose his friendship with Eustace if he had to work with him every day."

Indeed, that sort of proximity does seem to try most souls. Particularly during apprenticeships. It doesn't help, of course, that the would-be apprentices who come to Turtle Island are often a little emotionally vulnerable to begin with.

"Some of people who want to come and live here," Eustace told me once, "are the most antisocial and maladjusted and miserable people in society. They think that Turtle Island is the place that will finally make them happy. They write me letters saying how much they hate humanity . . . Jesus Christ, can you imagine trying to organize a work detail out of people like that? Teenage runaways want to come here. There's someone in the state prison system writing me letters right now about wanting to come here. These are the kind of dissatisfied outcasts that I attract."

When I visited Eustace in August of 1999, he had a young apprentice whom he'd nicknamed Twig. Twig was from some disaster of a dysfunctional family in Ohio and kept getting thrown out of homes and in trouble with the law. Eustace accepted Twig because it is the very cornerstone of his philosophy that anyone can handle this primitive life if he is fully willing and properly taught. Twig was a major pain in the ass, though. He was a belligerent and untrustworthy little punk, and several of the other apprentices (there were three other young men and women there at the time, about the normal number each year) asked Eustace to dismiss the kid, because he was so disruptive to the spirit of their work. And, needless to say, Twig didn't have a single hard skill. But Eustace wanted to give Twig a chance, and he invested hours in working with him and calming him down and teaching him how to use tools and trying to show him how to get along with people.

There had been some major improvements. Twig came to Turtle Island weak and pale and lazy. In time, you could see every muscle in his chest and his back while he was working hard. (This transformation from feebleness to fitness plays out all the time at Turtle Island, and it is perhaps Eustace's favorite thing to witness.) And this screwed-up kid could now hitch a plow to a horse and tend to pigs and cook over an open fire. One evening he even made me soup out of yellow jacket larvae—an ancient Cherokee recipe. But the magnitude of what Twig had yet to learn was positively numbing to think about.

One evening, I went to a distant field with Eustace to watch him teach Twig how to use a disc plow. They had to drag the plow out to this field about half a mile through the woods with a mule and draft horse, using a sturdy old Appalachian sled to carry the machinery. Every aspect of the job spoke of potential physical danger—the ungainly and willful animals, the unsteadiness of the sled, the flying chains and leather straps and ropes, the razor-sharp edges of the heavy old plow. And yet knowing all this, and having lived at Turtle Island for six months, Twig elected to show up for this job wearing flip-flops.

"Personally, I wouldn't run a disc plow in a rocky pasture using a mule as temperamental as Peter Rabbit while wearing flip-flops," Eustace told me, as we watched Twig work, "but if he wants to lose a foot, I'll give it to him."

"You're not going to say anything to him?" I asked.

Eustace looked exhausted. "Ten years ago, I would have. I would have given him an earful about the proper footwear for farming and about protecting yourself around animals and heavy machinery, but I'm tired now, I'm tired of dealing with people who don't have one molecule of common sense. I could correct Twig on this, and I could correct him seven hundred times a day on stuff like this, but I've reached the point where all I have the energy for is to keep people from killing themselves or me or each other. You know, when Twig first came here, he begged me to throw him right into the wilderness, because he wanted to live close to nature. The reality is that he's ignorant. He wouldn't last five goddamn minutes in the real wilderness. He doesn't even know how much he doesn't know. And I have to deal with this stuff all the time—not just from Twig, but from hundreds like him."

Then, to Twig, who had begun to plow the vast field in weird and tiny little circles, Eustace said: "Here's an idea, Twig. Every time you turn the animals, you're putting pressure on their mouths and pressure on yourself and on the machinery. Try to think of a more streamlined way to plow instead of making so many tight turns. How about making long runs with the plow, all the way from one end of the field to the other, keeping in one direction for as long as you have the momentum going? You understand what I'm saying? You might even want to plow this slope here, but I'd recommend coming at it from below, since you're still inexperienced and you don't want to have to worry about running over your animals with your plow."

As Twig headed off, sort of doing what he'd been told, Eustace said to me, "This is going to take him forever. I'd rather be in my office right now taking care of the seven hundred letters I need to write and the seven hundred tax bills I need to pay. But I have to stay here and watch him, because I can't trust him yet with my animals or machinery. So why do I bother? Because my hope is that someday he'll learn how to handle this chore and then I can send him out by saying, 'Go plow that field,' and he'll know exactly what to do and I'll be able to trust that the job will be done right. But we're a long way from that. I mean, the boy is wearing flip-flops! Look at him.'"

Actually, he was wearing flip-flops and shorts and no shirt, and he had a cigarette tucked behind his ear.

"I like to think I'm teaching these people skills that they'll someday use in their own lives, but when I think of the hundreds of people who have come through here over the years, I can't imagine one who could manage a primitive life right now all alone. Maybe Christian Kaltrider will someday. He was brilliant. He's building a log cabin on his own land right now, and that's good to see. He learned all that here. There's a kid named Avi Aski, who was a terrific apprentice. He's looking for land to buy in Tennessee, and maybe he'll make it work. Maybe."

Twig came toward us with the plow, churning up a wobbly path of soil.

"You're doing a good job," Eustace told him. "Much better than I expected."

Eustace delivered the compliment with an expressionless face and an even tone. But underneath the praise I could hear the scary traces of controlled anger and impatience and disappointment that I usually hear in Eustace's voice at this time of evening, when the sun's going down and the chores haven't been done and somebody's screwing up again. Around this time of evening, it's pretty obvious that what Eustace really wants to do is line up the lot of us in a neat row and bitch-slap some sense into our stupid heads.

Of course, he would never . . .

"Nice work, Twig," he said instead. "Thank you for your focus."

Eustace regularly gets apprentices who have never before held a bucket. He'll give them the simplest task in the world—*go fill this bucket with water*—and then he'll watch in horror as they try to carry the filled bucket. They don't know how. They hold the heavy bucket as far away from their bodies as they can, keeping their arm stretched out in front of them, parallel to the ground, wasting energy and strength just holding their burden. It makes him wince in pain to watch it. Or hammers. Eustace gets young people up at Turtle Island who have never before met a hammer. They have no sense of how a hammer works. They come to him because they claim they want to live "self-sufficiently," but when he asks them to hammer in a nail, they grab the hammer in a tightened fist, way up by its head, and then they *punch* at their target.

"When I see that," Eustace says solemnly, "it makes me want to lie down and die."

When he's teaching young children in public schools, he sometimes tries to play this old Indian game with them, where you roll a hoop and try to throw sticks through it as it tumbles along. But he finds again and again that whole classes of American children are incapable of figuring out how to roll a hoop.

"It's a crazy thing for a child not to know how to roll a hoop!" he rants. "I show them how to do it and I hand them the hoop and they drop it. They kind of randomly throw the hoop and, of course, it lands flat on the ground, two feet away from them. So they stare at it. *Why isn't it moving?* They don't get it. Even after I've showed them once, they can't figure it out. After a long time, some child might figure out that a wheel needs momentum to roll, and if I'm lucky, some genius might think, *Ah! Let's try to spin it!*

"I see this played out over and over. I watch these kids and I think, 'Can this unbelievable crisis be real?' What kind of children are we raising in North America? Listen, I can guaran-damn-*tee* you that every child in Africa knows how to roll a fucking wheel. It's a question of understanding natural law. The world is ruled by a few basic physical laws—leverage, inertia, momentum, thermodynamics—and if you're out of touch with these fundamental principles, then you can't hammer a nail, carry a bucket, or roll a wheel. That means you're out of touch with the natural world. Being out of touch with the natural world means you've lost your humanity and that you live in an environment that you completely do not understand. Can you even begin to imagine my horror at this? Can you begin to comprehend what's been forgotten in just a few generations? It took mankind one million years to learn how to roll a wheel, but it only took us fifty years to forget."

We've forgotten, of course, because of the oldest natural law on the books: Use it or lose it. Kids can't manage the simplest tools because they have no need to learn. It serves no purpose in their comfortable, well-appointed lives. Their parents can't teach them this kind of physical dexterity, because they, by and large, don't have it, either. Don't need it, never learned it, no call for it anymore. But we know things weren't always this way. Even a century ago, for instance, there wasn't a man in America who didn't carry some kind of knife with him at all times. Whether it was for skinning bears or trimming cigars, a man needed a knife as a basic tool for living, and he knew how to take care of it and sharpen it and handle it. Who needs a knife now?

For that matter, who needs a horse? Who even needs to know what a horse is? Eustace found on his horse journeys that it was the people in their seventies and eighties who were likely to be comfortable around the animals, having grown up with working livestock as children, or hearing stories about it from their parents. But to each successive generation the idea of a horse was increasingly foreign, exotic, unthinkable. The younger people had no idea how to behave around the animals, how to protect themselves, how to grasp the concept of another living being.

"And what will *their* children think?" Eustace wondered. "Twenty years from now, a horse will look like a camel to people, like some crazy zoo animal."

So it is that the incompetence widens with each generation. Still, Eustace feels he could handle this incompetence if it weren't for the one big flaw he sees in modern Americans of all ages: people don't listen. They don't know how to pay attention. They don't know how to focus. Even if they claim that they *want* to learn, they have no discipline.

"The hardest thing is to get young people to trust me and do as I say," Eustace said. "If I have four people up here working with me and I say, 'OK, everyone. Let's roll this log on the count of three,' one will start rolling the log immediately, two will *pull* the log on the count of three, and the fourth will wander off somewhere and pick his nose. And they're constantly questioning my authority. They always want to know *Why are we doing it this way, why are we doing it that way?* Listen, *I* know why, and that's all that matters, and I don't have time to explain every decision. They never believe me when I say I'm right. If I say I'm right, then you can be sure I *am* right, because I don't make mistakes. If I'm not sure of something, then I'll say I'm not sure of it, but most of the time I am sure. People get mad and say, 'Eustace thinks his way is the only way.' Well, that's true. My way *is* the only way. And I believe the best work is done when people surrender to one authority, like in the military. That's the most efficient and streamlined way to produce labor. If I was the general of an army, for instance, the discipline would be more organized and I could insist that everyone do exactly what I said, and then things would run properly."

To make Turtle Island function, Eustace ends up taking control—as his grandfather did with his campers and staff—of every aspect of his apprentices' lives.

"It gets to the point," said one apprentice, "where you feel you have to ask Eustace's permission to take a shit. Because God forbid you should be off in the woods taking a shit when he needs to teach you how to use a foot-pedal grinder or forge a horseshoe."

Yeah, Eustace wouldn't deny that. I've heard him lecture his apprentices on the proper way to tie their shoes, because why should people waste time having their shoes come untied when there's so much work to be done? But that's how American utopian communities—the ones that lasted more than a week—have always been run. Discipline, order, and obedience make them endure. In the bedrooms of female Shakers, back in the nineteenth century, you would have found this instructive sign:

"Each person must rise from her bed at the sound of 'first trumpet.' Kneel in silence on the place where you first placed your foot when getting out of bed. No speaking in the room unless you wish to ask a question of the sister having the care of the room. In that case, whisper. Dress your right arm first. Step your right foot first. At the sound of 'second trumpet' march in order, giving your right side to your superior. Walk on your toes. Fold your left hand across your stomach. Let your right hand fall at your side. March to the workshop in order. Ask no unnecessary questions."

Lord, how Eustace Conway would love that kind of order around

Turtle Island. But there's only so much control he can assert each day. For now, it's all he can do to get his apprentices to roll a log on the count of three.

Most of the apprentices live in fear of Eustace, to be perfectly honest. They talk about him whenever he's out of earshot—hushed and somewhat desperate conversations—huddled like courtiers trying to read the king's motives and moods, passing on advice for survival, wondering who will be cast away next. Too intimidated to deal with Eustace directly, the apprentices, unsure of how to please this demanding master, seek advice from Eustace's girlfriends or brothers or close friends, asking these privileged associates: *What does he want from me? Why am I always in trouble? How can I keep him happy?* Eustace knows this chattering goes on behind his back, and he loathes it. He considers it the ultimate of insubordination.

That's why he nailed this letter on the Turtle Island community bulletin board in the summer of 1998:

"Turtle Island staff, residents, and associates. I, Eustace Conway, am pissed off. My girlfriend Patience has been here for five days, and she has been approached by many of you in discussion about your problems with me. This is a challenge and an unnecessary burden for her and our young relationship. I resent this approach to 'reaching me.' If you have a problem with me, approach me with it, NOT her. If we can't solve it or you can't find satisfaction, DON'T work through her. If you can't stop talking about negative aspects of your relationship with me, please resign or leave now. I am intolerant of this behavior. I am hurt, saddened, and full of grief that such would ever happen. I personally would rather beat the living shit out of you than have you work your problems with me through Patience. If this seems overreacting, well, that is a social-emotional burden that I will carry. I hope I have made myself clear of my need. Grateful and respectful of your consideration, humbly yours in trust, Eustace Conway."

No Shirt. No Shoes. No Fucking Backtalk.

It might seem from all this that the only people who could survive on Turtle Island are those who have no self-will, who are wimpy and easy to push around, who will meekly do as they're told for months without a peep of complaint. But this isn't true. Wimpy people crumble here and they crumble fast. They try hard to please Eustace, and when they realize they'll never get the validation they crave, they break down in mourning, devastated by how violated they feel. (These apprenticeships generally end in tears: *I gave and gave and gave, but it was never enough for you!*) The only people who crumble faster than the wimps are the cocky individuals with chips on their shoulders who stubbornly refuse to bend. They're the ones who believe they will be personally exterminated if they have to live under someone else's authority for even a minute. (These apprenticeships generally end in a big fight: *I am not your slave!*)

But the people who thrive here—and there aren't many of them— are an interesting species. They are among the most quietly self-aware people I've ever met. They have in common a profound psychic stillness. They don't talk a lot, and they don't seek praise, but they seem confident of themselves. They are able to make themselves vessels of learning without drowning in it. It's as if they decide, when they come here, to take their fragile and sensitive self-identity, fold it up tight, tuck it away someplace safe, and promise to retrieve it two years later, when the apprenticeship will be over. That's what Eustace Conway's all-time star apprentice Christian Kaltrider did.

"I came here in a very humble state," Christian explained, "but also extremely fired up and interested, and I was a big-time sponge. It was my intention to learn, and that was all. Eustace would teach me something, and I'd go off and do it. I didn't spend any time talking—just listening and watching and doing what I was told. Of course, he had control over me all the time, but I didn't let that frustrate me. I told myself, 'I am letting him have this control for the purpose of my education. And he is in control only of my education, not of my identity.' That's a subtle distinction. Are you giving yourself to Eustace, or are you letting him take you? I made the decision to give myself over as a student, and that's why my experience was so different from the experience of many others who come here. Other people come here worshipping Eustace. They want to please him, so they let him take over their entire *selves*, and that's when the resentment starts to build. It builds slowly, over time. What wears people down here isn't the physical labor but the psychological stress of losing their identity. I was never in danger of that."

"If you don't protect yourself from Eustace," explained Candice, another Turtle Island apprentice determined to make her experience successful, "then he'll suck you dry. You have to keep some part of yourself—your ego, I guess—where he can't reach it. And you have to be quietly stubborn about it. I've made my decision. I'm staying here for the full two years of my apprenticeship, no matter how hard it gets. I refuse to become just another DETI."

" DETI?" I asked.

"Disgruntled Ex-Turtle Islander," she clarified. "Look, I came here to learn, and I am learning. And I find Eustace to be fair and patient, even when I'm an idiot. I try to be quiet and private, and that's the only way to do the work around here and get something from it. He's the boss, and you do have to accept his decisions. You have to take his leadership seriously, but you can't take it personally."

It's the same thing that makes a good soldier—not mindless obedience, but mind*ful* obedience. Which is probably why one of the most successful Turtle Island apprentices was a young woman named Siegal, who, before coming to North Carolina, had served in the Israeli military. Perfect training! Siegal survived Eustace Conway the same way she survived her military service. "You must make yourself very small," she explained, as if that's such a simple thing to do.

It's not at all simple, though. Not many people can subdue their egos. The talent for submission is especially hard for modern American kids, who are raised in a culture that has taught them from infancy that their every desire is vital and sacred. Their parents, their teachers, their leaders, their media, have always asked them, "What do *you* want?" I used to see this when I was a diner waitress, of all things. Parents would interrupt ordering food for the entire table to hover around their toddler and ask, "What do *you* want, honey?" And they'd stare moon-eyed at the child, waiting desperately for the answer. *Oh my God, what will he say? What does he want? The world holds its breath!* Eustace Conway is right on target when he says parents did not give their children this kind of power a hundred years ago. Or even fifty years ago. I myself can declare with all honesty that on the rare occasions when my mother and her six Midwestern-farm siblings ate in restaurants as children, if any of them had dared to make a personal demand of their father . . . well, they just wouldn't have.

But Americans are raised differently now. And the "What do *you* want, honey?" culture has created the kids who are flocking to Eustace today. They undergo enormous shock when they quickly discover that he doesn't give a shit what they want. And between 85 and 90 percent of them can't handle that.

And then there's the food.

One of the things that makes a Turtle Island apprenticeship challenging is that the food up on the mountain can be . . . well, inconsistent. I have enjoyed some of the finest meals of my life there, after a day of steady labor and a invigorating wash in the creek, sitting around the solid oak table with my workmates, eating fresh produce from the garden and a flank off one of Will Hicks's famous pigs, all sopped up with hot cornbread out of a cast-iron pot lifted right off the coals. It's nice. I have eaten gorgeous handfuls of wild morel mushrooms at Turtle Island, irritating Eustace to the point of madness by saying, after every bite, "Do you know how much these things cost in New York?" ("No," he says. "Do you know how delicious these things *taste* in North Carolina?") But I also spent a week at Turtle Island in January when we had the same venison stew for three meals a day. And it was skanky, old, tough venison. Heat it up every night, try not to *taste* the burn and rust from the bottom of the pot. And the only other ingredients of the stew were apparently an onion and five beans.

While the paying guests—the special groups and the young campers who visit Turtle Island—get excellent food served by wonderful cooks hired for the occasion, no such arrangements are made for the apprentices, so the food situation can get pretty grim sometimes, especially in the winter. The squash, for instance. Squash is the staple of the winter diet of the apprentices. They turn squash into everything they can imagine—squash bread, squash pie, squash lasagna, squash soup. And then they give up and eat squash mush until the garden starts up again in the spring. It's as if they're sixteenth-century sailors and the squash is their hardtack, their last provision. There have been mutinies over the squash alone. There have been tearful meetings where apprentices who have endured every other physical challenge will wail to Eustace, in a unified protest, "The squash must stop!"

They don't get a lot of sympathy from him, though. Because it's not as if he's holing up there in his cabin sucking the marrow out of *duck a l'orange* while his long-suffering apprentices shovel more squash down their gullets. If squash is all there is to eat, it's what he eats, too, and let there be no whining about it. There is—as with everything at Turtle Island—nothing he asks of his apprentices that he himself will not endure. (He's no Peter Sluyter, the utopian shyster who ran a strict Labidist homestead in seventeenth-century upstate New York. Fire was forbidden to his followers, though Sluyter always had one roaring comfortably in his own home.) No, Eustace Conway is cold when his people are cold; he's hungry when his people are hungry; he's working when they're working. Although he's usually also working when his people are asleep, for that matter. Eustace has been in hungry places in his life, places where squash mush would have been an epic feast, so he's not too sympathetic. Anyhow, if they get really desperate, they can always head down into Boone for some Dumpster Diving.

Dumpster Diving is a Conway family tradition. It's something (maybe the most fun thing) the Conway boys learned from their father. Big Eustace Conway is a lifetime salvage artist. It appeals to his sense of frugality and of adventure to pick apart the garbage of others. There is no garbage too foul for him to look through in search of a great find. Eustace and Walton and Judson inherited the skill from their father, but they refined it to the point that they learned to look in other people's garbage not only for old record players and air conditioners, but for food. Delicious, decadent food. The Dumpsters behind the huge supermarkets of the American dream, it turns out, are the free-as-the-wind buffets of the truly resourceful.

Eustace Conway, naturally, has made Dumpster Diving into an art. He supported his appetites through college by subsidizing his blowgun game catches with the juicy remains of the supermarket alleys. And he perfected his system because, you can be sure, if he's going to do it, he'll do it flawlessly, like everything else.

"Timing is crucial," he explained. "You want to pick exactly the right moment of the day to start foraging in the Dumpster. It's best to hang around the store a bit and scope things out, see what time each day the food goes out so that you can get it at its freshest. It's also important to walk back to the Dumpster as though you belong there, moving with speed and confidence. Stay low to the ground and don't dawdle. I always look immediately for a sturdy, wax-covered cardboard box with nice handles, and I grab it and jump into the Dumpster. Leaning over the side and poking around is not an economical use of your time. I waste no time with any produce that is poor quality. Just because you're eating *out* of the garbage, doesn't mean you need to *eat* garbage. I fly through the produce, throwing aside anything that's rotten or of low quality. If there's a crate of spoiled apples, I may find the three perfect apples in there and toss them into my cardboard box. You can often find one perfect melon in a box of smashed melons, and sometimes you can find a whole crate of grapes that were thrown out because they're off the stem. And meat! I've brought home dozens of sirloin steaks, all nicely wrapped in plastic, that were tossed out because they're one day over expiration. I can almost always find whole trays full of yogurt—I love yogurt—that are perfectly good and were thrown out for the same reason. Isn't that a sin, what gets wasted in this country? It reminds me of what my old Appalachian neighbor Lonnie Carlton said: 'We used to live on less than what folks throw away these days.' "

One famous incident occurred when Eustace went into a Dumpster in Boone all alone, on a quiet and routine sortie. Looking confident, keeping low, finding his special cardboard box, he was making quick progress through the Dumpster and compiling "the nicest arrangement of fruits and vegetables you ever saw" when he heard a truck pull up behind the store. Then footsteps. Shit! Eustace ducked down into the corner of the Dumpster and made himself as tiny as he could. And then a man, a nice-looking older gentleman in clean clothes, leaned over the Dumpster and started poking around. A fellow Diver! Eustace didn't breathe. The stranger didn't notice him, but it wasn't long before he did notice Eustace's sturdy, wax-covered cardboard box filled with the finest produce money can't buy.

"Hmm," said the stranger, pleased with the discovery.

He leaned far over, picked up the box, and walked away with it. Eustace heard the truck start up again and sat there, huddled like a rat in the corner, thinking this over. Should he hide until the truck was gone? Play it safe? Start his search over? But, wait. That man was stealing *his* produce! It had taken him a good fifteen minutes to find those goods, and they constituted the best food available that day. Eustace couldn't stand for that. You can't let a man take food from your mouth! He leaped out of the Dumpster as though he were on springs and took off after the truck. He waved the guy down, yelling as he gave chase. The stranger pulled over, ashen, trembling at this wild apparition that had emerged, running and yelling, from the bowels of a supermarket Dumpster.

"Good afternoon, sir," Eustace began, and released one of his most charming smiles. "I have to tell you, sir, that those are my fruits and vegetables you've taken."

The stranger stared. He seemed to be considering having a heart attack.

"Yes, my friend, I collected all that food for myself, and it took me some time to do it. I'm happy to share it with you, but I can't let you take it all. Why don't you wait here while I find you a box of your own, and I'll split it up for the two of us?"

Then Eustace ran to the Dumpster and found another sturdy, wax-covered cardboard box. He ran back, jumped into the bed of the stranger's pickup, and quickly and evenly divided the produce into two even caches. He grabbed one box for himself, hopped out of the truck, and returned to the driver's side window. The man gaped at him, dazed. Eustace let fly another big smile.

"OK, then, sir. You've got yourself a nice box of groceries now, and so do I."

The stranger didn't move.

"You're good to go now, sir," Eustace said. "And have a nice day."

Slowly, the stranger drove away. He'd never once said a word.

So. There comes a time in the residency of any Turtle Island apprentice when the skill of Dumpster Diving is introduced. Most of the apprentices take to it like rats to a junkyard, enjoying the opportunity to get into town for a field trip and to stick it to society once more in a subversive way. They call these little shopping expeditions "visits to the Dump Store," and when the squash mush has been served up for the fourth consecutive week, that forbidden fruit from the A&P starts to look pretty good. This helps account for the odd variety of food I have experienced at Turtle Island. Yes, there is the fine homemade gingerbread with homemade peach butter. Yes, there is the superb spinach, fresh from the garden. But I've also dined up there on such decidedly non-Appalachian fare as pineapples, coconuts, chocolate pudding cups, and, on one memorable occasion, something I found in a Styrofoam package labeled "white and dainty cream-filled pastry horns."

"In all the months I've lived here," Candice the apprentice told me, "I've never once figured out how we survive. I honestly don't know how we live. Dumpster Diving can take you only so far, you know, and in the winter we starve. Sometimes people bring us food, which is great, because we're not allowed to buy anything. I've been in charge of the cooking most of the time that I've been here, and I've only ever spent Eustace's money twice, on real staples, like cornmeal or oil or pepper. Other than that, we scrounge."

I once asked Candice what she used for her excellent bread, and she replied, "Whole wheat. Plus"—and ran her fingers through a sandy grain she kept stored in an old coffee can—"I always throw in some of this weird stuff. I got it from one of the horses' feed bins in the barn. I don't know what it is, but you can't taste it in the bread, and it makes the wheat last longer."

Another afternoon, I was hanging out with Candice in the outdoor kitchen, helping her cook, when Jason wandered in.

"Hey, Jason," she said. "Can you move Barn Kitty for me?"

Barn Kitty was Turtle Island's most excellent mouser, a hardworking cat that could usually be found in the granary or on the topmost shelves of the outdoor kitchen. I realized that I hadn't seen Barn Kitty in a while.

"Where is she?" Jason asked.

"Yeah," I said. "Where is she?"

"Under the water trough," Candice replied. "The dogs keep rolling in her and moving her around, and she smells awful."

I looked under the water trough. Oh, that's why I hadn't seen Barn Kitty in a while. Because Barn Kitty was now a matted, reeking, legless corpse. Candice explained that a bobcat got to Barn Kitty one night a few weeks earlier. Since then, Barn Kitty's battered remains kept showing up all over Turtle Island, dragged around by various other living creatures. Jason picked up the remains with a stick and threw them up on the tin roof of the kitchen, where the sun could bake them dry and the dogs couldn't reach them.

"Thanks, Jason," Candice said, and added under her breath, "Jeez, I don't know why we didn't just eat that old cat. Eustace makes us eat every other damn thing that dies around here."

I overheard Eustace one day talking on the telephone to a young man who had called all the way from Texas because he wanted to sign on as a Turtle Island apprentice. The kid sounded promising. His name was Shannon Nunn. He'd been raised on a ranch and claimed to have done farm labor his whole life. He also knew how to fix automobile engines. And he was a star athlete of enormous personal discipline. Eustace tries not to get his hopes up about people, but these few factors alone made Shannon Nunn sound about 1000 percent more promising than the scores of idealistic, romantic, and incompetent college kids who often arrive at Turtle Island "unable to open a car door." Shannon said that he'd read about Eustace in *Life* magazine and was calling because he wanted a new challenge for himself. If he could learn how to live off the land, maybe he'd escape a life in shallow modern American culture, where "everyone is drowning in complacency."

Sounded good so far.

Still, Eustace spent an hour explaining to Shannon what he could expect at Turtle Island. It was a lucid and patently honest speech.

"I'm not a normal person, Shannon," I heard him say. "Many people find that I'm not easy to get along with or work for. My expectations are high, and I don't give my workers much praise. People sometimes come here thinking they already have a lot of valuable skills to offer, but I'm rarely impressed. If you come, you'll be expected to work. Turtle Island is not a school. There are no classes here. This is not a survivor's course. I'm not going to take you in the woods for a certain number of hours a day and teach you an organized program of wilderness skills. If that's the kind of experience you want, please don't come here. There are plenty of places where you can find that, places that will put your needs and desires first. Outward Bound is good for that, and so is the National Outdoor Leadership School. You pay them; they'll teach you. I am not about that. I'll never put your needs or desires first, Shannon. The needs of this farm always come first. A lot of the chores I'll give you are repetitive and boring, and you'll probably feel you're not learning anything. But I can promise that if you stay with the apprenticeship program for at least two years, and if you do what I say, you'll acquire the hard skills that will give you a degree of self-sufficiency almost unknown in our culture. If I see that you're willing to learn and able to work, I'll devote more time to you individually as the months go by. But it will all come very slowly, and I'll always maintain my authority over you.

"I'm telling you this because I'm tired. Tired of having people come here with preconceptions that are different from what I've just explained to you and then leave in disappointment. I don't have time for that, so I'm trying to make myself extremely clear. I'll demand more of you than you've ever had demanded of yourself. And if you aren't ready to work hard and to do exactly what I say, then please stay home."

Shannon Nunn said, "I understand. I want to be there."

Shannon showed up a month after this conversation, ready to work. He was more excited, he said, than he'd ever been about anything. He was a young man seeking spiritual wholeness in the woods, and he believed he had found his teacher. He was looking, he said, "to drink of that water that—once you find it—you will never thirst again."

Seven days later, he packed up his bags and left Turtle Island, deeply angry, hurt, and disappointed.

"I went there," Shannon told me over a year later, "because I thought I understood the deal. Eustace promised me that if I worked for him, he'd teach me how to live off the land. I thought he would be teaching me survival skills, you know? Like hunting and gathering. Like how to build a shelter in the wilderness and how to make fire—all the stuff he knows. I'd invested a lot of time and energy to go to Turtle Island. It was scary, because I'd left everything—my home, my family, my school—to go there and be taught by him. But all he had me doing was mindless menial labor! He didn't teach me anything about living off the land. He had me building fences and digging ditches. And I told him, 'Man, I could be digging ditches back home and getting paid for it. I don't need this.' "

Shannon was so disappointed that within a week of his arrival, he went to Eustace to discuss his problems with the apprenticeship program. Eustace heard the boy out. His response was: "If you don't like it here, go." And he walked away from the conversation. This made Shannon furious to the point of tears. Wait a minute! Why was Eustace walking away from him? Couldn't he see how upset Shannon was? Couldn't they talk about it? Work something out?

But Eustace had already talked and didn't feel like talking anymore. He'd had this same conversation again and again with many different Shannon Nunns over many years, and he had nothing more to say. Eustace walked away from the conversation because he was tired and because he had to get back to work.

He sleeps only a few hours a night.

Sometimes he dreams about Guatemala, where he saw children who were adept with a machete by the age of three. Sometimes he dreams about the orderly farms and quiet families of the Mennonites. Sometimes he dreams of dropping his agenda for saving the human race and, as he wrote in his journal, "changing Turtle Island into a private 'for me' sanctuary to try to survive the ridiculous nature of the world today."

But then he dreams about his grandfather, who once wrote, "More enduring than skyscrapers, bridges, cathedrals, and other material symbols of man's achievement are the invisible monuments of wisdom, inspiration, and example erected in the hearts and minds of men. As you throw the weight of your influence on the side of the good, the true and the beautiful, your life will achieve an endless splendor."

And he dreams about his father. He wonders how much more backbreaking success he'll have to achieve before he earns one word of praise from the old man.

And then he wakes up.

Every morning, he wakes up to the same thing, to a national crisis. An impotent nation reflexively ruining everything in its path. He wonders whether there's any hope of repairing this. He wonders why he's thrown his life into the breach to save everybody else's life. Why he allows his sacred land to be overrun by clumsy fools who treat the place so roughly. He wonders how it came to pass that, when all he ever wanted was to be nature's lover, he feels he has become her pimp instead. He tries to comprehend the difference between what he's obligated to do with his life and what he's allowed to do. If he could do only what he truly wanted, he might sell off this whole heavy burden of Turtle Island and use the money to buy a broad parcel of land somewhere in the middle of New Zealand. There, he could live in peace, all alone. Eustace loves New Zealand. What a spectacular country! Free of every kind of poisonous creature, sparsely populated with honest and trustworthy people, clean and isolated. To hell with America, Eustace thinks. Maybe he should drop out of the mountain man rat race and leave his countrymen to their fate.

It's a gorgeous fantasy, but Eustace wonders whether he'd have the resolve to act on it. Maybe when he dreams about moving to New Zealand he's like one of those urban stockbrokers who dreams about cashing out and moving up to Vermont to open a hardware store. Maybe, like the stockbrokers, he'll never make the shift. Maybe, like them, he's too invested in his lifestyle to ever change.

"Maybe I'm too late with my message," he says. "Maybe I'm too early. All I can say is that I think this country is suffering through a mortal emergency. I think it's a nightmare and that we're doomed if we don't change. And I don't even know what to suggest anymore. I'm tired of hearing myself talk."

CHAPTER NINE

We are great, and rapidly—I was about to say fearfully—growing!

—*John Caldwell Calhoun, 1817*

I get drunk with Eustace Conway sometimes. It's one of my favorite things to do with him. OK, it's one of my favorite things to do with almost anybody, but I particularly enjoy doing it with Eustace. Because there's some measure of peace that the alcohol brings to him—those famous sedative properties at work, I suppose—that tamps down the fires within. The booze helps turn down his internal furnaces for a short while, which lets you stand close to him without getting singed by the flames of his ambitions and blistered by the buckling heat of his worries and convictions and personal drive. With a little whiskey in him, Eustace Conway cools out and becomes more fun, more light, more like . . . Judson Conway.

With a little whiskey, you can get Eustace to tell his best stories, and he'll whoop in delight as he remembers them. He'll imitate any accent and spin the most outrageous yarns. He will laugh at my dumbest jokes. When Eustace Conway is drinking, he's likely to crack himself up by peppering his dialogue with distinctly un-Eustacian modern phrases he's picked up over the years, such as "Yadda-yadda-yadda," or "You da bomb!" or "That's a win-win situation," or—my favorite—upon receiving a compliment, "That's why they pay me the big Benjamins!"

"So, I'm hiking around Glacier National Park one summer," he'll say, soon after the bottle has been opened, and I'll smile and lean forward, ready to listen. "I'm high up above the timberline, walking across a snowbelt. Nobody knows where I am, and I'm not even on a trail; just a ridge of snow and ice as far as you can see, with steep drop-offs on either side. Of course, I don't have any decent equipment; I'm up there messing around. So I'm walking along, and suddenly I lose my footing. And it's so goddamn steep that I start sliding right down the slope, skating down the sheer ice on my back. Most people hiking up there would've brought an ice ax, but I don't have one, so I can't stop my fall. All I can do is try to dig all my weight down into my backpack, to slow myself, but it's not working. I'm digging my heels into the ice, but that's not working, either! Then the snow and ice turn to gravel and loose rock, and I'm speeding *thumpa-thumpa-thumpa* across the boulders at top speed. I keep falling and falling, and I think, *I'm gonna die for real this time!* and then—THUD. I slam to a halt. What the hell? I lift my head and realize I have just slammed into a dead mule. I swear to God! This is a dead motherfucking mule! This is a freeze-dried, mummified carcass of a mule, and it's what stopped my fall. Slowly, I stand up and look out over the mule, and right there, on the other side of his body, is a sheer cliff, dropping down about two thousand feet into the middle of Glacier National Park. I start laughing and laughing, almost hugging the mule. Man, that dead mule is my hero. If I'd dropped off there, nobody would've even found my body! Not for a thousand years, until some hikers came across it and then wrote a damn *National Geographic* article about me!"

A few more sips of whiskey, and Eustace will talk about Dorothy Hamilton, the black woman who came running out of the fast-food restaurant in rural Georgia when the Long Riders rode by, flapping her apron and kissing the Conway boys and demanding to talk into their tape recorder journal. She knew the Long Riders were riding all the way to California—she'd seen them on TV—and she had a loud message for the West Coast: "*Hellllloooo all you surfers out theah in California!*"

Eustace keens away in his cabin, summoning up this woman's joyful voice. "*This is a big hello from yo' friend, Dorothy Hamilton, the girl in the CHICKEN shop!!!*"

One night, Eustace and I walked down the holler in the snow to visit his dear old Appalachian neighbors Will and Betty Jo Hicks. Will and Eustace set to talking about some old "double-*burl*" shotgun Will used to own. I tried to eavesdrop, but realized, as I do on every visit to the Hickses that I can't understand one word in ten that Will Hicks drawls. He says "hit" for "it" and "far" for "fire" and "vee-hickle" for "car," but I can't decipher much more than that. Between his missing teeth and his backcountry euphemisms and his molasses inflection, his speech remains a mystery to me.

Back in Eustace's cabin that night, over a bottle of whiskey, I complained, "I can't make any sense of that damn Appalachian accent. How can you communicate with Will? I guess I just need to study me that Appa-*language* a little closer."

Eustace howled and said, "Woman! You just need to Appa-*listen* harder!"

"I don't know, Eustace. I think it's gonna take me an Appa-*long* time before I can understand the likes of Will Hicks."

"Heck, no! That old country boy was just tryin' to teach you an Appa-*lesson!*"

"I reckon we can discuss this Appa-*later*," I said, giggling.

"You're not Appa-*laughin'* at old Will Hicks, are you?" Eustace said.

By this time we were both Appa-*laughin'* our fool heads off. Eustace was busting up, and his big grin was gleaming in the firelight, and I loved him like this. I wished to heaven I had ten more bottles of whiskey and as many hours to sit in this warm cabin and enjoy watching Eustace Conway let go of his fierce agenda and Appa-*loosen* the hell up for once.

I said, "You can be so much fun to hang out with, Eustace. You should show people this part of yourself more often."

"I know, I know. That's what Patience used to tell me. She said the apprentices wouldn't be afraid of me all the time if I'd let them see my spontaneous and fun side. I've even considered trying to figure out how to do that. Maybe every morning before we start work, I should institute a practice of having five free minutes of spontaneous fun."

"*Five* minutes of spontaneous fun, Eustace? Exactly five minutes? Not four? Not six?"

"Argghhh . . ." He gripped his head and rocked back and forth. "I know, I know, I know . . . it's crazy. See what it's like for me? See what it's like inside my brain?"

"Hey, Eustace Conway," I said, "life isn't very easy, is it?"

He smiled gallantly and took another long swig of hooch. "I've never found it to be."

There is still ambition in Eustace. He's not finished yet. Back when he was really young, back when he first walked around Turtle Island with his girlfriend Valarie, he pointed out, as though reading from a blueprint, what he would make of his domain. Houses here, bridges there, a kitchen, a meadow, a pasture. And he has made it so. All over his land now, standing physical and real, is the evidence of what Eustace had originally seen in his mind. The houses, the bridges, the kitchen— everything is in place.

I remember standing with Eustace over a nearly cleared pasture on my first visit to Turtle Island. It was nothing but a field of mud and stumps, but Eustace said, "Next time you come here, there'll be a huge barn in the center of that pasture. Can't you see it? Can't you picture all the grass growing up green and healthy and the horses standing so pretty, all around?" The next time I went to Turtle Island, there was, as though by some enchantment, a big beautiful barn in the center of the pasture, and the grass was growing up green and healthy, and the horses were standing so pretty, all around. Eustace walked me up a hill to give me a better view of the place, and he looked around and said, "Someday there'll be an orchard right here."

And I know the man well enough to be certain there will be.

So, no, he's not done with Turtle Island yet. He wants to build a library, and he's looking to buy a sawmill so that he can produce his own lumber. And then there's his dream house, the place where he'll live. Because after all this time—after more than twenty years in the woods, after working himself numb to acquire a thousand acres of land, after building more than a dozen structures on his property—Eustace still doesn't have a home of his own. For seventeen years he lived in a teepee. For two years he lived in the attic of a toolshed. And recently he's taken to living in a small rustic cabin he calls the Guest House—a fairly public place, where all the apprentices and guests gather twice a day for meals in the wintertime when the outdoor kitchen is closed. For a man who claims to want, more than anything, isolation, he has never given himself a truly private space on Turtle Island. Everybody else, from the hogs to the apprentices to the tools to the books, must be housed first.

But there is a home he has been designing in his mind for decades. And therefore you can be sure that it will exist someday. He made the first drawings of it when he was in Alaska, stranded on an island for two days, waiting for the rough seas to subside enough so that he could kayak safely back to the mainland. And when I asked him one afternoon if he could describe it for me in detail, he said, "Why, yes."

"The fundamental philosophy of my dream house," he began, "is similar to my feeling about my horses—you go beyond the necessary because you have a love for the aesthetic. This house is a bit showy, but I'm not going to sacrifice quality for anything. If I want slate shingles, I'm going to have slate shingles. Also beveled glass, copper trim, hand-forged ironwork—anything I want. The house will be built with large wooden timbers, and I've already picked out some from the woods around here. Big logs and lots of stone, with everything overbuilt for strength and longevity.

"When I open the front door, the first thing I'll see is a stone waterfall that goes up over thirty feet, with a stone pool at the bottom of it. The waterfall is powered by solar electricity, but also heated, so it contributes to the heating of the house. There will be a stone or tile floor, something that feels good to the eye and feet. The main room looks straight up to a cathedral ceiling over forty feet tall. At the back of the room will be a big sunken fire pit, made of stone, with stone benches built into it. I'll make fires in there, and my friends can come over on cold winter nights and warm their bodies and backs and butts on those warm stones. To the left of the great room is a door leading to my workshop, twenty feet by twenty. The exterior wall is really just two massive doors on five-foot-long iron hinges that swing out wide and open into the outdoors, so when I'm working in my shop during the summer, I'll have the air and sun and birds singing.

"Next to the great room are two glass rooms. One is a greenhouse, so I'll can have a plethora of fresh greens and vegetables all year. The other is a dining room, simple and perfect. There's a place for everything, just like on a ship. A big wooden table and benches and a wraparound couch. And windows everywhere so that I can look down into the valley, where I'll see the barn, the pastures, and the garden. Behind the entrance to the dining room is a door leading to the kitchen. Marble countertops, handmade cabinets with antler handles, open shelving, wood-burning stove—but also a gas range. Sinks with running cold and hot water, all powered by solar, and all kinds of handmade this and hand-forged that and cast-iron cooking ware. And there's another door leading to an outside kitchen, where I can cook and eat in the summertime, with a sheltered deck and a table and outdoor sinks with running water and shelves and stoves, so that I don't have to keep going inside all the time for supplies. The deck looks out over a beautiful drop-off in the ravine, and there'll probably be propane lighting out there.

"Upstairs are two small loft bedrooms and—this can be seen from the great room—a balcony opening out from the master bedroom. The master bedroom is the size of the workshop below, but it won't be all cluttered. Just open space, clean and beautiful. Down the hall from the master bedroom is a composting toilet and a sauna and the loft bedrooms. There's also an outdoor sleeping porch with a bed on it, but if I have to sleep indoors, there's a king-size bed with a skylight over it so that I can look at the stars all night. And, of course, there will be huge walk-in closets.

"There will be art everywhere in my home. Over the balconies will be hanging Navajo rugs. It'll be a little like that Santa Fe style everyone likes so much these days, but full of real and valuable art—not the art-i-fakes people collect because they don't know better. This home will have lots of art, lots of light, lots of space, peaceful, safe, underground on three sides, useful and beautiful. I'm telling you, *Architectural Digest* would love to get its hands on this place. And I know I could build it myself, but I won't even break ground for it until I have a wife, because I will be *damned* if I'm gonna build this house without the right woman beside me."

He stopped talking. Sat back and smiled.

I myself was unable to speak.

It wasn't that I was wondering where the hell Eustace had ever picked up a copy of *Architectural Digest.* It wasn't that I was shocked that Eustace, who has preached for decades about how little we need in the way of material surroundings to live happily, had just described his desire to build a rustic mansion suitable to the aesthetic standards of a retired millionaire oilman. It wasn't that I was contemplating how much Eustace suddenly sounded to me like Thomas Jefferson—a civic-minded but solitary idealist, momentarily letting go of his obligations to the Republic in order to lose himself in the decadent reverie of designing the perfect home away from society. It wasn't even that I was wondering where those thirteen kids Eustace keeps planning to sire are going to sleep in a house that has only two spare bedrooms. I could handle all that. Didn't faze me one bit.

My shock was much more basic.

It was merely that, despite all the surprising twists of character I'd come to expect over the years from this most complex and modern of mountain men, I still could not *believe* I had just heard Eustace Conway utter the phrase "huge walk-in closets."

Here is Eustace Conway, looking down the *burl* of the shotgun that is age forty. If the actuary charts of the insurance industry are to be believed, he is halfway finished with his life. He has achieved much. He has seen more of this world than most of us will ever read about. He has, about seventy-five times a year, done things that people told him were impossible to do. He has acquired and protected the land he always wanted. He has paid attention to the laws of the universe, and that attention has rewarded him with proficiency in a dazzling range of subjects. He has instituted an organization of teaching and preaching founded in his exact image. He has become a public figure of considerable renown. He is venerated and he is feared. He's at the top of his game. He even calls himself a Type-A Mountain Man, and, indeed, he has become a Man of Destiny in action, the World's Most Public Recluse, the CEO of the Woods.

But there are cracks. And he can feel the wind blowing through them. Just as when he was thirty, he can't seem to make his relationships with other people work as well as he would like. The folks he labors with at Turtle Island are always angry with him or misunderstanding him. Virtually every apprentice I met at Turtle Island ended up leaving Eustace long before his or her time was officially up, and usually in tears. Even Candice, who was fiercely determined not to become just another Disgruntled Ex-Turtle Islander, left the mountain abruptly as a DETI, frustrated by Eustace's refusal to give her more control over the garden.

And Eustace fares no better with his family. Foremost in his consciousness, of course, is that disparaging father—looming over his every breathing moment, critical and disgusted and angry. Forever it has been the case in Eustace Conway's life that when he looks for love and acceptance from his father, he goes nearly snowblind from the blankness he sees there.

Although something strange did happen this year.

Eustace called me on his thirty-ninth birthday. We had a normal conversation, talking for an hour about Turtle Island business and gossip. He told me about his new apprentices and about work on the barn and the birth of a beautiful new colt named Luna.

And then he said, in a strange tone, "Oh, there's something else. I got a birthday card this week."

"Oh, yeah?" I asked. "From who?"

"From my father."

There was a long silence. I put down the tea I was drinking and found myself a chair.

"Tell me," I said. "Tell me everything."

"I'm holding the card right here in my hand."

"Read it to me, Eustace."

"It's kind of interesting, you know? My dad . . . um . . . he drew the card himself. It's a drawing of three little balloons floating up to the sky. He drew the balloons with a red pen and drew a bow around the strings of the balloons with a green pen. He used a blue pen for the message."

"What message?"

Eustace Conway cleared his throat and read: *"It's hard to believe that thirty-nine years have passed since you were born and started our family. Thank you for the many blessings you have brought us over the decades. We look forward to many more. Love, Daddy."*

There was another long silence.

"Run that by me again," I said, and Eustace did.

Neither one of us spoke for a while. Then Eustace told me that he'd received the card two days earlier. "I read it once and folded it up and put it back in its envelope. I was so upset by it, my hands were shaking. It's the first kind thing my father has ever said to me. I don't think any-one can know how that makes me feel. I didn't look at it again until right now. It took me two days to get the courage to open it up again and read it over. I was afraid to even touch it, you know. I wasn't sure it was true. I thought maybe I dreamed it."

"Are you OK?" I asked.

"I don't know. Oh, my God, I don't know how to open my fearful heart and even think about it. I mean, what the hell is this about? What does this mean, Dad? What the fuck are you up to, Dad?"

"He may not be up to anything, Eustace."

"I think I'm going to hide this card away for a while."

"Go ahead," I said. "Maybe you can read it again tomorrow."

"Maybe I'll do that," said Eustace, and he hung up.

This tiny but startling thaw between the two Eustaces reminded me of an obscure word I'd learned recently. I'd discovered it one day when I was paging through a dictionary on a whim, trying to find Eustace's name, to see if I could learn its derivation. There was no *Eustace* in my dictionary, but I did discover *Eustasy*, which is a noun. And here's what *Eustasy* means: "a worldwide change in sea-level, occurring over many millennia, triggered by the advance or retreat of glaciers."

A slow and epic melting, in other words. Which is what it would take, I suppose, to effect even a marginal alteration on the level of an ocean.

And then there are the other members of the Conway family to consider. Eustace's relationships with them are unsettled, too. He adores his mother, but he mourns her sad and arduous married life with an intensity that corrodes his own ability to seek happiness. He cares for his little brother Judson more than he cares for anyone, but it's cruelly obvious to the most casual observer that the brothers are not as close as they had once been. Not since the Long Riders journey. Judson lives near Eustace now, residing just over the holler from Turtle Island in a small log cabin that he built himself and now shares with his totally kick-ass fiancée (a tough and independent soul who hunts for deer with a bow and arrow, and who works as a lumberjack, and whose name is— get this!—Eunice). Judson could easily ride his horse over to visit Eustace every day if he felt like it, but he doesn't feel like it. The brothers rarely see each other. Eustace wants much more access to Judson than he is offered, but Judson carefully and affably keeps an arm's length between them.

"I saw it when we rode across America," Judson told me. "Eustace is like my dad. He's too fucking intense and hard to be around. He and my dad both pride themselves on being great communicators. They think they operate at this higher level of intelligence and communication than anyone else. At least Eustace does try to listen to people, and he comes across all gentle and equal, but the bottom line's the same—he has to get his way all the time, and there's no talking through it. Hey, I love my brother, but I don't know how to deal with that. That's why I keep my distance. I don't have any choice. And it makes me really sad."

Walton Conway, the middle brother, also lives nearby, less than an hour from Turtle Island. Brilliant and multilingual and reserved, he lives in a comfortable modern home, his bookshelves filled with Nabokov and Dickens. Walton teaches English and writes quiet fiction. He runs a business out of his home, importing and selling handmade crafts from Russia. His wife is a generous and lively woman with two daughters from a previous marriage, and they've since had another daughter. Walton's life is tranquil now, but he did a good bit of rough traveling in his youth. Back then, he was always writing letters home to his big brother Eustace, whom he admired deeply and whose respect he so clearly wanted.

"I hate to say it," Walton wrote to Eustace back in 1987, after a long stay on a farm in Germany where he'd found work, "but you might be proud of me. When I was working, my hands would get good and grimy, and I've got calluses now in places I'd never discovered before."

Or this letter from Russia in 1992: "Had a great change of pace digging a cucumber bed way out of the city last weekend. Good shovel work all day long. Thought of you and Tolstoy and of that summer you did construction work—sweeping?—down in hotter-than-hell Alabama. (You see, I've lived all your adventures vicariously, through little peepholes.) In general, though, you would hate it here in Moscow. I am surrounded by filth. It is pitiful to see the city, what man has done to himself, what lives are doled out at the front of the lines. I can't imagine you here. I dream of Turtle Island."

But now that Walton lives so close to Turtle Island, he hardly ever visits his brother. This kills Eustace, who dearly wants to spend time with Walton, and who feels wounded because his brother won't take a larger role in his life.

"It's the ego that keeps me away," Walton said, by way of explanation. "I can't stand it. Some mornings I wake up and I think, *God, wouldn't it be great to have a brother with all the skills and interests of Eustace, but who was humble, too?* I'd love to spend time with somebody like that, to learn from him. I'd like to go hiking with Eustace someday and have a quiet interaction, but this ego thing is really difficult to get around. I always want to say to him, 'Imagine if one day you went for a horse ride and didn't have to tell everyone about it? Does every moment of your life always have to be such a public show?"

As for Eustace's only sister, Martha? Well, I consider her the most inscrutable of all Conways. She lives so far outside the bold and adventuresome world of her brothers that it is sometimes easy to forget her existence. The big joke in the Conway family is that Martha was a changeling and that nobody can understand how she "got that way." Martha lives with her husband and two daughters in a tidy suburban development, in a house so clean and sterilized you could use her kitchen as an operating theater.

"You know how most parents have to hide all the breakable stuff in their house when they have little kids around so that nothing gets wrecked?" Judson asked me, when trying to describe his sister. "Well, in Martha's house, it's not like that. She leaves the breakable stuff sitting right out there on the coffee table and tells her daughters not to touch. And you'd better believe they don't touch."

Martha is a devout Christian, considerably more religious than either of her parents. She is also a keenly intelligent woman with an MBA from Duke. I'm certain she could be running General Motors right now if she wanted to, but she focuses all her acumen and organizational ability on being a faultless housewife, an exacting mother, and a vital member of her church. I don't know Martha well; I spent only one afternoon with her. But I liked her. I found her to be more gentle than I had expected, after hearing reports from her brothers about her famous rigidity. I was moved that she welcomed me into her home, considering how sacred that place is to her. I could see in her eyes how hard it was for her to let me in. I could see the painful edge in her, where her profound sense of Christian hospitality sparred against her cherished sense of privacy.

When I asked Martha to define herself, she said, "The most important thing in my life is my walk with Jesus Christ. It reflects on everything I do—how I raise my children, how I honor the commitment to my marriage, how I struggle not to put myself first, how I struggle to deal with my emotions and control my voice. Every choice I make is based on my faith. I teach my children at home because of my faith. I don't want my children in public schools. I feel there are a lot of evils there, ever since they took prayer out of school. I want my children to grow up with serious faith, and they can get that only here with me. Out there in the world, everything is based on relativism, and I don't want my children to learn that. Out there, nothing is an absolute anymore. But I still believe in absolutes. I believe there is an absolute right and wrong way to live, and I can teach my children that, right here in this house."

The other big joke in the Conway family is to point out how different Eustace and Martha are. "Wait until you see how she lives," I was warned. "You won't believe that she and Eustace are related!" But I respectfully disagree. As soon as I walked into Martha's living room, I thought, *Sorry, folks. These two are the exactly the same.* Eustace and Martha both found the world "out there" to be corrupted and repulsive, so both designed their own worlds, worlds so stubbornly isolated from the greater society that they may as well be living under glass domes. They preside over their personal worlds with an unconditional power, never having to suffer the sting of compromise. Eustace's world just happens to be a thousand acres, and Martha's world is closer to a thousand square feet, but they rule with the same impulse. It's all about absolutism.

And absolutism is great for getting a lot of work done, but when absolutisms collide, it can be a loud and fatal train wreck. Which is why Eustace and his sister have never managed to be close. This is made sadder because both want to work out some kind of relationship. But they only vex each other. Eustace believes he makes every effort to respect Martha's values and tightly scheduled life by giving her plenty of warning before he visits and by reading Bible stories to her children and by trying not to mess up her cherished house. Still, she accuses him of being rude and self-centered, which hurts him all the more, considering his perception that Martha—who has brought her family up to Turtle Island only twice, despite repeated invitations—seems to take no interest in his life. Martha, on the other hand, is routinely hurt by what she perceives: a domineering brother who demands that the entire world stop and drop at his feet to worship him whenever he breezes through town. Out of pride, out of habit, Martha refuses to bow.

So, no, Eustace's interactions with his family aren't satisfying. Not on any front. He can't get past that. What bothers him even more, though, is that he hasn't begun a family of his own. Now, as when he was thirty, he scans his empire and is shocked to notice that, while he has accomplished much through sheer force of will, he still doesn't have a wife and children. At this point in his life, he should be well into a family, deep into the process of childrearing and heartily comforted by the solidity of marriage. Where does Eustace go wrong on this? He can't figure it out.

Eustace and I drove down his mountain one day to visit his horse mentor, the old hillbilly farmer and genius animal trainer, Hoy Moretz. We had a good afternoon in Hoy's kitchen, eating cornbread with his wife, Bertha, and listening to wild old lies and paging through Hoy's photo albums, which contain nothing but pictures of mules, bulls, and horses. Hoy is funny and sly. (When I met him for the first time, I said, "How do you do, sir?" and he said, "Fat and lazy. How 'bout you?") He's not book-read—his daddy had him driving teams of bulls at the age of six for the saw mill—but he's an inspired farmer. His land is three hundred acres of the neatest and sweetest pastures and fields you ever saw. Hoy has no children of his own, and so, over the kitchen table, Eustace got to asking him what would become of that gorgeous land after he and Bertha both passed on. Hoy said he didn't rightly know, but he imagined "Uncle Sam'll take it over and sell it to them developers who just put nine hundred houses up on the other side of my mountain."

In the car later, I asked Eustace whether he would want Hoy's land. The Moretz farm is only forty-five minutes from Turtle Island, and it's gorgeous, and, yes, Eustace said, of course he would want it and of course he would hate to see it developed into a graveyard of suburban homes.

"But that's the pattern of the world," he went on. "First come the roads and then come the farms and then the farmers sell out to developers who chop it up and rape it and put in more roads until it's all chewed to pieces. I can't save every acre in North Carolina. I don't have the power for that."

"But what would you do with Hoy's property if you could get it?" I asked, thinking he might use it for hayfields or as a place to graze his ever-increasing kingdom of horses.

"I'd save it and then give it to one of my sons when he was grown so that he could make it a traditional heritage farm," Eustace said.

That sentence hung awkwardly in the air for a long moment. There were several assumptions at play here: that Eustace will someday have a bunch of children; that there will be boys among them; that any one of these boys will grow up to give a shit about heritage farming; that Eustace will not find *his* sons to be as mammoth a disappointment ("the antithesis of what I had expected!") as his grandfather and his father found their sons to be; that any of his land will still be around in twenty-five years. Even Eustace seemed to hear these doubts.

"My *sons*," he said finally, in self-disgust. "Listen to me talk. Where am I going to get sons?"

Where, indeed? And with whom as a mother? This is the trillion-dollar question in Eustace's life, the question that haunts not only him but everyone who knows him, to the point that it's like a national pastime for people to sit around speculating about who (or if) Eustace Conway would someday marry. Every member of the Conway family has taken me aside at some point in the last few years to utter his or her secret desire that Eustace will never marry and certainly never have children, because he would be, as Martha fears, "way too scary as a father."

But Eustace has other friends who are constantly trying to set him up with one mountain-climbing, peace-loving, dark-skinned, modern nature girl after another. Some friends think he should go back to Guatemala and marry the prettiest and quietest fourteen-year-old Mayan girl he can find. Others think he needs the world's toughest and most modern ballbuster to come in and kick his ass around Turtle Island for a while. And he has one friend, a blunt woman artist, who never stops challenging him with this accusation: "Hey, Eustace. Why don't you just admit that you don't really like children? You can't get away from them fast enough when they're in the room with you."

Like everyone else, I have my own opinions about Eustace's romantic life. It seems to me that what he really needs is a woman who is both strong and submissive. This may sound like a contradiction, but it wasn't always the case. Strength combined with submission in women was the norm for centuries, especially on the American frontier. Take a look again at Davy Crockett's wife, whose thorough competence in the wilderness was matched only by her subservience to her husband. That's what Eustace needs. But that was 1780. Times, as we've all surely noticed, have changed. And so it is my personal opinion that Eustace Conway is not going to have much luck finding himself a wife (or, as he sometimes puts it, "a mate"). As an urban friend of his bemoaned once, in a fake folksy drawl, "A century of goddamn feminism done spoilt all the brides!"

Like many impressive Men of Destiny before him, it is only in this one most delicate operation of intimate partnership where Eustace doesn't succeed. All his energies and all his talents become useless in the face of it. As the unhappy Meriwether Lewis wrote to his dear friend William Clark, a few years after they'd crossed and mapped the continent, "I am now a perfect widower with respect to love . . . I feel all that restlessness, that inquietude, that certain indescribable something common to old bachelors, which I cannot avoid thinking my dear fellow proceeds from *that void in our hearts* which might, or ought to be better filled. Whence it comes I know not, but certain it is, that I never felt less like a hero than at the present moment. What may be my next adventure God knows, but on this I am determined, *to get a wife*."

It's not as though Eustace doesn't have plenty of options. The man has a powerful effect on women and has access to loads of them, isolated though his world may seem. There is no end of beautiful and starry-eyed female dreamers who dance through Turtle Island every year as campers, apprentices, and day-trippers, many of whom would be more than happy to have a thrilling roll in the duff with a real mountain man, given the invitation. If all Eustace was after in life was hot sexual gratification, he could easily pick himself an endless supply of lovers, as if picking berries off a bush. He must be given credit, though, for never having used Turtle Island as a personal Free Love Utopia. He has never exploited that crop of lovelies for short-term sexual pleasure. On the contrary, he consciously detaches himself from the many young girls who idolize him for his rugged image, because he doesn't think it's appropriate to take advantage of their adoration. Instead, what he endlessly searches for is a robust and sacrosanct monogamous union of Olympian dimensions between two heroic figures. It's a search informed and inspired by a conception of romantic love that remains doggedly—indeed, heartbreakingly and unbelievably and almost belligerently—naïve.

"It was so intriguing to meet you and have a chance to share with you," he wrote in an early letter to one woman who never hung around long enough to even be legitimately listed as one of Eustace Conway's girlfriends. "I don't know exactly what you must think about me, but I hope we will have a chance to get to know each other. I am looking for a mate—an energetic, intelligent, adventuresome person like yourself is really attractive to me. I would like to live out my fantasies of a sacred relationship that was filled with a lifetime of love and compassionate care and understanding. I want that 'perfect' love-filled American dream 'fantasy' relationship, if you will. I am holding out for nothing less than that . . . I have been interested in marriage for 10 years. I have been looking but haven't found the 'right one' yet . . . If you have the vision to see and the care to investigate, you will find me a deep and caring person who is capable and willing to offer you more than you have ever dreamed about in the way of meaningful partnership through this journey of life, 'the human experiment.' I offer you that. Please take me seriously on this and not let another protective mechanism keep you from finding in me what your heart truly desires. Insofar as I can offer you my love, truest sentiments, Eustace."

But this "stand-in-the-wind-tunnel-of-my-love" approach hasn't worked, there, either. And it baffles Eustace, this absence, this loss, this failure to create an ideal family to erase his brutal childhood. He's all too aware that he's running out of time. Just recently, he got involved with Ashley, a twenty-four-year-old beautiful hippie he's known for years. She is as warm and loving as any human being I've met. Eustace first ran into her six years before, at a party, and stared at her all night, watching her talk to others, thinking that "she was so alive, so full of love, like a waterfall spilling all over the room with the mist boiling up around her, so captivating. I took one look at her and thought, *This is the one. I need to marry that girl.*"

But Ashley, all of eighteen at the time, already had a lover. She was on her way out of town, about to step into the world for some wild traveling and adventures, and was in no way ready to be Eustace Conway's woman. But she has since returned to Boone and she's single now. Eustace has fallen in love with her once again, and she with him.

Eustace thinks Ashley is an angel, and it's not hard to see why. She emanates kindness and humanity. Ashley was driving me through Boone one afternoon when a homeless man approached her car at a red light and asked for money. Ashley, who has been barely surviving for years on food stamps and hope, dug around in the car for spare change, but could find only a few dimes.

"I can't give you much money," she apologized to the homeless man, "but I promise I will give you all my prayers."

"Thank you," he said, smiling as if he'd been handed a hundred-dollar bill. "I believe you."

Ashley has a heart big enough to absorb all the love and need and hunger that Eustace thrusts at her without even flinching. But there's a glitch with Ashley. Somewhere along her journeys she managed to acquire three young children—a five-year-old son and toddler twin daughters.

When I heard about them, I said, "Eustace, I always thought you wanted thirteen kids. Looks to me as if you've got a good start here, buddy. Three down, ten to go."

Eustace laughed. "Sure, but the *concept* of thirteen kids is a lot different from the *reality* of three."

Ashley is calm, affectionate, funny, attentive, and steady. She brings a much-needed sense of peace and hospitality to Turtle Island. And she can gracefully handle that way of life. She spent several years living on a scrappy Rainbow Gathering commune that made Turtle Island look like a Hilton Resort. This is a woman who went through two pregnancies without seeing a doctor. ("You know when you're healthy," she explains, "and I didn't need anyone to tell me I was doing fine.") This is a woman who delivered her twins outside in the middle of the night on the cold Colorado ground, barely sheltered under a tarp. This is a woman who could definitely manage a life of hog-butchering and Dumpster Diving.

Eustace swears he would marry Ashley in a minute if she didn't already have a family. He has strong reservations about bringing up another man's freewheeling children, particularly when that other man is a hippie who still has a considerable presence in his kids' lives. Eustace doesn't want an undisciplined influence like that anywhere near children he himself might someday be raising. Although he is not as frightened, it should be said, by Ashley's twin daughters as he is by her energetic and willful young son.

"How could I adopt that boy when he's already begun to be formed? He's already seen too many corrupting things that I can't control or erase. I had the worst relationship with my father, and if I'm going to have a son, I have to be sure that the relationship is perfect right from the beginning. I don't want there to be a moment of anger or trouble between us. For all I know, I could spend ten years showing Ashley's boy the proper path, and then he could turn on me when he's fourteen and say, 'Fuck that, Dad. I'm gonna go get high.' "

"Eustace," I said, "nobody can promise you that your own biological children wouldn't say the same thing someday. In fact, I can almost promise you that they will. You do know that, right?"

"But the odds would be better with my own children, because I'd be there from the beginning to teach them what's acceptable and unacceptable behavior. The odds just don't look good with Ashley's kids. They're already undisciplined. Ashley's a great mother but her children manipulate her and cause all kinds of havoc and destruction. It's really hard to have her kids around all the time, because they're not trained. They're always getting into everything and demanding her attention. She brings them up here and I do things with them, like take them horseback riding, but it's no fun. It's fun for *them* but not for me."

Eustace can't quite let go of Ashley, because she's beautiful and kind and gives him the deliciously unconditional love he's been starving for. But he can't keep her around, either, because she brings too many terrifying variables into his exacting and well-ordered cosmos. He's been trying to help her bring more order and discipline to her family; he's lent her books from his library written by the Amish about how to properly "train up" a child, very much as one would train up a horse. Ashley, who is indeed run ragged by her children, studied the books carefully and gratefully, and has taken much of the advice to heart. She's even passed these old-fashioned lessons about childrearing along to her hippie friends who are mothers, to help them create some stability within their own disorganized families. And it's been a largely successful education. Using the strict old Amish system, Ashley has gotten her children on a more solid schedule, and there are fewer tantrums and meltdowns. But the children are still a handful, of course. Because there are three of them and because they are children.

So Eustace doesn't know what to do about Ashley. In the end, his decision will almost certainly be a showdown between the two things he craves most: absolute love and absolute control. It's a tough call. Historically, love has always been a pretty fierce contender, but some people in this world need more than love. Eustace has lived without love before; that's a familiar sensation for him. Whereas he has never lived a moment of his adult life without control.

So he remains alone and single. And full of questions about what kind of woman he should seek. After all these years, he's come to think that he should be more careful about whom he selects to love. Maybe he's been too random in his choices; maybe that's why it never works out. Taking on the challenge as he would take on any organizational task, Eustace recently sat down and efficiently listed the requirements for his perfect woman. If he could evaluate prospective candidates in each category, he should be able to choose wisely, and surely he would never be hurt or lonely again.

Very healthy, his list (set forth in no particular order) begins. Then:
Capacity for intimacy.
Beautiful.
Confidence with and passion for sexuality.
Spiritual belief/direction.

Excited and motivated to live each day completely and with sacred
  appreciation for it.
Nurturing, giving, caretaking, traditional woman sides to personality.
Leans toward nonmaterialistic lifestyle, <u>values</u>.
Emotional, confident, centered, energy, positive support, and <u>social</u>
  <u>skills</u>.
Independently able self, with capacity to bond deeply in sacred
  marriage union.
Multilingual.
Involved with or appreciation for arts—dance, theater, literature,
  visual, etc.
Passion for family a priority.
Appreciates judicial money management.
Likes to work at tasks, i.e., farm/land/garden management.

The list goes on and on. So you can see the problem. You can see
how God himself might shake his head when handed such a invoice
and say, *Sorry, pal, we don't carry that in stock.* But Eustace is way more
optimistic than God. And way more lonely than God, too.

When Eustace first showed me this love list, I handed it back and
said, "I'm really sorry, Eustace, but this isn't how love works."

"I don't know how else to *do* it," he said, sounding, for once, helpless.

It's true that this list testifies to how enormously unequipped Eustace Conway is when it comes to handling intimacy. Look, we all seek
certain traits in a lover, but this list looked to me like a cheat-sheet for
an exam that most of us don't need to study for. Most of us don't need
to match up people's qualities with an inventory printout; we can tell
when we're in love. But Eustace isn't sure that he can tell. He has too few
of the basic skills to face the mountains and valleys and unpredictable
weather patterns of real love between flawed and wonderful human
adults. He is, by his own admission, too damaged and sensitive, and I
find it astonishingly brave of him to continue trying to open his heart
to others at all.

Whether these troubles can be blamed on the hard-driving masculine iconography he's absorbed from American culture or whether it's the fallout of his traumatized childhood, I do not know. But when I see Eustace Conway heading off into the wilderness of intimacy, clutching that exhaustive checklist of his, he looks to me an awful lot like the chubby suburban guy who just bought out the Orvis catalogue for a weekend hunting trip: overpacked, underskilled, and scared to death.

One of Eustace's regular gigs over the years has been at Merlefest, a well-established festival of folk music and arts held every summer in western North Carolina. Eustace doesn't travel and speak as much as he used to; he prefers to stay home at Turtle Island away from the masses. But he still works at Merlefest every year, setting up his teepee on the fairgrounds and speaking to people about natural living. It's a good job. It pays well and draws an earnest crowd, and Eustace gets to spend the weekend listening to live folk music from Appalachian heroes of his like Doc Watson and Gillian Welch.

I went to Merlefest with Eustace in the summer of 2000, and saw, in his manner with the public, more world-weariness than I'd ever seen in him before. It wasn't as if he were telephoning in his performances with people, but he wasn't the firebrand I remembered from speaking engagements in years past. And it wasn't hard to understand, during the course of this weekend, why a man could lose his spark in the face of the world's reality.

Eustace had been told well in advance that he was to share the stage at Merlefest with another headline speaker, "a real Indian Chief from the Florida Everglades" named Chief Jim Billy. For weeks, Eustace was somewhat nervous and apprehensive about this encounter.

"I know a lot of Native Americans and I'm usually welcome," he explained. "But sometimes Indians have a bad reaction to me, like, *Who's this white guy in the teepee pretending to be*? Especially with politicized native people, I can be seen at first as offensive. Of course I understand their hesitation, so I'm always a little cautious; careful to be extra respectful."

In this case, he needn't have worried. Chief Jim Billy turned out to be a big friendly guy in blue jeans with the wide smile and hearty handshake of a born salesman. His tribe had just gotten a massive windfall in the form of gaming profits, and the chief carried himself with the satisfied ease of well-fed wealth. His act, which he did just for fun these days, now that he didn't need the cash, was to get on stage and sing "rock 'n' roll–inspired inspired songs for kids" about all the cool and scary animals that live down in the Everglades.

"Hey, parents!" he warned between songs. "Don't let your kids go into the woods alone, 'cuz there's animals back there that will bite you! Bite you? Heck, down in the Everglades, they'll *eat* you!"

When his act was over, Chief Jim Billy sat in the audience and listened attentively to Eustace's compelling and sober presentation about how to live in harmony with nature. Eustace showed the audience how to weave rope with grass and with their own hair, and displayed baskets and clothing that he had made from natural materials. Chief Jim Billy approached Eustace after the show, extremely impressed.

"I'll tell you something, man," he said, hugging Eustace. "You're great. The stuff you know how to do? It's great. You gotta come down to Florida and teach my people all this stuff, because nobody down there knows how to do these things anymore. You're more Indian than any of us! Hell, the only thing people in my tribe know how to do is fly up to Miami and get a tan! I'm just pullin' your leg here, buddy. But seriously, you should come down and see us on the reservation. We're doing real good these days. We run a little safari that goes right through the swamp for the tourists, and the tourists would love to see you. You could be a real good attraction, because those people are looking for something authentic, something genuine, and that's what you got. We try to give them a taste of genuineness on our swamp trip, but we like to have some fun, too. We have one guy who dresses up in a black hairy costume and runs alongside the boat, jumping out at people. I tell you, man, you'd love the hell out of it. Any time you want to come down and visit, just call me. I'll take care of you, treat you like a king. You got a telephone back there in the woods, Tarzan? Good. Call me. I'm serious. I'll pick you up in my plane, fly you down for the weekend. I got my own jet, a real nice G-4. It's even got an indoor outhouse! You'll love it!"

Then Chief Billy hugged Eustace again and smoothly handed over his business card.

"Everything you need to know about me is on this card," said this gregarious Chief of the Seminoles to Eustace Conway. "Phone, cell phone, beeper, everything. Call me anytime, man. You're awesome."

Together, Eustace and I walked in silence away from the stage and back toward his demonstration teepee, which was set up on the midway, across from the concession stands. There were two nine-year-old boys playing inside when we arrived, dirt bikes parked by the smoke flap, and they nearly tackled Eustace when he showed up.

"We heard you can teach us how to start fires!" one of them said. One boy was dark-haired and small for his age; the other was overweight and blond, wearing a T-shirt that said EARTHDAY.

Accommodating them, Eustace took two sticks and explained to the boys that "trees hold fire. They get their fire from the sun. Inside every tree is a little bit of the sun that you can release with your own energy." Eustace ground the sticks together until he got a small bright ember, which he dropped into the center of a tiny nest of dry tinder, cupped in his hand. "What we have here is a baby ember, a newborn piece of fire. If we don't treat it right and feed it the nice food of oxygen, it will die." He encouraged the dark-haired boy to blow gently on the tinder, and, like magic, suddenly there was flame. The boy cheered. Then there was a loud electronic squawk in the teepee. The chubby boy in the EARTHDAY shirt pulled a walkie-talkie out of his back pocket.

"What?" he shouted into the receiver, deeply annoyed.

"Where are you, Justin? Over," came a woman's voice.

"I'm in a teepee, Mom!" Justin yelled back. "Over!"

"I can't hear you, Justin. Where are you, Justin?" the walkie-talkie repeated. "Over."

Justin rolled his eyes and screamed, "I said I'm in a *teepee*, Mom! Over! A *teepee*? A *teepee*, Mom? Get it, Mom? Over!"

I stepped outside, away from the clamor, thinking how much work Eustace has ahead of him if he's really intent on saving this culture. Outside the teepee, I found a middle-aged man in a flannel shirt looking over Eustace's structure with interest. We set to talking.

"My name is Dan," he told me. "I come here to Merlefest every year from Michigan and always try to find Eustace. I like listening to him talk about his life. It appeals to me, although it makes me envious, too. God knows, I'd move into the woods in a minute if I could. But I can't. I've got five kids in school to support right now. I've got a good job at Sarah Lee, I've got alimony to pay, and I don't see how I could leave the financial security and health insurance and live like Eustace, but I wish to God I could. I think about it every year when I come here, whenever I meet him. He's pretty compelling, you know? And look how healthy he is, living in that natural way. Not like the rest of us."

Here, Dan smiled with sweet embarrassment and patted his heavy stomach. He continued. "Eustace is always, like, *you can do it, you can do it*. But I don't see how I can do it. We just built a big house, you know? It's full of so much damn stuff, I don't even know where it came from. I swear to God, I don't understand how it happened that we own all this stuff. Sometimes I look at my house and wish I could burn it to the ground, walk away from everything, start over somewhere else with nothing. Lead a simple life out in the woods, away from the world. You understand that feeling at all? You ever get that desire? You ever wanna disappear off the face of the earth?"

"Of course," I said. "Everyone gets that desire."

"Not Eustace Conway, I bet."

"Don't lay your money on it, Dan."

All of which is to say that, looking toward the age of forty, Eustace must admit that he has not exactly provoked the kind of change in our world that he hoped to when he was younger. (Indeed, that he was certain he would provoke.) The waves of eager citizens following him into the woods never quite materialized as he'd expected when he was twenty. The world remains what it was, maybe worse.

Looking back two decades, he told me, "I honestly believed I could change things. My feeling was *Just give America to me; let me take it; I'll fix it myself!* I thought all it would require was conviction and hard work, and I knew I was capable of working harder than anyone. I didn't think the whole country would come streaming back to a more natural way of living, but I figured maybe sixty or a hundred people a year would come to Turtle Island and then take their lessons back to their communities and the message would spread like ripples in a pond and the effect would keep expanding. But I see now how hard it is to make a major difference in this country if you don't happen to be the president or an important senator and if you have no resources except your energy. How can one person make a difference? It's impossible and it's improbable and, most of all, it's damn tiring."

And America's obsession with devouring land continues, faster and more efficiently than ever. Eustace is glad to see that environmental awareness, once a radical and fringe concept, is now "totally pop and hip." Still, he can't see that a little recycling fever is any match for the famished momentum of industry and overpopulation and rampant consumerism that define our culture. It may be that Turtle Island will, a century from now, be as Eustace once imagined it: "A tiny bowl in the earth, intact and natural, surrounded by pavement and highways. People will climb up to the ridges around Turtle Island and peer inside, and they'll be able to see a pristine and green example of what the whole world once looked like."

Maybe that's true. Maybe what Eustace is doing by saving this little patch of Appalachian forest is what medieval monks once did by copying all those ancient texts. In a dark time, one that does not value knowledge, he is steadfastly preserving something small and precious in the hope that a more enlightened future generation will be grateful to have it. Maybe that's all he's doing.

People used to say to Eustace, "If you touch only one life, you've had an effect on the world!" But Eustace was never satisfied with that. It was his intent to alter the very destiny of humanity and never to settle for the meager accomplishment of touching a random life every now and again. He runs into people sometimes these days who'll say, "You're Eustace Conway! I remember you! You spoke at my high school fifteen years ago! You were amazing! You changed my life!"

Then Eustace gets all excited, until the person clarifies that. "Yeah, ever since I heard you speak, I don't run the water anymore while I'm brushing my teeth. I'm conserving resources."

Eustace can only laugh, covering his face with his hands and shaking his head. "I mean, don't get me wrong," he'll tell me. "I want to say to these people, hey, I'm glad you're not running the water while you're brushing your teeth. Honestly, I am. That's a very nice way to conserve a precious resource and that makes me really happy. But you know what? I kinda had bigger plans for you."

Eustace has lost, too, his youthful notion that he could teach absolutely anybody to live in the woods. When he was younger, he never considered turning away a would-be apprentice from Turtle Island. He never believed there was a single person in this country who couldn't master a more natural life with a little training. But now he's more cautious, more selective. He doesn't automatically welcome the ex-convicts and barely recovering drug addicts and angry teenage runaways anymore, because it saps the system to have such people around.

He's also found it useful to formalize the apprenticeship program more. It used to be a loosey-goosey, sealed-on-a-handshake relationship, the details of which altered from person to person, from year to year. Basically, all a young man or woman had to do was show up at Turtle Island and express some eagerness, and Eustace would sign the kid up, asking only that the apprentice promise to work hard and keep a positive attitude throughout the stay. These days, though, Eustace screens all potential apprentices through a fairly rigorous application process that demands resumés, references, background information, and a written essay. Moreover, tired of the Eustace Conway Whiplash Effect that decimated the morale of his workforce, Eustace now hands out this memo (simply entitled "Re: Relationship With Eustace") to every applicant:

"Please don't expect to develop a close friendship with Eustace or be disappointed by anything other than a working boss, leader, and director-type of friendship. People are attracted to aspects of Eustace's warm and generous personality and often want a more personal contact than can be expected, or than Eustace is comfortable in allowing. Apprentices have been disappointed when they did not get enough social contact with Eustace. Eustace is comfortable with extending his time to you on a mutually agreed upon expectation level. This clearly defined relationship is between a leader and those who are learning about the chores, methods, and needs of a farm and educational center."

Lately, Eustace has suffered such crushing disappointments with his workers that he's considering altogether giving up the apprenticeship program. Two of his apprentices quit this spring after serving out only six months of their year-long contracts, abandoning Turtle Island with the usual complaints that the work was too hard, they were having trouble with Eustace's leadership, the experience was not what they'd expected, and they "needed to follow their bliss," even if it meant not honoring their commitments.

"Does it mean nothing to anybody anymore to sign an agreement?" Eustace asked in wonder. "Is it naïve of me in my antiquated way to think that people should do what they say they're going to do? How could these kids walk away after six months without caring that they'd promised to stay a year? They had no sense of the bind that put me in, or the fact that I might have made plans around their commitment. They bailed out early and left me high and dry. And why does this keep happening, time and again?"

What devastated Eustace about the loss of these two young people was not only that their stay at Turtle Island followed such a familiar trajectory (enthusiastic hope followed by bitter disillusionment) but that one of the apprentices, a thoroughly competent and reliable woman named Jennifer, had been, to Eustace's mind, possibly the best worker he'd ever had. She even rivaled the legendary Christian Kaltrider with her potential. She was smart, dedicated, and uncomplaining, with a serious commitment to learning about primitive farming. She'd been raised in the mountains and had brought skills to Turtle Island that even Eustace didn't have. He'd trusted her enough to turn over to her the management of the Turtle Island garden (an act of faith he'd made with no small amount of suffering, and largely as a self-experiment, to see whether he could handle the loss of control). And Jennifer had made the garden thrive, even as she was learning about the care of horses and the construction of buildings. She was perfect, and Eustace had come to respect her and rely on her. And now she had up and quit.

"Look up the word *heartbroken* in the dictionary and you'll see a picture of me next to it," he told me on the phone a week after Jennifer had left. "I was so depressed when she left, I didn't get out of bed for two days. If somebody like Jennifer can't make it here for a whole year, who can? Who am I kidding? Why am I bothering? What is Turtle Island for, if that's how it's always going to end? It's something I pour my lifeblood into for the benefit of others, but it's not working, and the people I'm doing it for keep quitting and failing. I'm closer to giving up than I've ever been. I've been having fantasies of hanging a little sign on the gate that says: *Turtle Island closed. Go away.* Of course, I won't. Or maybe I will. I don't know anymore . . ."

And so it goes that Eustace, by hard necessity, is narrowing his vision as he ages, winnowing out some of his youthful ideals, giving up some of his boldest dreams. His latest aspirations are strikingly modest. For now, he's not taking on any new apprentices but is concentrating his energy on getting a horseback-riding program instituted at Turtle Island. He's been running ads in the Boone newspapers, inviting people to come up to his property for day trips around his woods. He's hoping that the money he makes by taking people on horseback rides will help defer the expenses of keeping all those lovely horses of his. And it's a refreshingly simple human interaction—the customer pays, Eustace provides a simple service, he doesn't try to convince anyone to move into the forest with him, and everyone goes home at the end of the day satisfied.

OK, he thinks now, *maybe I can't change the world*. Maybe Eustace's influence will be more modest, affecting small groups and scattered individuals—people like the motorists he waved to from his horse on the Long Riders trip, the kindergarteners he buried up to their necks in the forest, the drug dealers in Tompkins Square Park whom he left to ponder the curious fact that a man can make his clothing from the materials of this earth . . .

Or consider the young campers who were exploring Turtle Island one day and discovered a beaver dam and were encouraged by their counselors to swim inside the dam through the beaver's tunnels until they reached the inside of the beaver's lodge—warm, dry, sacred, and hidden. How many boys in this century have been inside a beaver lodge? That event must have sent an immeasurable and lasting tremor through the consciousness of those boys. To Eustace Conway, with his grand architect's vision of a transformed America, that may not seem like much. But in this age of increasingly mindless conformity, even the faintest suggestion that the world can be looked at from another vantage point for one fleeting moment, it is *much*. And maybe that doesn't satisfy Eustace, but that may be all he gets. He is, in the end, a teacher. And like all teachers, he may have to accept the reality that only a few of his students over a few decades will truly be affected by a few lessons.

There was once a kid, for instance, named Dave Reckford.

He was raised outside Chicago, a suburban child with a physician father and a mother who expressed her vaguely hippie leanings by sending her son to Quaker schools and feeding him health foods. When Caterpillar Tractor closed its Illinois factory, Dave's hometown turned from boom to bust, and his parents moved to North Carolina, where Dave was sent to an expensive private school packed with children from the oldest families in the South. And then his life turned upside down. Dave's father fell in love with another woman and split. The family was shattered into chaos. Eventually, those shattered bits were re-ordered. After a few hard years, his mother pulled her life together and married a wealthy and kind man, but somehow Dave was left behind in all this. He was thirteen years old and shaken to his guts. Profoundly sad. And searching.

A few years later, a modern-day mountain man named Eustace Conway came to teach a nature class at the private school where Dave Reckford was a student. "He was all dressed up in buckskin," Dave remembers, "and he didn't smell very good. And he started talking, in his quiet way, about his teepee and his blowgun and his life in the wilderness. I was enthralled. He talked about going to the bathroom in the woods. He got on this diversion about how squatting is the natural way to go to the bathroom and how sitting on a toilet seat puts an unnatural strain on the organs of digestion, and we were shocked—this whole room of elite Southern teenagers. We'd never heard anything like it.

And then he said, 'In fact, when I have to go to the bathroom someplace where all they have is toilets, I just jump up on the toilet seat and squat on it like this—' and he hopped up onto a desk in a squat to show us. He was laughing and we were laughing, and somehow he made it all seem OK and interesting without freaking us out."

Later, Eustace set to talking with Dave, and, sensing the level of desperation in the kid, invited him to visit Turtle Island. Dave immediately agreed, and drove his "little rich-boy Mercedes coupe" up there for a weeklong visit. This was in the early, early years. There wasn't much to Turtle Island yet, except Eustace's teepee. He hadn't cleared any land and he didn't have any livestock. It was still primitive. When Dave showed up, Eustace was sitting by his teepee, talking "with a really pretty woman. He asked me if I could please excuse myself for a half hour so that he could be alone with this girl in his teepee, and then he slipped off with her to have—it was pretty obvious—sex. I was pretty amazed by the openness of his sexuality. He finally came out of the teepee, and the girl left, and then he began to teach me. The first thing he showed me was a bed of coals in his fire pit. He explained that if you keep your deep-set coals warm all the time, you'll always have fire ready at hand and not have to strike up a new flame."

Then he set Dave to work rebuilding the forge in the blacksmith shop. Next, they began digging the foundation for the toolshed Eustace was building. He taught Dave how to make shingles, which was "really hard work, with a sledgehammer." And so it went, day after day, hard manual labor from a boy who had never experienced such a thing.

"It wasn't what I'd expected," Dave said, "from the quiet-warrior, soft-spoken, Zen-master teacher I thought I had followed up the mountain. He was a slave driver. He was relentless and obsessive about detail, and the work made me cry and almost broke my back. It was so hard, I was afraid each day that I wouldn't survive. But every night, I got to sleep near Eustace in his teepee, on the animal skin rugs by the warm fire, and that was the best and safest sleep I'd had since I was a child. He made me great food and listened to me talk about my family. I don't think anyone gets this kind of access to Eustace Conway anymore, but this was in the years before he had apprentices and campers everywhere and all his public duties. He was twenty-seven years old and I was a fatherless kid, but it was a profound experience to spend time with a grown man who wanted to talk to me and teach me things."

Eustace used his time with Dave to try to have him understand the fundamental essence of his philosophy, which centered on mindfulness. There is no way, Eustace said to Dave, that you can have a decent life as a man if you aren't awake and aware every moment. Show up for your own life, he said. Don't pass your days in a stupor, content to swallow whatever watery ideas modern society may bottle-feed you through the media, satisfied to slumber through life in an instant-gratification sugar coma. The most extraordinary gift you've been given is your own humanity, which is about consciousness, so honor that consciousness.

Revere your senses; don't degrade them with drugs, with depression, with willful oblivion. Try to notice something new every day, Eustace said. Pay attention to even the most modest of daily details. Even if you're not in the woods, be aware at all times. Notice what food tastes like; notice what the detergent aisle in the supermarket smells like and recognize what those hard chemical smells do to your senses; notice what bare feet feel like; pay attention every day to the vital insights that mindfulness can bring. And take care of all things, of every single thing there is—your body, your intellect, your spirit, your neighbors, and this planet. Don't pollute your soul with apathy or spoil your health with junk food any more than you would deliberately contaminate a clean river with industrial sludge. You can never become a real man if you have a careless and destructive attitude, Eustace said, but maturity will follow mindfulness even as day follows night.

Eustace told Dave tragicomic stories about some of the teenage American boys who'd visited Turtle Island and were so oblivious of their environment that they literally didn't have the sense to come in from the rain. A storm would come up, and the boys would stand there in the downpour, as stupefied as a flock of overbred sheep, unable to reason that they should transport their bodies to a shelter. Or there was the boy Eustace had seen step in a yellow jacket's nest and then stand stock still and confused as the swarm gathered around him. The boy was patently unable to think that he should get himself out of this situation until Eustace shouted, *"Run!"*

Be awake, Eustace said, (laughing at the very simplicity of it), and you will succeed in this world. When it rains, find shelter! When you're being stung by yellow jackets, run! Only through constant focus can you become independent. Only through independence can you know yourself. And only through knowing yourself will you be able to ask the key questions of your life: *What is it that I am destined to accomplish, and how can I make it happen?*

What Dave remembered more than anything about that week, though, was the transformative, almost religious, experience of watching Eustace build a fence.

"Building a fence up here in this rocky soil is hard work. First you have to pound into the ground this metal post, slamming it with a sledgehammer and making a hole for your black locust stake. I almost cut my leg off once, trying to do it. Then you stick that black locust stake into the hole and whale on it with that heavy sledgehammer, drilling it in. I did six of these in a row, and I swear to God I almost died. I can't describe what hard work that was. I collapsed on the ground and felt that my heart would explode. Eustace then took over for me, and while I tried to catch my breath, he put in the next twenty stakes without pausing once, without even breathing hard.

"I studied him as he worked. How could he do this? He's not as big or muscular as I am. I'm a triathlete and I'm big, and I couldn't do it. His arms are lean. How can it work? But as I watched him, I realized he had an intimate physical relationship with his tools. When he swung that sledgehammer, he didn't use just his arms; he swung it in one perfectly economical motion, using his whole body. His hips helped him hoist the sledgehammer up, and then he arched back and put all his momentum behind the blow. It was beautiful. It was complete physical attention to one task. It was like watching a dance. The dance of manual labor. And I knew that this was why Eustace could do everything faster and better than everyone else, because of that intensity and grace and perfection of focus."

Dave remembers watching Eustace on another day hammering

nails into wood—fast, rhythmic, and perfect—and asking, "How come you never miss the nail?"

"Because I made up my mind a long time ago that I'd never miss the nail," Eustace replied. "So I don't."

In the end, the grueling pace of the work at Turtle Island was such a shock to Dave's body that he collapsed. He became physically ill from the eleven-hour days of labor. Eustace, seeing this, stopped the work for a day and drove Dave down to town. "Let's take a fun trip," he said casually. He took the kid into a bar and got him a beer—his first. Eustace laughed and joked with the bartender and never mentioned the work that was left behind. On the way back up the mountain that night, Dave broke down and told Eustace he didn't think he could stay any longer.

"I told him I wanted to go home. I was probably crying. I'm sure I was homesick, because I was just a kid. Eustace was calm and thoughtful. We sat in his truck and he talked about life and about what it takes to become a man. He imparted wisdom and kindness to me, taking me seriously at an age when nobody ever took me seriously. He told me that one of the reasons people are so unhappy is they don't talk to themselves. He said you have to keep a conversation going with yourself throughout your life to see how you're doing, to keep your focus, to remain your own friend. He told me that he talked to himself all the time, and that it helped him to grow stronger and better every day. He suggested some books I should read. Then he hugged me."

Fifteen years later, Dave Reckford still couldn't tell this part of the story without tears brimming up.

"Listen," he said, "it was a real hug, long and strong. It was a bear hug. It was the first time I had ever been hugged by a man, and it seemed to cure something inside me that was lonely and hurt. He told me I was free to go home and he wished me luck. But he also told me I was free to come back and stay with him on Turtle Island any time I wanted to, because I had done a good job and because I was a good person. And I did go home, but when I got there, I found that something had changed in me. And the rest of my life was changed."

Every man in Dave Reckford's family is a lawyer, a doctor, a businessman, or a diplomat. That's what is expected, the way of the family.

It's not Dave's way, as it turns out. Dave is thirty years old now and has been roaming around, looking for his place. He's studied history and music. He's tried his hand at writing. He's traveled to Cuba and Europe and across America and even joined the Army, trying to find where he should place himself for his short time on earth.

Recently, he finally landed. He solved it. He asked the woman who tends to his parents' gardens to take him on as her apprentice. She agreed. So now Dave Reckford has become what he believes he was intended to be: a gardener. He takes care of plants. He spends his days thinking about soil and light and growth. It's a simple relationship, but he is rewarded by it. He tries to understand what plants need and how to help them. He tries to make his every movement careful and precise, to honor his work. He talks to himself all the time, keeping in contact with his personal essence. And every single day of his life he thinks about perfection of focus and about the singular grace of human labor.

Which means that, every single day of his life, he thinks about Eustace Conway.

EPILOGUE

You can't fix it. You can't make it go away.
I don't know what you're going to do about it,
but I know what I'm going to do about it. I'm just
going to walk away from it. Maybe
a small part of it will die if I'm not around
feeding it anymore.

—*Lew Welch*

The history of Eustace Conway is the history of man's progress on the North American continent.

First, he slept on the ground and wore furs. He made fire with sticks and ate what he could hunt and gather. When he was hungry, he threw stones at birds and blew darts at rabbits and dug up roots from the ground, and so he survived. He wove baskets from the trees in his domain. He was a nomad; he moved on foot. Then he moved into a teepee and became a more sophisticated trapper of animals. He made fire with flint and steel. When he mastered that, he used matches. He began to wear wool. He moved out of the teepee and into a simple wooden structure. He became a farmer, clearing the land and cultivating a garden. He acquired livestock. He cut paths into the woods, which became trails and then roads. He improved the roads with bridges. He wore denim.

He was first an Indian, then an explorer, then a pioneer. He built himself a cabin and became a true settler. As a man of utopian vision, he now sustains himself with the hope that like-minded people will buy property around Turtle Island and raise their families as he will some-day raise his. The neighbors will till their land with animal-drawn ma-chinery and come to each other's aid in the time of harvest and join each other for bursts of recreational dancing, and they will ride to each other's homes on horseback and trade goods.

When all that happens, Eustace will have become a villager. That's what he wants—to create a town. And when that is all firmly in place, he will build his dream home. He'll move out of the cabin and into a large and expensive show house full of walk-in closets and appliances and family and *stuff.* And he will have finally caught up with his time. At that point, Eustace Conway will be the paradigm of a modern Amer-ican man.

He evolves before our eyes. He improves and expands and improves and expands because he is so clever and so resourceful that he cannot help himself. He is not compelled to rest in the enjoyment of what he already knows how to do; he must keep moving on. He is unstoppable. And we are also unstoppable. We on this continent have always been unstoppable. We all progress, as de Tocqueville observed, "like a deluge of men, rising unabatedly, and driven daily onward by the hand of God." We exhaust ourselves and everyone else. And we exhaust our re-sources—both natural and interior—and Eustace is only the clearest representation of our urgency.

I remember driving back to Turtle Island early one evening with him, after a visit to his grandfather's old empire of Camp Sequoyah. We were almost home, passing through Boone, and stopped at an intersec-tion. Eustace suddenly spun his head and asked, "Was that building there two days ago when we left for Asheville?"

He pointed at the skeleton of a small new office building. No, I hadn't noticed it there two days earlier. But it looked almost finished. Only the windows needed to be popped in. A battalion of construction workers were leaving the site for the day.

"Couldn't be," Eustace said. "Can they really put up a building that fast?"

"I don't know," I said, thinking that, of all people, he ought to know. "I guess they can."

He sighed. "This country . . ." he said.

But Eustace Conway *is* this country. And, that being the case, what remains? What remains after all this activity? That's the question Walt Whitman once asked. He looked around at the galloping pace of American life and at the growth of industry and at the jaw-clenching rush of his countrymen's ambitions and wondered, "After you have exhausted what there is in business, politics, conviviality, and so on—have found that none of these finally satisfy, or permanently wear—what remains?"

And, as ever, dear old Walt gave us the answer: "Nature remains."

That's what Eustace is left with, too. Although, like the rest of us (and this is his biggest irony), Eustace doesn't have as much time as he wishes to celebrate the natural world.

As he told me one winter evening over the phone, "We had a snowstorm up at Turtle Island this week. A friend of mine came to visit and said, 'Hey, Eustace, you've been working too hard. You should take a break and build a snowman. Ever think of that?' Well, hell, of course I'd already thought of that. All I had to do was take one step outside my door that morning to see that it was perfect snow for a snowman. I'd already visualized the snowman I would build, if I were to build one. I quickly analyzed the consistency of the snow and decided exactly where to put the snowman for best presentation, exactly how big it would be, and where in my blacksmith shop I could find charcoal for the eyes. I pictured every detail of the snowman right down to the carrot nose, which I had to think about for an instant: *Do we have enough carrots to spare that I could use one for this snowman? And after the snowman is over, could I get the carrot back and put it in a stew so that it wouldn't be wasted? Or would an animal get at the carrot first?* I ran through all this in about five seconds, estimated how much time it would take out of my busy day to build the snowman, I weighed that against how much pleasure building a snowman would bring me—and decided against it."

More's the pity, because he does enjoy being outside and he might have gotten more pleasure from the snowman than he was able to logically calculate. Because he does love nature, for all his commitments and obligations. He loves it all—the cosmic scope of the woods; the stipple of sunlight slanting down through a verdant natural awning; the loveliness of the words *locust, birch*, and *tulip poplar* . . . More than loving it, he needs it. As Eustace's grandfather wrote, "When the mind is tired, or the soul is disquieted, let us go to the woods and fill our lungs with the rain-washed and the sun-cleansed air, and our hearts with the beauty of tree, flower, crystal, and gem."

The best man that Eustace can be is the man he becomes when he is alone in the woods. That's why I drag him out of his office whenever I come to Turtle Island and make him lead me on a walk. Even though he generally doesn't have time for it, I make him do it, because we don't get ten steps into the forest before he says, "That's bee balm. You can make a straw out of its hollow stem and suck moisture up from pebbles in streams where it might be too shallow to drink."

Or, "That's Turk's Cap, a flower that looks a lot like a tiger lily, only more exotic. It's extremely rare. I doubt there are five of these plants on all thousand acres of Turtle Island."

Or, when I complain about my poison ivy, he takes me down to the river and says, "Come join me in my pharmacy." He pulls up some jewelweed, and opens it to the ointment inside, spreads it on my bumpy wrist, and suddenly everything feels better.

I love Eustace in the woods because he loves himself in the woods. It's that easy. Which is why, one day when we were walking, I said to him out of the blue, "Permission to introduce a revolutionary new concept, sir?"

Eustace laughed. "Permission granted."

"Have you ever wondered," I asked, "if you might benefit the world more by actually living the life you always talk about? I mean, isn't that what we're all here for? Aren't we each supposed to try to live the most enlightened and honest life we can? And when our actions contradict our values, don't we just fuck everything up even more?"

I paused here and waited to get punched. But Eustace said nothing, so I continued.

"You're always telling us how happy we could be if we lived in the woods. But when people come up here to live with you, what they end up seeing is your stress and frustration at having so many people around and being overwhelmed with responsibilities. So of course they don't absorb the lesson, Eustace. They hear your message but they can't *feel* your message, and that's why it doesn't work. Do you ever wonder about that?"

"I wonder about it constantly!" Eustace exploded. "I'm totally fucking aware of that! Whenever I go into schools to teach, I tell people, 'Look, I am not the only person left in this country who tries to live a natural life in the woods, but you're never going to meet all those other guys because they aren't *available*.' Well, I am available. That's the difference with me. I've always made myself available, even when it compromises the way I want to live. When I go out in public, I deliberately try to present myself as this wild guy who just came down off the mountain, and I'm aware that it's largely an act. I know I'm a showman. I know I present people with an image of how I *wish* I were living. But what else can I do? I have to put on that act for the benefit of the people."

"I'm not so sure it's benefiting us, Eustace."

"But if I lived the quiet and simple life I want, then who would witness it? Who would be inspired to change? Only my neighbors would see me. I'd influence about forty people, when I want to influence about four hundred thousand people. You see the dilemma? You see my struggle? What am I supposed to do?"

"How about trying to live in peace for once?"

"But what does that *mean*?" Eustace was roaring now, laughing and totally losing it. "What does that fucking *mean*?"

Of course, that's not my question to answer. All I can tell with any certainty is when the man *appears* to be most at peace. And that usually isn't when he's firing apprentices or spending six straight hours on the telephone haggling with tax lawyers, school boards, newspaper reporters, and insurance companies. When he appears to be most at peace is when he is experiencing the closest and most personal liaison with the wilderness. When he is right inside nature's stupefying theater, he is closest to happy. When he is—as much as is humanly achievable in our modern age—living in communion with whatever is left of our frontier, he gets there.

Sometimes I'm lucky enough to have a glimpse into that best part of Eustace Conway in the most unlikely instances. Sometimes the moment just finds him. There was this one evening when we were driving back from Asheville, trucking along in silence. Eustace was in a quiet mood, and we were listening to old-time Appalachian music, taking in the sad twang of hard men who had lost their farms and hard women whose husbands had gone down into the coal mines and never returned. It was drizzling rain, and as we moved from superhighway to freeway to two-lane macadam to the dirt road of his mountain, the rain lightened up, even as the sun was going down. We bounced and trundled up toward Turtle Island under the gloom of steep, overgrown hollers.

Quite suddenly, a family of deer leaped out of the woods and onto the road before us. Eustace hit the brakes. The doe and her fawns skitted sideways into the darkness, but the buck stayed, staring into our headlights. Eustace honked. The buck stood. Eustace jumped out of the truck and let out a loud whoop into the damp night, to chase the buck back into the woods, but the buck stood where it was.

"You're beautiful, brother!" Eustace shouted at the deer.

The buck regarded him. Eustace laughed. He made fists and shook them wildly in the air. He whooped and howled like an animal. Again, Eustace shouted to the buck, "You're beautiful! You rule! *You da bomb!*"

Eustace laughed. Still the buck held his ground, unmoving.

And then Eustace, too, stopped moving—enchanted into a temporary paralysis. For a long while he stood as stock still and silent as I'd ever seen him, barely illuminated by the spilled bath of his shadowy headlights, staring at that buck. Nobody budged or breathed. In the end, it was Eustace who broke first, throwing his fists up into the air again and shouting out into the night with all the voice he could summon:

"I love you! You're beautiful! I love you! I love you! I love you!"

Acknowledgments

I would like to thank the extraordinary Conway family for their openness and hospitality during this project, and particularly Eustace Conway for his courage in letting me proceed with this work unfettered.

It has been an honor to know you all, and I have tried to honor you here.

There have been many people in Eustace's life—past and present—who gave generously of their time to help me formulate the ideas behind this book. For their tolerance in being incessantly interviewed, I thank Donna Henry, Christian Kaltrider, Shannon Nunn, Valarie Spratlin, CuChullaine O'Reilly, Lorraine Johnson, Randy Cable, Steve French, Carolyn Hauck, Carla Gover, Barbara Locklear, Hoy Moretz, Nathan and Holly Roarke, the Hicks family, Jack Bibbo, Don Bruton, Matt Niemas, Siegal Kiewe, Warren Kimsey, Alan Stout, Ed Bumann, Pop Hollingsworth, Patience Harrison, Dave Reckford, Scott Taylor, Ashley Clutter, and Candice Covington. And a special note of thanks to Kathleen and Preston Roberts, who are not only lovely and gracious people, but who let Eustace and me sit on their porch and drink beer and shoot off guns all night long. ("I never fired a gun when I was drunk before," Eustace said, and Preston shouted, "And you call yourself *Southern?*")

I am grateful to the authors of the many books and histories that have guided this endeavor. Among others, I found inspiration in John Mack

Faragher's biography of Daniel Boone, David Roberts's biography of Kit Carson, James Atkins Shatford's biography of Davy Crockett, David McCullough's biography of the young Teddy Roosevelt, Rod Phillips's analysis of forest Beatniks, and Stephen Ambrose's compelling account of Lewis and Clark's journey to the Pacific.

Anybody interested in reading more about American utopias should get Timothy Miller's encyclopedic *The 60's Communes: Hippies and Beyond*, and anybody interested in a surprisingly funny book that happens to be about American utopias should hunt down a copy of Mark Halloway's brilliant *Heavens on Earth: Utopian Communities in America, 1680–1880*. The statistics quoted in Chapter Seven on the decline of males come from *The Decline of Males*, by Lionel Tiger. I also owe thanks to R. W. B. Lewis for his wise study *The American Adam*, and to Richard Slotkin for his equally wise *The Fatal Environment*. And my bottomless thanks (and eternal admiration) go to the living library that is Doug Brinkley, for telling me to read all these books.

Thanks also go to Powell's Bookstore of Portland, Oregon, for having—when I was seeking books about the impressions of nineteenth-century European visitors to America—an entire shelf labeled "Impressions of 19th Century European Visitors to America." There is no better bookstore in America, and this proves it.

I am fortunate to have great friends who are also great readers and editors. For their help and valuable assistance in editing various versions of this book, I thank David Cashion, Reggie Ollen, Andrew Corsello, John Morse, John Gilbert, Susan Bowen (the speed-reading Georgia Peach), and John Hodgman (who invented just for me the essential new editing abbreviation CWRBS, meaning "Cut the Will Rogers Bullshit"). I thank John Platter, who found the strength to read an early draft of this book in his final days of life, and whom I miss terribly every time I walk to my mailbox and remember that I will never receive another letter from him.

I thank Kassie Evashevski, Sarah Chalfant, Paul Slovak, and the hugely incredible Frances Apt for their sure-footed guidance. I thank Art Cooper at *GQ* for believing me four years ago when I said, "Trust me— you just gotta let me write a profile about this guy." I thank Michael Cooper for saying long ago, when I was in doubt about writing the book,

"Wouldn't you rather make a mistake by *doing* something than make a mistake by *not* doing something?" Again, I thank my big sister Catherine for her preternatural genius about American history and for her steadfast support. Again, I thank my dear friend Deborah for being open twenty-four hours a day to dispense her wisdom on the human psyche. This book would be virtually barren of ideas without the inspiration of these two amazing women.

There are not enough thanks in the world to offer the Ucross Foundation for giving me 22,000 acres of privacy in the middle of Wyoming during what I will probably always remember as the most important thirty days of my life.

And lastly, there are not enough ways in the world for me to say this: Big Love